EMERGENT CURRICULUM

by Elizabeth Jones
and John Nimmo

A 1993-94 NAEYC Comprehensive Membership benefit

NATIONAL ASSOCIATION FOR THE EDUCATION OF YOUNG CHILDREN
WASHINGTON, DC

Illustrations: The illustration on page 83 was drawn by Marie Chu. Illustrations that appear on pages 34, 40, 81, 106, and 110 (top) were drawn by Lura Schwarz Smith based on the original art of Elizabeth (Betty) Jones. The remainder of the art in this book was contributed by Betty Jones and children she has known over the years. Special thanks to Nicholus White for his artistic contributions.

Photos: © Hildegard Adler (p. x); © Marietta Lynch (p. 4, 58); © Bunny Rabiroff (p. 15); © Robert Bowie (p. 27); courtesy John Nimmo (p. 44); © Nina Pratt (p. 67); © Carolyn Kozo (p. 76); Marilyn Nolt (p. 84); © Peggy Snyder (p. 97); © Cleo Freelance Photo (p. 127); © Nancy P. Alexander (p. 130); © Renaus Thomas (p. 139).

Cover design: Betty Jones and John Nimmo.

National Association for the Education of Young Children
1509 16th Street, N.W.
Washington, DC 20036–1426
202–232–8777   800–424–2460

The National Association for the Education of Young Children (NAEYC) attempts through its publications program to provide a forum for discussion of major issues and ideas in our field. We hope to provoke thought and promote professional growth. The views expressed or implied are not necessarily those of the Association. NAEYC wishes to thank the authors, who donated much time and effort to develop this book as a contribution to our profession.

Library of Congress Catalog Card Number: 94-068321
ISBN Catalog Number: 0-935989-62-5
NAEYC #207

Editor: Carol Copple. *Book design and production:* Jack Zibulsky, Penny Atkins, and Don Harris. *Copyediting:* Millie Riley. *Editorial assistance:* Beth Panitz and Stacey Chevalier.

Printed in the United States of America

Contents

List of Boxes

Foreword

Emergent curriculum in early childhood education is not new. There have always been classrooms in which the curriculum took shape week by week and day by day, with the teachers thoughtfully making plans that drew on the children's interests and activities rather than mapping out everything months in advance. But it was not until 1970 that Betty Jones introduced the term *emergent curriculum* (in her introduction to the NAEYC publication *Curriculum Is What Happens*, edited by Laura Dittman). Having a concise, apt phrase to describe such early childhood programs has proven to be very helpful.

Each word in the phrase *emergent curriculum* has an important point to make. *Emergent* emphasizes that planning needs to emerge from the daily life of the children and adults in the program, particularly from the children's own interests; it re-minds us that spontaneity always has a place in the settings where young children play and learn. Yet, as the word *curriculum* conveys, there *is* also teacher planning in such settings, there *is* a curriculum. Both aspects of emergent curriculum—the spontaneity and the planning—come to life in this book. Betty Jones and John Nimmo have struck on a fresh and effective approach to convey the essentials of emergent curriculum and show us what it looks like in action: they draw us into the spirited conversations that take place in staff planning sessions during a year in a child care center—and into the center's lively classrooms. And as we the readers witness the ongoing life of one group of teachers and children, we cannot help but grapple with vital issues in teaching and living with children.

—*Carol Copple*

About the Authors

Elizabeth (Betty) Jones

John Nimmo

Elizabeth Jones and **John Nimmo** are members of the faculty of Pacific Oaks College, Betty in human development at Pasadena, California, and John in human development and education at Pacific Oaks Northwest in Seattle, Washington. In the course of graduate work at the University of Massachusetts at Amherst, John, an Australian, became interested in Reggio Emilia and became part of an ongoing research team focusing on children's collaboration. He is a contributor to the *The Hundred Languages of Children: The Reggio Emilia Approach to Early Childhood Education*. For several years he has been exploring and writing about the development of classroom community. By an interesting coincidence, John left Australia for California in the same semester (the fall of 1986) that Betty was working on emergent curriculum ideas as a visiting fellow in South Australia. They connected the next spring and discovered they liked thinking together.

Betty's books include *Growing Teachers: Partnerships in Staff Development, Teaching Adults: An Active Learning Approach, The Play's the Thing: Teachers' Roles in Children's Play* (with Gretchen Reynolds), and *Dimensions of Teaching-Learning Environments* (with Elizabeth Prescott). Betty and John are consulting editors for NAEYC. Both authors have spent many years in early childhood programs, as teachers and as observers.

Acknowledgments

To Stephanie Feeney—thank you for pushing!

To the teachers whose real-life stories found their way into this book:

Theresa Barrios	Joyce Mortara-Shoop
Suzanne Bush	Trish Myers
Beni Campbell	Joan Newcomb
Susan Corbin	Michelle Payne
Mary Durall	Ann Pelo
Steve Goldenberg	Margaret Pollard
Marilyn Haywood	Sandra Rangel-Lizer
Suzanne Jones	Doug Tolbert
Mamie King	Georgina Villarino
Jacqueline McMurray	Connie Wortham

And, especially, to Laurie Read, an extraordinarily playful emerger of curriculum, to whose memory this book is dedicated.

1

Introduction: A Year in the Life of a Child Care Center

For a long time we've wanted to write about emergent curriculum, but figuring out how to do it has been the challenge. You can't just present an emergent curriculum as a plan or a product. It's a *planning process* that takes place among a particular group of people, and so, we realized, it has to be told as a story unfolding over time.

We have decided to tell a story about a year in the life of a child care center—a composite center drawn from our varied experiences. We have invented this story, just as a writer of fiction does. It isn't fact, but it could have happened this way. It's been said that "Fiction is a lie that tells the truth."

Although we began the writing with an overall plan for the book project as a whole, several plans emerged as we went along. Simply put, emergent curriculum asks that we be responsive to particular people, in a particular place, at a particular time. What you encounter in this book has developed a life of its own, just as real curriculum does. In the head of an experienced teacher of young children, even internal dialogue invents itself in unexpected ways.

Emergent curriculum is sensible but not predictable. It requires of its practitioners *trust in*

the power of play—trust in spontaneous choice making among many possibilities. Good programs for young children encourage children to become competent players. Children's programs that are also good for teacher growth encourage teachers as well to become competent players, choosing among possibilities and thus constructing their own hands-on understanding of the teaching–learning process.

We introduce ourselves, Betty and John, into the story as observers of staff meetings and children's program. We're teacher educators at a nearby college, where this child care center's director is enrolled part-time in a graduate program in early childhood education. Intrigued by seminar discussions of emergent curriculum, she proposes documenting her center's planning process as the topic for her thesis. For ourselves we see an opportunity to gather field data on our own burning questions about inventing curriculum while supporting Ruby, the director, in her staff-development efforts as well as her thesis research. We also weave into this story our ongoing, real-life debates about how spontaneity and planning can best come together in creating a curriculum for young children. We don't always agree on how an emergent curriculum should proceed, and we find this creative conflict essential to our continued learning together.

In documenting what's going on and sharing our observations and questions with staff as co-researchers,[1] we are taking on the role of *external facilitator* or *storyteller* for teachers,[2] a role with which we're familiar and about which we're enthusiastic. We think it adds another dimension to the story, while offering the sort of support helpful to a director in working with staff.

The setting

Manzanita Children's Center is a nonprofit child care center located in the urban area of a large Southwest city in the United States. When Ruby became head teacher of this center 10 years ago, there were 45 three- and four-year-olds in a multipurpose auditorium of the community center. At that time Ruby led the staff of five teachers in the challenge of making this difficult space work for them and the children.[3]

The surrounding neighborhood is mixed, both in people and land use—small houses interspersed with small businesses and light industry further west. The first people to move in during the 1950s were Anglo-Americans and Latinos; in the decades since, the neighborhood has attracted successive waves of in-migrant families looking for relatively affordable but stable housing after getting their first start in more transient neighborhoods. These families have included African Americans, Asians, and Central Americans; the newest families are from the Middle East.

Although the region's population is growing, the school-age population has declined in parts of the city, and some older, smaller schools have been closed. The school district leases space in school buildings to other community groups, and this summer Manzanita Children's Center moved into the early childhood wing of one of these schools. The center has five classrooms for the children, a multipurpose room for adults, and an adjacent outdoor space. Other rooms in the building are rented by a legal aid office, an infant program for adolescent parents, and an adult education center.

At its new site, Manzanita continues to serve the same ethnically diverse, mostly middle- and low-income community as it did before. Spanish and English are the primary languages of the families. Enrollment has been expanded by 25, including children both older and younger than those of the initial group; now there are 2s and 5s as well as 3s and 4s. In response to this growth, Ruby has moved to full-time director, and four new staff positions have been added.

As a matter of philosophy and policy, the child care center tries to reflect the neighborhood population in its staff hiring. Two staff members are African American; three are of Latin heritage, but they do reflect different generations and nationalities. The one Asian teacher speaks Japanese; however, different Asian languages are spoken at home by several families. None of the full-time staff are personally familiar with the cultural traditions of the several Middle Eastern families who have recently enrolled; staff will need to learn more. Not all families with children in the center live in the neighborhood. The center has developed a well-deserved reputation for quality, and a number of families from more upscale areas find it conveniently located on the way to their downtown offices. Diversity is an important source of the center's curriculum as well as of the challenges in building relationships and developing skills for conflict resolution. In fact, Ruby has been heard describing one of her tasks as "supporting healthy conflict maintenance,"[4] believing that the airing of genuine differences among people is a source of continuing growth and learning.

The characters

Ruby has been at Manzanita for 10 years, first as head teacher and now, this year, as director. She has a bachelor's degree in early childhood and is working on her master's. She previously taught at a Head Start center. She's committed to staff participation in decision making.

———

Yoshiko is a recent arrival from Japan, where she was head teacher in a large preschool. Her own children are grown, and she is in the United States because of her husband's work. She will be teaching the 2-year-olds.

Mayella, Yoshiko's partner with the 2s, has been at the center for a long time. She's a grandmother, experienced but not formally trained. Ruby has been trying to persuade her to work on her Child Development Associate (CDA) Credential. She's been resisting.

———

Sally has an associate degree in early childhood education and five years' experience at Manzanita. She'll be in charge of the younger 3-year-olds.

Bob will be working with Sally. New to the staff, he's a recent college graduate in environmental studies, with a previous summer's experience in child care. He likes children and speaks a little Spanish.

_____

Marnie has a bachelor's degree in child development. Last year she taught in the laboratory preschool of her university, where she learned the curriculum framework on which she relies. She's teacher of 3s and 4s.

Gloria, who has just earned her CDA Credential, has been working at an inner-city feminist cooperative day care center and is one of its founders. She'll be working with Marnie.

_____

Sandra has her associate degree and is a part-time student in an early childhood bachelor's degree program with a strong developmental focus. She has been at this center for two years and is teacher of the older 4-year-olds.

Dolores, who joined the staff the year the center began, lives in the neighborhood and has raised a large family. She's working with Sandra and began work on her CDA Credential last year.

_____

Bethany is the 5-year-olds' teacher. She has a bachelor's degree in psychology and discovered early childhood education as a parent in a cooperative preschool. She has since then taught preschool in assorted settings and recently become a grandmother. Last year she was with Dolores and the 4s.

Staff meetings

Finding time for staff meetings in full-day child care is always a challenge. Children's naptime may work for short meetings of part of the staff, but evenings or weekends are the only available times in most programs when real meetings can be scheduled.

Manzanita Center staff meet one evening a month directly after work, beginning with shared supper. While this timing makes meetings somewhat problematic for staff on early shift, Ruby, the director, offers those affected some opportunities for time off when she is able to cover in their classrooms. Meetings are defined as staff development, and theory and practice are discussed within the context of program planning. Attendance at these meetings and at the two Staff Days that begin the year is specified in staff's job descriptions and is paid for accordingly.

What this book is for

This book is a story about taking your own ideas and other people's ideas, bouncing them off each other, and trying them out with children. It's about empowering teachers as planners of curriculum through a divergent, open-ended process that enables people to negotiate their differences. That's what young children do in cooperative play. We think teachers can do it, too.

Many administrators and teachers are looking for curriculum formulas, following the example of elementary education, which has relied heavily on the formulas provided by workbooks, texts, and tests. There are plenty of formulas available. "If you do it this way, it will work," promise many of the commercial exhibits at early childhood conferences. Many conference goers want to believe it; they're shopping for magic.

There is no magic except the magic we create for ourselves. Humbug magicians play tricks and, in doing the same tricks over and over again, astound each new audience. Today's young children spend hours as members of the TV media audience, astounded by the magicians on the screen. Some teachers are tempted by this starring role. But young children, as learners, are active, not passive; they are protagonists in their own spontaneous dramas. They are not waiting for us to entertain them, rather *they* are the wizards, inviting us to join them in their magic making.

In this book we write about curriculum planning as adult play. Like improvisational theater, it requires practiced skills of movement, voice, and response, but there is no script to be memorized. The play really begins only when we meet the children. For young children, new in the world as they are, potential curriculum is infinite; it's everything in the world. As caring adults, we make choices for children that reflect our values; at the same time we need to keep our plans open-ended and responsive to children. As active learners, children are busy

Magic in the Making

How's this for "play that sustains itself?" Yesterday after days of downpour we finally had some glimmer of sunshine and only occasional showers as we played in the yard. Twelve kids were at the gym and all the rest (21) were in the yard. No pushing, shoving, serious fighting at all for two whole hours, even when the "big" kids came back from the gym and joined us. That yard really works!

Wesley and Bing had brought two little plastic containers to school, and indoors they had played with them in various ways, with varying degrees of appropriateness. At one point I had seen these toys flying off the loft and figured it was just a matter of time before a teacher took them away from the boys. But outdoors, in the woods, five boys played a game of hide-and-seek and Easter-egg hunt for just about forever. Someone would hide their eyes and others would hide the toys and then everyone would look for them—these seemed to be the original game rules, with infinite variations.

Kaleb to *Bing,* who was hiding his eyes: "Count to 26."

Bing: "One, two, three . . . I don't know how to count to 26. I'll count to 10."

Kaleb: "No, that's not long enough. Count to 26!"

Bing: "21, 22, 26. I'm ready!"

And so it went. Planning, negotiating, running, yelling, inventing, laughing—on and on and on. I watched and wondered if play of this sort could be captured on video. I doubt that it could, which is too bad because it embodies all the things we have talked about regarding play and much of what Piaget says about real learning (Kaleb *knew* the connection between the length of time in counting to 26 vs. counting to l0), with peer interaction and *no adult needed.*

And it freed me to watch a lovely connection develop between Laine and Bonnie, in which Laine built a "jail" for Bonnie, who repeatedly wandered off only to be sought out again by Laine. Though they wandered all over the map, each one always knew where the other was and wove this game around many other diversions.

Meanwhile, up on the east 40, mass birthday cakes were being concocted of sand and water—strawberry, raspberry, burgerberry, all with quite original candles. And on the giant spool was a "store" which sold juice. You could choose between purple and purple. And the trees were full of kids. And under the trees, Ethan knew, were trolls and snakes and one more woofie.

Reprinted from "From Here to There and Back Again: Settings That Work in Children's Programs" (pp. 131–32) by B.A. Sweeney, (master's project), 1991, Pasadena, CA: Pacific Oaks College. Copyright © 1991 by the author. Used by permission.

making choices for themselves, and the capacity to make wise choices is one of the most important life skills we can give them.

Teaching is a complex task with hard-to-predict outcomes. It is misleading to pretend it can be made simple and rational (though some approaches to lesson planning ask us to pretend that we're really going to do what our plans say). We get better at it with conscientious practice. But none of us ever learns to write the perfect script because teachers' improvisational theater is played out with child actors who are busy writing scripts, too. The socio-dramatic play of young children is quite different from prewritten scripts or games with rules. It is open-ended and continually negotiated by the players, who keep learning through the exchange of worldviews with their peers—and with us. Good teachers are skilled negotiators with children.

No teacher invents curriculum from scratch; we borrow from every possible source and then try to invent moderately functional systems for finding resources when we need them. This isn't a book of formulas, but there are lots of "borrowables" in it. As you read these teachers' story, you'll be doing your own planning of possible curriculum; alert teachers do that all the time. You may think, "I wouldn't do *that*." Or you may think, "Oh, that's a good idea," and try it with the children you teach. By the time you and they are finished with it, it will be a collection of new ideas. That's as it should be.

In an emergent curriculum we take the children as our models and our coplayers. We *are* the stage directors; curriculum is teachers' responsibility, not children's. People who hear the words *emergent curriculum* may wrongly assume that everything simply emerges from the children. The children's ideas are an important source of curriculum but only one of many possible sources that reflect the complex ecology of their lives. Teachers need to have both the ideas and a vision of where the players might adventure together. The teacher, the responsible adult, is the organizer who sets the stage, times the acts, and keeps the basic drama together. On those days when all the parts come together, the result is truly magic.

2

September Staff Days— First Day:

Identifying Interests and Webbing Ideas

During Manzanita Children's Center's move to a new site, it closed for two weeks. Teaching staff had a week's vacation followed by a week of setting up the new environment and getting acquainted with their teaching partners, four of whom are new to the center this fall. The two days at the end of the week have been designated as shared planning time—Staff Days. Ruby has put a lot of thought into structuring them. (Marnie's partner, Gloria, hasn't been hired as yet and misses this planning time. She joins the staff the following week.)

Our plan as observers at this meeting is to keep a low profile, though we may find ourselves drawn into conversation along the way. While we know Ruby well, and she has assured us that the staff have agreed to our presence, some staff members are new and everyone shares the anxiety inherent in a move to new space. And so the two of us arrive a little early, settle ourselves in opposite corners of the room, and prepare to take notes as unobtrusively as possible.

Thursday morning: Identifying interests

Walking in on Thursday, staff are greeted by these directions posted on the wall:

What did you like to do as a child?

Find a partner. Talk to her/him about it.

Go with your partner to write the things you liked to do on the big paper on the wall.

Cover the whole paper with the things everyone liked to do.

People put off the task for a while, getting coffee, chatting, some of them resisting the game, but gradually they pair off.

"Ruby? What age child?" asks someone.

"Any age," says Ruby. "Talk about what you especially remember."

"Well, paper dolls, all over the living room floor," says Bethany to Bob, as she settles herself on the floor, leaning on a cushion, and

Empathy and Perspective Taking

When teachers are encouraged to get in touch with both their own childhood feelings and the feelings of children, they are able to evaluate potential activities in this light.

Empathic teaching requires practice in being in touch with (1) one's own remembered feelings from childhood, (2) one's adult feelings, and (3) the feelings of the children in one's care.

In drawing on one's childhood memories, Bowman and Stott remind us of the risks of making assumptions about the experience of growing up:

> Personal knowledge is a two-edged sword: because teachers can connect with their own feelings and memories of their child-

hood, teachers can draw on a reservoir of emotions and thoughts to inform their understanding of the world of children. But teachers are misled when they use only their own experiences as the hallmarks for the experiences of others, when they fail to recognize the differences between themselves and others. Teachers always run the risk of having their own personal issues evoked by particular children, but when teachers and children do not share cultural experiences, the markers for development are even more difficult to apply.[1]

The cultural diversity that is represented in the Manzanita staff and the dialogue they are encouraged to engage in enables these teachers to appreciate that not all childhoods are alike.

pushes her glasses onto her smooth, greying hair. "I did those mostly by myself. And I had a dollhouse my dad made out of two crates; I really liked that, though it always bothered me that it didn't have any stairs. My cousin's dollhouse did; it was the kind you buy. But mine was bigger.

"When we went camping, my friend Jo and I used our tin cups to make sand cakes we placed all over a big rock next to the stream. We decorated them with grass and flowers and little cones. I still remember how delighted our mothers were when we invited them to come and see.

"We played in vacant lots a lot and along the train tracks behind my house. We chewed grass stems and made whistles out of them—I wonder if I could still do that? And we walked on the tracks and had grass bomb fights when other kids came around."

"We did too," says Bob. He's looking a little tousled this morning, and his jeans have holes in both knees; he'd be right at home in a grass-bomb fight. "And

sometimes we had rock fights. We used to hide a lot in the tall grass and in the bushes, and we'd smoke cigarettes we stole from the store. We traded baseball cards . . ."

As people talk to each other, Ruby is printing "As A Child, I Liked To" on a big sheet of paper. She tapes it on the wall and puts a box of markers on the table. "Are you ready to write?" she asks after a while. Some pairs aren't through talking, and they just ignore her. But gradually it gets crowded around the paper, so she adds another one next to it. Pretty soon it looks something like this.

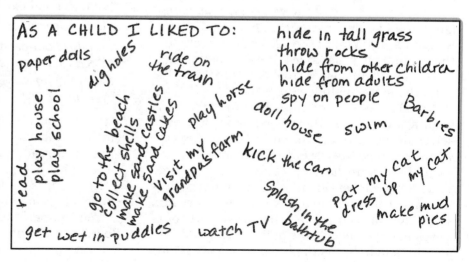

AS A CHILD I LIKED TO: paper dolls / dig holes / ride on the train / play house / play school / read / go to the beach / collect shells / make sand castles / make sand cakes / play horse / visit my grandpa's farm / doll house / kick the can / splash in the bathtub / swim / pat my cat / dress up my cat / make mud pies / Barbies / hide in tall grass / throw rocks / hide from other children / hide from adults / spy on people / get wet in puddles / watch TV

Before the paper is full, Ruby gives one of her shrill whistles—the kind kids do. (We smile at each other from across the room; this is clearly one of her talents.) As people look up, Ruby points to a new set of directions she has added to the wall:

Find another partner. Tell her/him about the things you like to do now as an adult.

Go with your partner to write the things you like to do now on the other big paper on the wall. Cover the paper with everyone's interests.

When this second round of conversations is done, and the "As an Adult I Like To" is filled, Ruby points to *more* directions on the wall.

When you're through writing, stand back and look at all the things people have written on both papers. Is there any overlap—that is, are there any things that people liked to do as children that they still like to do as adults?

Of the things that people like to do now, which of them would be appropriate to do with preschool children? Circle any of the ones you think are appropriate.

Then sit down, and let's see what we've got.

"Let's just sit down. I'm tired of all this fun and games. Ruby sometimes goes a bit overboard, for my taste," says Dolores.

We notice that Bethany, who clearly enjoys Ruby's fun and games, thinks they're playful and stimulate thinking, but doesn't say so. She just sits where she can see "As an Adult I Like To . . ." and watches as Bob and Sally busily circle things—Sally's short ponytail bobbing with her energy.

People are milling around, getting tea and coffee, chatting about other things; and Ruby doesn't rush them. We guess that she thinks getting acquainted shouldn't be all structured activities.

Gradually they sit down. It is almost quiet when Ruby starts to talk.

"Look at the adult like-to-do paper," she suggests, "and at the things people have circled as appropriate to do with children. What do you think?"

"It makes a difference whether it's at home or at the center, doesn't it?" asks Sally. "I watch TV with my nephews at their house, but we don't have TV at the center."

"Other day cares have TV," says Mayella. She's settled comfortably on the couch, her ample lap an invitation for a cat or a child—but there are no children or cats here today. "How come we don't?"

"We've got us," says Ruby. "We're interesting enough for kids."

Mayella mutters, and Dolores pats her, smiling her gentle broad-faced smile. This issue of TV is apparently an ongoing argument, and Ruby steps clear of conflict for the time being. She continues with, "The things we do with young children come from all sorts of sources, including things we like to do ourselves. Where we begin, in curriculum planning, isn't as im-

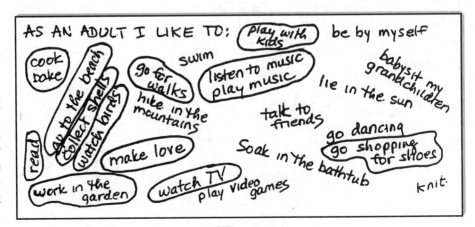

portant as where we go with it and where children go with it.

"I do expect you to plan. But rigid lesson plans are often deceptive; they can't predict what *really* happens, particularly if you're responsive to children's ideas. Why get boxed in by your plans? I think webbing is a more useful planning approach, because it's playful and open-ended. It keeps growing."

"Please, what is that word *webbing?*" asks Yoshiko, picking up her dictionary. She's dressed carefully in a slim, dark skirt and crisp, white blouse for this first meeting with strangers. Sitting erect on a straight chair, Yoshiko pays close attention to Ruby's words.

"Oh, I'm sorry," says Ruby. "A web is what a spider makes. It begins in the middle and goes out in all directions. Only spiders aren't very imaginative; they make the same web every day. We're imaginative, and so we can make webs any way we like. I'll show you. And staff who were here last year have done this before, so they can help." Ruby looks at the papers on the wall.

"'Collect Shells' is something some of us liked to do as children and like to do as adults, too. Suppose you went to the beach this summer, and now you have a collection of seashells. You really like them, but they aren't something you need to keep forever. You think maybe you'd like to share them with the children.

"There are many ways you could do that," Ruby continues. "Some teachers put shells on a science display table, and they're there to look at but not to do anything else with. Some teachers talk about shells at circle time, but 'talk about' isn't how young children learn mostly.

Staff Diversity

Disequilibrium is a predictable outcome of diversity; people with different worldviews and styles of being in the world keep challenging each other's assumptions. New learning is one outcome of disequilibrium; resentment and conflict are others. Just as good early childhood programs devote energy to helping children name their feelings and resolve their conflicts, the adult staff in such programs must learn to do the same, with each other and with parents. The goal is not avoidance of conflict but getting it out in the open and learning to see it through.[2]

"Suppose you've decided that the shells can be played with. What do you think are all the things that might happen, starting with seashells, growing out of both your ideas and the children's? Let's see! We agree that 'curriculum is what happens', " Ruby continues.

"On this big sheet of paper (isn't it good that I brought a lot of paper?) I'm going to write Seashells in the middle. Pretend you're 4 years old and you've just discovered my seashells. What do you want to do with them?"

"Shells belong in the sand. I want to put them in the sandbox," says Sandra, lighting up.

"Me too," says Sally. "I'm going to bury mine so you can't find them."

"Yes, I can. I'll pour water on the sand and make waves to uncover them . . ."

"And then I'll grab them . . ."

"And then I'll hit you . . ."

"And then I'll come and tell you to play nicely," says Dolores. "Behave yourself, you two." They subside with grins. Ruby has been writing some of the teachers' ideas on the paper (though we notice she can't possibly catch them all). Other people volunteer more ideas, and after a while the paper is filled.

Some of the conversation sounds like this:

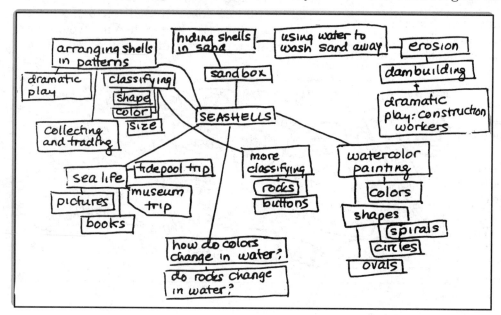

"I brought in seashells last year," says Dolores. "I didn't let children take them outside, but they could play with them on the table. I remember that Lydia and Amalia really got into arranging them in patterns and pretending they were families—Daddy, Mommy, and children. That took me by surprise! Later, some of the kids started claiming some shells for their own, and then they started trading them."

"Did you ask them to classify the shells—like white ones and pink ones and black ones or big ones and little ones?" asks Marnie. Her face has a freshly scrubbed look; she's a bit like a seashell herself.

"Yes, I tried that," smiles Dolores, "but they liked Mommy and Daddy and baby better."

"Couldn't you get into a whole study of sea life? We've got some picture books; I think I remember one about a hermit crab,"[3] Bethany says.

"How about taking kids to the tide pools? I love tide pools," says Bob.

"With a dozen little kids, you love tide pools? You've got to be out of your mind! And what about the insurance?" exclaims Mayella.

"The wonderful thing about brainstorming," Ruby reminds the teachers, "is that the sky's the limit; no idea is too wild. It's a chance to play, and that's what we're doing right now. Webbing doesn't commit us to doing all the ideas on the web; it couldn't. There are always too many of them. So, I'm going ahead and writing down all ideas even if some are impractical."

"Is it OK if we lose the shells along the way?" asks Sandra. "I can imagine that if kids started bringing water to the sandbox, they'd want the hose in the sandbox, and then we'd get erosion on a large scale. We'd have to build dams to keep the water from going all over the yard, and by that time no one would care about shells any more. They'd need trucks and hard hats!" continues Sandra, twisting her long braid and shaking her dangly earrings.

"Isn't that the point of webbing?" Bethany asks. "It makes a picture of the way in which ideas really do connect with each other. And it names all the different pieces of curriculum that just naturally emerge."

"So if I plan a unit on shells and it turns into dam building, that doesn't mean I'm an awful teacher who keeps losing control?" asks Sandra.

"No, it means you're a teacher who's paying attention to children's interests, who's flexible and creative," says Bethany.

"Isn't it lunchtime yet? I'm hungry," says Sally.

Thursday afternoon: Webbing

With lunch over, some people look as if naptime might be their next priority. But Ruby, poised and smiling warmly, is ready with more directions.

Why Do Webbing?

Why do webbing? It gives a staff of adults the chance to explore the possibilities of any material or idea in order to make decisions about use: Is it worth doing? Is it likely to generate developmentally appropriate activities? What are the ways we might want to enrich the activity by being prepared with other materials or questions? How long might children's interest continue?

A web is a *tentative* plan. It doesn't tell you exactly what will happen or in what order. That depends in large part on the children's response. So, first you plan and then you start trying your ideas, *paying attention to what happens,* evaluating, and moving on with further activities.

Make a group of three (exactly three, please, so we come out even). You can go anywhere you like, but take some paper and markers with you. Do three things together:

1. Make a long list, all together: "What have you done with children because it was something you liked to do?"

2. Web at least three of the items on your list. Do more if you'd like to.

3. Put your webs up on the wall in the livingroom; there's tape on the table. And then look for a sign explaining what to do next.

Sandra looks eager. Marnie, sitting next to her, looks doubtful. "When are we ever going to get down to real planning?" she asks. "I thought this was going to be our planning day."

Sandra throws her a what's-the-matter-with-you? glance but says nothing, and Marnie misses it. Bethany joins them with paper and markers, and they decide to go outside on the porch.

"I'll write the list," volunteers Sandra. "What have you done because you liked it?"

"Read stories," Bethany begins, "especially to my own kids at home. I've always said that I had all those kids so I could spend years reading children's books and going camping—though again, that was mostly with my own kids. But we used to go camping with the primary class I taught, too. I like taking kids on moonlight walks—no flashlights allowed. In the daytime I like taking them up steep rocky places."

"Really?" says Sandra. "That's not my thing at all. I like being in cozy rooms with kids. I like singing and dancing with them. I love cooking for my family, and I like cooking with kids too. Last year we even baked bread and made pizza from scratch."

Bethany has clearly been thinking. "I like giving kids real challenges. I like building obstacle courses. One year at a summer camp with 6- and 7-year-olds, I introduced campfire building. I thought that was an important skill for older kids to learn before we went on our overnight; but really what I liked was the drama of it and the reality of the need to keep it safe. I got to be a meaner "teacher" than I usually am (usually I'm a pushover), and my insistence on rules made sense to the kids; fire is *important* stuff."

"I'd never thought about that aspect of cooking—the reality part about keeping it safe—but I like that too," says Sandra. "And I like giving parties; when we bake bread, I make snack time into a real celebration. I also like dressing up; so do the kids, and they think it's pretty crazy when I do it, too."

"I like bringing snakes to school, and lizards," Bethany remembers. "My family gave me a gopher snake for Christmas one year, and he lived at school for a while. It was interesting seeing which kids liked to hold him and which ones were scared."

Marnie hasn't said a word, but they haven't given her much of a chance.

"How about you, Marnie?" Sandra asks. "What do you especially like to do?"

"What's going on?" Marnie bursts out. "I don't understand all this stuff about just doing things to have fun with children. Doesn't anyone here ever do real planning? I learned to plan activities from cognitive objectives and to think about the reasons for each activity I provide. We might do cooking, sure, but not just because I like to cook. Cooking gives children sensory experience and opportunities to count and classify and see transformations."[4]

Curriculum Is What Happens

In early childhood education, curriculum isn't the focus, children are. It's easy for teachers to get hooked on curriculum because it's so much more manageable than children. But curriculum is *what happens* in an educational environment—not what is rationally planned to happen, but what actually takes place.

The teacher's lesson is on the color blue, and she has several children absorbed in finding things that are blue. But Marguerite is absorbed in fingering the fringe on her collar, and Paco is watching the squirrel in the tree outside the window, and Danny is planning his "Let's see if I can make my teacher mad" curriculum, which may well succeed in displacing hers, at least momentarily. Following an emergent curriculum—for teachers and children—things would begin to look different. If Paco says, "Hey, look at that squirrel!" and other children's interest is caught, the teacher may well decide that blue can just as well happen tomorrow. Or perhaps, children's interest in squirrels and other creatures will be sustained, to the point that it becomes the group's shared focus for the day or week or more.

Still, regardless of what the teacher does, Danny's, Paco's, and Marguerite's actions will be part of what actually happens—the curriculum. Traditional school-type lesson plans, the kind that go in a straight line from objectives to activities to evaluation, oversimplify the teaching–learning process. While practice in identifying the developmental objectives and intended outcomes of each activity is one way to become more purposeful as a teacher, it's an inadequate model of the complexity of the planning task and leaves out altogether the playfulness of it. Moreover, linear planning can lead teachers to ignore the reality of all the significant interactions that happen but never show up in plans at all. An emergent curriculum is a continous revision process, an honest response to what is actually happening. Good teachers *plan and let go*. If you're paying attention to children, an accurate lesson plan can be written only after the fact. It is important to be accountable for what really happens, as distinguished from one's intentions. Teachers are often hoodwinked by their good intentions.

"It surely does," agrees Sandra. "It's always a relief to me when I stop to think about that, that the things I like to do with children are important for their learning. But frankly, I don't usually *begin* by thinking about what children will learn even though that's what I was taught to do. I start with the interesting things in the world, and then I observe children while they're exploring the activity to see what they know, what they're learning, and what their interests are."

"That sounds so casual—almost irresponsible—to me," insists Marnie.

"I've found that too much analysis upfront can get in the way of creating curriculum," offers Bethany. "Creation is playful: What will happen when I put these things together? I don't know until I try it. I try it, and *then* I can analyze: What did happen, and what do I know now that I didn't know before?"

Marnie looks puzzled. Evidently, Bethany's insights aren't helping to clear up her concerns. "When do you meet to plan?" she asks anxiously.

"We're going to have an evening meeting every month for two hours," Sandra explains. "We get paid for it."

"Once a month?" Marnie is incredulous. "How does anyone know what's going on?"

"Staff in each room will do their own planning," replies Sandra, "usually at naptime, or whenever there's a moment during the day. It isn't easy. Some weeks are better than others. Have you taught in day care before, Marnie?" askes Sandra.

"No, I worked at the lab school at my college. Children were there for half-day sessions, and we planned and evaluated daily. I don't know if I'm going to like being with children *all* day."

"You have to know something about working with children, you have to be resourceful and you can't take it too seriously," Sandra advises. "You're not *teaching* children all that time. You're *living with* children. So it's important to meet some of your own needs as well as theirs and to enjoy being with them." [5]

Marnie doesn't seem convinced. We sense that this discussion is far from finished, but Bethany steps in to return their focus to the task at hand.

"What does our list look like? We're supposed to pick some things to web," Bethany reminds the other two. After some discussion they agree on cooking, Legos® (Marnie's contribution), and snakes. Marnie and Sandra aren't sure they want to think about snakes, but Bethany does. So they begin with snakes to get it over with.

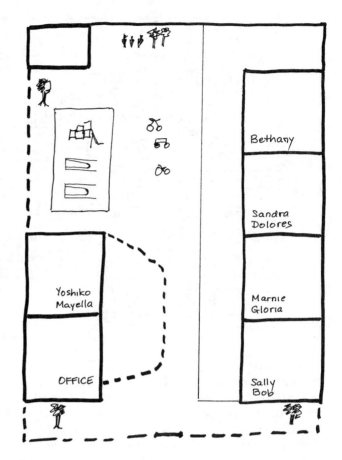

"*Why* do you like snakes?" asks Sandra. "I think they're gross."

"I like the way they slither," explains Bethany, "and the feel of their muscles when I'm holding them. I think they're beautiful; they're so smooth. So why do you think they're gross?"

"Well, for one thing they're dangerous. Some are deadly dangerous!" says Marnie.

"Not all the snakes that live here," answers Bethany. "Sure, rattlesnakes are poisonous, but they're easy to tell from other snakes. I want to teach children the differences, not just teach them to be scared."

"But they *are* scared," Sandra says. "They'll tell you snakes are gross, too."

"Well, some will, and some won't. Some kids are like me. It sounds to me as if we have some good, solid curriculum here on being scared, on what you can do when you're scared—crying, and running, and hiding, and finding someone to take care of you—and on what things are dangerous. I remember a 6-year-old who made a whole book about things that were dangerous. He was learning to write, and he worked very hard on it because it was so important to him."[6]

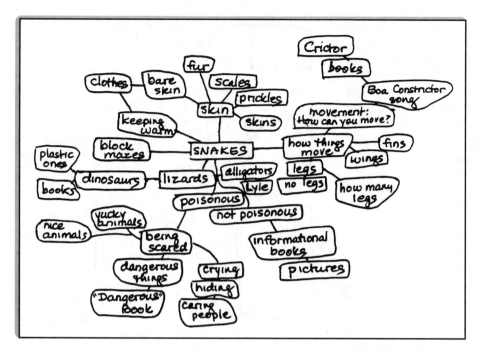

The web diagram contains the following labels: Crictor, books, Boa Constrictor song, fur, scales, prickles, skins, Clothes, bare skin, skin, movement: How can you move?, keeping warm, how things move, fins, plastic ones, block mazes, SNAKES, legs, wings, books, dinosaurs, lizards, alligators, Lyle, no legs, how many legs, poisonous, yucky animals, not poisonous, nice animals, being scared, informational books, dangerous things, crying, hiding, pictures, "Dangerous" book, caring people

time I got interested in the alphabet, seeing the pictures of the snake making the letters," says Marnie.

"Snakes like to be held because people's hands are warm," Bethany mentions. "Cold-blooded and warm-blooded are hard for young children to understand, but they can think about ways to keep warm—like people wearing clothes and animals wearing fur."

"Well, I like some of these ideas, but I still don't like snakes," decides Marnie. "If I did any of this I'd begin with plastic dinosaurs. Can we do Legos now?"

And so they web Legos, and Marnie, back on familiar territory, is enthusiastically involved (see chapter 6 for what happened with Legos.) Now they move on to Sandra's idea: cooking.

"OK, we can have recipe picture cards," Sandra begins. "Or we could try what my friend Deanna did in her class—she gave a small group of 5-year-olds cups of powdered sugar and milk and vanilla and said, 'Here, invent the frosting for our carrot cake.'[9] They did, too, with lots of great conversation."

"I like that. But I don't want to have foods with sugar. So I talk with kids about foods that are good for you," says Marnie.

"Careful of those talkabouts!" Bethany warns.

"It's never just talking. We get into conversations while they're doing. All those skills to be practiced—stirring, pouring, and . . ." Sandra explains.

"Cooking takes so much adult supervision though. If you're cooking with a group, how do you manage the rest of the room?" asks Marnie.

"With 4s and 5s I often set up 'uncooking' with picture recipes and ingredients that don't need cooking," says Sandra. "You know, peanut butter on celery and things like that. I help kids the first few times and then they know how to do it.

"Last year a couple of children had big sisters who liked coming in after school to help. So we did major cooking projects in the late afternoon—soup (the kids had loved reading *Stone Soup*,[10] and that set us off) with all kinds of vegetables, then different kinds of rice and the different ways you can eat it."

"You know, I have a friend in Australia," Sandra pipes up, "and there most snakes *are* poisonous. She says that kids are fascinated by snakes because they're scary. I suppose that good curriculum makes kids feel, as well as think. Besides, if you start with snakes, you'll get into other reptiles, won't you? Lizards. And dinosaurs—endlessly. And alligators. And you can read *Lyle Lyle Crocodile*.[7] At this point, we both realize that Sandra is beginning to find her own way into "snake" curriculum.

"When I brought in my snake, the kids wanted to watch it move along the floor," Bethany remembers. "They built it mazes out of blocks. They wanted to build it houses out of blocks, too, but that made me nervous. I was afraid it would get squished."

"They could build the house for the plastic dinosaurs. That would be safer," says Marnie.

"But not as interesting," says Sandra, "because the dinosaurs won't try to get out. But then again, maybe they would. I've seen some pretty convincing dinosaur play in my classroom."

"Snakes don't have legs, so they move differently. There's a whole study unit on how things move," Marnie adds.

"As long as we don't just talk about it. Kids need to see it, and *do* it. How can you move?" comments Sandra. She looks ready to move, herself. "Can you move like a snake? A kangaroo? A dinosaur?"

"We could sing 'I'm being eaten by a boa constrictor.' And we could read *Crictor*.[8] I loved that story when I was 4. My mom says that's the first

"Didn't you say you'd done baking, too, Sandra?" Bethany asks. "That's more than I'd want to tackle; but then my yeast bread turns out to be pizza. I don't think I have the knack."

"With baking powder it's easy. But we've done yeast baking when we had a volunteer grandmother. We've made *masa*, too, and some pretty unusual tortillas."

"It's lucky for children that different grown-ups like to do different things, isn't it?" says Bethany.

The teachers look at each other, in agreement about this point at least. It is time to return for a wrap-up discussion. The other groups have already taped their webs to the wall and are looking at the potential curriculum generated by their colleagues.

"We're webbed out," Dolores calls to Ruby. "It's a useful tool and we'll keep using it—you'll make sure we do! The walls look like the spiders have been having a field day."

The teachers laugh. Bethany, though, is looking uneasy and remarks, "You know, with all these ideas we could enrich kids' experience for months. But isn't it too soon to be worried about enriching? We're moving a program into a whole new space, with some new adults and kids. Shouldn't we be keeping it simple for a while?"

"You're absolutely right," agrees Ruby. "And beginning with teachers' interests as a source of curriculum certainly isn't how you do that. We're all too complicated! I chose that focus today to help us get better acquainted with each other and to encourage you all to do some of the things you like to do simply *because* you like to do them. Hopefully, this will become part of your curriculum as the year goes on.

"To get started, I like to begin with the physical environment, and that's what we'll be looking at tomorrow. If we set up an environment for children to explore—richly provisioned—and if we pay attention to what they're interested in, that's how our curriculum will start to grow. Our own interests will come in as they connect with children's interests or as we find that children aren't bringing up something we think is important for them to understand."

"Or even, as the year goes on," adds Mayella, "when we just get worn out and bored and want to try something new."

Ruby nods in agreement. She sees this is a good time to bring the day's discussion to a close. Knowing the skills of her staff, she has asked Sally and Dolores to share a song from a workshop they recently attended. Sally somewhat nervously takes the lead from Ruby. "This is one we particularly liked. We'll need your help, though!"

While walking on the beach, I looked at the sky,
I saw a seagull flying by.
Thought to myself, oh me, oh my,
Oh I wish I could fly . . . .

While riding in my boat, I looked in the water,
Saw myself a big grey otter.
Says to myself, oh me, oh motter,
How I wish I could swim like an otter.

While walking in the grass, I looked around,
Saw a gopher tunneling in the ground,
Says to myself, oh me, oh munnel,
How I wish I could tunnel . . . .[11]

It turns out to be an emergent song, of course. Bob was walking in the swamp, a little bit later, saw himself an ol' alligator. Sally went to the garden, started to dig, and who should come along but a big, fat pig? Just the sort of on-the-spot inventing that teachers of young children need to practice! But this isn't practicing, it's having fun for themselves. And adults who work with children do need to do that together.

3

September Staff Days— Second Day: Environment As a Source of Curriculum

Friday morning: Beginning with the environment

"As I said yesterday," begins Ruby, "when I'm teaching, I start with the physical environment. Do you?"

"That makes it easy," says Marnie. "You just set up your areas. The house area, the block area, the . . ."

"I don't think it's that easy," says Dolores. "Why a house area? And how do you know what to put in it?"

"I was trained in a curriculum that develops specific cognitive concepts," explains Marnie. "It's all very clear what you do and why."

"I've read something about that," Bethany says. "I thought it sounded like a useful starting point. But the areas you're talking about are all indoors. What about the outdoors? Especially at this time of year, that's where I want to be with kids. It's easier to stay cool, too, if there's lots of water play."

"I know sensory experience is important for children's learning," agrees Marnie. "But the

Environment As an Invitation

"The teacher's contribution to play always begins with the physical environment, with stage setting. Developmentally, physical knowledge comes first," advises *The Play's the Thing.*[1]

Teachers of young children begin by provisioning the environment with accessible, open-ended materials and tools, and an inviting aesthetic. In turn, the environment invites young children to action. Children in action can be observed by teachers, with the goal of getting to know them. Cassidy and Lancaster tell us that "Careful observation will reveal what is individually appropriate for each child in the class as well as interests that are shared."[2]

That's how the curriculum starts to grow.

really important environment is the classroom, isn't it?"

"Most teachers certainly think so," says Ruby. "In cold, winter climates that makes sense, but here we can be outside most of the year. That's new for you, isn't it, Marnie? You'd never know it was possible, though, looking at the schedule in public schools. Outdoors seems to be just for recess. And there's never enough to do at recess, so kids are always getting into trouble. Remember those yard teachers with their whistles? I hated recess when I was a kid."

"At the center where I worked last year, our yard was like that," volunteers Bob. "It was a child care program in a public school, and it had the usual asphalt playground with swings and climbers and slides. There was lots of sand but no tools or anything to use in it. Water was a no-no. Kids ran a lot and got hurt a lot. Adults yelled a lot.

"The most creative kids picked up trash. And they invented games with it—cups and plastic bags to put sand in, and pieces of cardboard to slide on. One day some of the boys invented and played a whole football game with a plastic bottle for the ball."

"How did you stand it?" Sally asks.

"Well, I'm not there any more, you notice!" says Bob. "Mostly, I organized ball games when

---

Emergent Football

For half an hour, up to seven boys are involved in a self-initiated football game, with a plastic detergent bottle for a ball. The teacher has appointed as referee, Christopher, who had recent hip surgery and is walking awkwardly.

"Hike, hike"—Christopher gets the bottle and throws it into play. A little later he gets a small toy to use as a whistle, and pretending to blow it, he shouts, "Listen to what the referee says. Gimme the ball, gimme the ball, OK?"

"You have to hike."

"It's his turn!"

"He already had a turn!"

It's clear that these 3- and 4-year-olds know a lot about football. Here comes the huddle, for the first time.

For the most part, the play continues smoothly and cooperatively, but teachers can be helpful. As a boy discusses the rules with a teacher, she clarifies, "No, you can't kick him. If you do, you get a penalty."

Reprinted from "Observation Notes: Play and Language Development" (v. 1) (n.p.) by E. Jones & G. Reynolds, Pacific Oaks Occasional Paper, 1989, Pasadena, CA: Pacific Oaks College. Copyright © 1989 by the authors. Used by permission.

---

the ball wasn't popped and chasing games—the other adults didn't approve at all. I was always getting in trouble for breaking the rules—just like the kids."

"Before I came here I had to work in a center like that, too," Dolores remembers. "But I couldn't leave until Manzanita came along; I needed the job. Even at Manzanita's old site our only outdoors was a parking lot! Ruby got us taking things outside. Remember, Ruby? We were brainstorming way back then.[3] Here we are with a new center, and I guess we're in for it again."

"You're right," says Ruby. "We'll certainly be getting to that. Today, though, let's begin with what we've got. You've all been in the yard, though the kids haven't yet. Think positive! What do you like about it?"

"It's big," says Bob. "There's room to run. Maybe it's too big—but I'm not supposed to say that now, am I?" Bob grins.

"It's got swings," says Mayella. "Kids like swings. I like pushing kids on swings; it's restful. You can just stand there and the swing goes back and forth, back and forth . . ."

"Just like your rocking chair," Ruby says. "I like swings, too. Kids get such satisfaction from learning to pump."

"I'm glad you like pushing swings, Mayella, because it's my least favorite thing to do," Bethany admits. "What I like is all the sand under the swings and especially under the climber and the slide where children can play in it. And I like the faucet being near the sand, so there can be water in the sand. You can do so much more with wet sand than with dry sand."

"I wish it had grass—sorry—but I'm glad it's got trees," says Dolores. "I saw a squirrel on one the other day, and there are birds. Children need living things, besides themselves, outdoors."

"I know people think chain-link fencing is awful, but when I was in school I liked it because you could see through it," says Marnie a bit shyly. "At the lab school we had a solid board fence; adults found it very attractive, and it kept out the street noises. But don't children like street noises and watching cars go by?"

"The little children, the 2-year-olds, need a small, safe space, I think," says Yoshiko thoughtfully. "Can we make that for them?"

"Yes. We'll be talking about that, and if I forget, remind me," answers Ruby. "First, though, let's try something else as we're thinking about what we like in an environment." Ruby continues, once again in charge. "This is a relaxation activity. Some of you look ready to go to sleep any minute, but don't, quite yet.

———

"Just stay where you are unless anybody would rather lie on the floor, but move your body around until you get comfortable. Relax. Shut your eyes. Rotate your neck slowly. Clench your fists —and let them go. Take a deep breath— let it out. Take another deep breath. Another."

Ruby is talking quietly and slowly, with long pauses between her words. She sounds as if she is breathing deeply, too.

"Now, go back in your memory and imagination to a place that was important to you in your childhood—some place you liked very much. Where did you like best to be?

"If you can't think right away, stay relaxed and just let your mind wander. Maybe a place will come to you.

"If you've found your place, settle down in it. Look around you. What do you see?

"What is touching your body? What does it feel like?

"Breathe in deeply. What do you smell? What does your place smell like?

"Listen! What do you hear? What are the sounds in your place or surrounding your place? Is it quiet? Noisy?

"What do you like to do in your place?

"Spend a few minutes being in your place, doing whatever it is you do there. Then, when you're ready, say goodbye and come back out of your memory, slowly, to your adult self in this room at this time. Don't hurry.

"When you're ready, open your eyes."

After a pause, Ruby goes on. "Some of you may really have been back in your childhood, but for others maybe nothing happened at all. That's all right; guided imagery doesn't work for everyone. You just got a chance to relax.

"If you did remember a place, would you like to talk about it?"

———

Sally is stretched out full length on the floor. "I had a little nest in the grass," she says dreamily. "Grass used to be so TALL then. I don't think it is any more; have you noticed that? And nobody knew I was there because the grass was so tall. I used to just lie there and watch the clouds. The grass smelled like grass—a wonderful smell. And it tickled. There must have been noises, but I don't remember any . . ."

"For some reason I remembered being under my house, though I don't think I went there

more than once or twice," Bethany says wonderingly. "My parents' house had a basement under part of the house, but the rest was just dirt, crawl space, and was it dirty! I guess my friend and I dared each other to explore it; we were sure there were black widow spiders, and there probably were. It felt forbidden and dangerous, and we got most splendidly filthy. I don't remember what our mothers said; maybe that's just as well."

"Oh, I got filthy climbing down a steep wall above the train tracks by hanging on to the honeysuckle vines," says Marnie. "My brothers played there all the time, and one day on the way home from school I joined them on the wall. I got spanked for getting my dress dirty, too.

"But that wasn't the place I remembered. I remembered the porch swing at my grandma's. It was one of those old striped-canvas ones with a metal frame and a chain suspending it from the frame. When I was there, it was my special place. I played with my dolls there, putting them to bed and giving them medicine. I liked having my dolls be sick. They cried when they were sick, and I rocked them on the swing and took their temperatures . . ."

There is more. Ruby asks just one question when everyone who wants to talk has talked: "How many of our places were indoors?" Only one, it turns out; the teachers agree that under-the-house doesn't count as indoors. All the rest were outdoors.

"That's interesting, isn't it? We've been remembering lying in the grass and getting dirty and finding bugs and taking risks and playing with dolls . . . . Are those important experiences for kids? Can we provide them for the children at the center?"

"There's no grass," says Dolores sadly.

"There's dirt, though," says Bob, "around the trees and along the fence."

"And lots and lots of asphalt and all that cement porch. I'm glad we have a covered porch," says Sandra.

"And sand. Lots of sand," adds Sally.

"So children can really experience a variety of surface textures, can't they?" says Ruby. "Is that important, do you think?"

"Yes," says Yoshiko, suddenly decisive. "Children need to get skills in using their bodies. The yard should not be all flat. Little children need to walk on hills and on rocks. On ground that has . . ." She gestures with her hands, and Dolores asks, "Bumps?" Yoshiko laughs. "Yes, bumps in it."

"Isn't that what climbing equipment is for?" asks Marnie. "That's designed for physical skill practice."

"Yes, but it is all the same," explains Yoshiko. "It is designed by people who plan and measure and make it all just right. Rocks are different. Each rock is a different shape. The child must learn to know each rock and learn the different ways to balance on different rocks."[4]

It is during this discussion that we begin to realize the important contribution Yoshiko's sensitive understanding of the environment could bring to the group. Indeed, each member of the staff brings with them skills and experience that Ruby seems adept in revealing.

"Man-made equipment is all predictable, isn't it?" asks Bob, thoughtfully.

"People-made," challenges Sally.

"I stand corrected," grins Bob. "Though it's mostly men who make it, and that's part of the problem, isn't it?"

"Yoshiko, thanks for giving me words for something I've only felt in my gut," Bob continues. "The manufactured parts of our environment are all standardized. Of course, that's useful, too. If a child pulls out half a dozen unit blocks, he or she will know they'll all balance neatly. But a child building with rocks or sticks

has to test each one to see how it relates to the others. I like thinking about that!"

"I do too," Bethany says. "So if we're analyzing our outdoor environment, we can look at what's natural and what's manufactured. Do we try for a balance of both?"

"I think so," says Dolores. "Isn't that the point, Ruby, that we try for a balance in almost *everything?*" Laughter follows. But Ruby nods.

"It's not a bad point," Ruby agrees. "At least trying for a balance keeps us thinking about all the possibilities.

"Let's make some more lists. We've got these surfaces:

> asphalt
>
> cement
>
> sand
>
> dirt

and we wish we had grass, so I'll put it on the list in parentheses:

> (grass)

What else do you wish we had? Yoshiko says 'rocks.' Shall we list hills, too? They're not exactly a surface, but . . ."

"Sure, we don't have to be purists. This is *our* list, after all," Bethany says. So Ruby adds

> (rocks)
>
> (hills)

"Then you have to have valleys," grins Sandra. And so they do.

> (valleys)

"The things at the top of the list are what we've got. The things in parentheses are challenges to think about," Ruby reminds them.

"OK, here's another challenge," Bethany says. "I want a jungle. I think children need a jungle—a wild place to explore. It would have dirt and grass; but the grass would be wild grass, and there'd be weeds and bushes and unexpected things."

"This list is getting pretty mixed," says Sandra. "Do the climbers and slide and swings go on it, too?"

"What do you think?" asks Ruby. "I was going to do it differently, but yes, I think they might as well. And I'll add wa-

OUTDOORS WE HAVE (WANT)

Play Places

~~Surfaces~~	Things to Do
asphalt	climb
cement	slide
sand	swing
dirt	run
(grass)	walk
(rocks)	crawl
(hills)	jump
(valleys)	balance
(jungle)	ride a bike
climbers	ride in a wagon
slide	pull a wagon
swings	dig
water	puddle
bikes	pour
wagons	scoop
	look through the fence
	watch squirrels
	watch birds
	listen to birds

Scavenger Hunt

This is a different sort of scavenger hunt—one in which you bring back descriptions of things rather than the things themselves. List what you find in each category below. Explore the whole environment. Try to see it from a child's perspective.

1. Find 3 places where you could go to be high up.

2. Find 3 places you might go to to get cool on a hot day.

3. Find 4 things that children could balance on.

4. Find 3 places where children are likely to run.

5. Find 3 places where children are likely to sit quietly.

6. Find 3 places where you could dig a hole.

7. Find 4 places you could go to be all by yourself.

8. Find 4 things (not made for the purpose) that children could use to make music.

9. Find 4 things children could build with.

10. Find 5 things children might use to learn about counting.

11. Find 4 activities that would be a physical challenge—a risk—for a young child.

12. Find 5 soft places.

13. Find 4 kinds of things from which a child might learn about differences in size.

14. Find 3 objects: (1) a pendulum, (2) an inclined plane, and (3) a lever.

15. Find 3 living things that children might want to investigate.

16. Find 4 activities that would be more interesting for a child to do with another child than alone.

17. Find 3 places that are good for watching what's happening inside the yard.

18. Find 3 places that are good for watching what's happening outside the yard.

19. Find the 1 place that seems most beautiful to you.

20. Find 1 place that's ideal for yelling. (Try it.)

---

ter, too, since that faucet is there, all ready to turn on."

climbers

slide

swings

water

"There are bikes and wagons in the shed," Dolores reminds her.

"And all we have to do is open the door. OK, on they go."

bikes

wagons

Ruby waits, but no one says anything more. "So now we have a list of play places, don't we? Can you make a list of activities to go with it? What can the children *do* in our yard?"

"Climb. Slide. Swing."

"Run." "Walk." "Crawl." "Jump." "Balance."

"Ride a bike. Ride in a wagon. Pull a wagon."

"Dig." "Puddle."

"Puddle?"

"Well, what *do* you call it when you pour water in sand and watch what it does?"

"Pour. Scoop." "Look through the fence. Watch squirrels. Watch birds." "Listen to birds."

The ideas slowed. "We certainly don't have everything listed. So, what are the kids digging and pouring with?" asks Ruby. "Shovels? Pitchers?"

"Sure, kids can dig with their hands, but we've got plenty of sand tools. What *are* you fussing about?" Mayella says impatiently.

"Am I fussing? Sorry," says Ruby. "It's just that we take for granted how things like sand tools add to children's play. How well an outdoor play environment works depends a lot on the availability of 'loose parts.' Those are things that children can move around and combine with other things. Sand tools are one kind of loose parts. They stimulate both sensory-motor play and dramatic play—cooking and road building and all that. What other kinds of outdoor loose parts can you think of?"

"Tires and crates," calls out Bethany, "and what about . . .?"

"Ruby, stop!" says Dolores firmly. "You're trying to get us to complicate everything again, just like you were yesterday. We haven't even *been* in this yard with children yet."

Loose Parts

"The presence of 'loose parts,' which can be combined by imaginative children or teachers as the need arises, contributes greatly to the potential richness and complexity of any learning environment," suggests a handbook for teachers on the dimensions of teaching–learning environments.[5]

Simon Nicholson's "theory of loose parts" says

> In any environment, both the degree of inventiveness and creativity, and the possibility of discovery, are directly proportional to the number and kinds of variables in it . . . most environments that do not work . . . do not do so because they do not meet the "loose parts" requirement. Instead, they are clean, static, and impossible to play around with. What has happened is that adults in the form of professional artists, architects, landscape architects, and planners have had all the fun playing with their own materials, concepts and alternatives, and then builders have had all the fun building the environment out of real materials. And thus has all the fun and creativity been stolen; children and adults and the community have been grossly cheated . . . .[6]

"Children, like adult designers and builders, need loose parts with which to design and build for themselves," concludes an article in *Child Care Information Exchange*. "In environments which offer the possibility of discovery and inventiveness, children's play sustains itself. In environments devoid of loose parts, children get into trouble. It isn't very difficult to change one environment to the other."[7]

Ruby subsides, her momentum suddenly blocked. Sally, thinking out loud, speaks up. "The outdoors is new to all of us," she says. "I think maybe, first thing, I'd like to take the kids outside on an 'expedition,' as Pooh would say, and let them find out what's there. We need to explore for a while before we start adding things."

"For 5-year-olds, yes. But that will not work at all for 2-year-olds," says Yoshiko. "The yard is very big for 2-year-olds. Little children need a small, safe space."

"You said that earlier, but I wanted to do something else then; I promised you we'd get to it, and here we are," says Ruby, pouncing on a promising tangent in the discussion. "How would you like to make a small, safe space, Yoshiko?" she asks.

"Can there be a little fence? In the space outside our door?" Yoshiko replies.

As observers, we could see how easily the needs of the younger ones could be swallowed up by preschool curriculum.

"Yes, there can," says Ruby in response to Yoshiko's request. "We have the loan of some snow fencing, and . . ."

"Pardon me? Fencing for snow?" Yoshiko is thoroughly puzzled. So, by the look on her face, is Sandra.

"Oh, sorry. It's flexible fencing that comes in big rolls . . . it's easy to move around. It's used in the mountains to keep snowdrifts off the roads; that's why it's called snow fencing." explains Ruby.

"I see," says Yoshiko politely. Though the English language remains a constant challenge for Yoshiko, what matters is that she will be able to create the space she has envisaged.

"Snow fencing will let us decide if and where we want fences without committing ourselves for a while. It's a loose part," Ruby adds with a smile. "I don't know any way to plan everything and have it work the way you all thought it would. So we'll be playing with our outdoors, just as the children do."

"And speaking of playing . . ."

"Oh, oh, here we go again," says Dolores, under her breath.

Ruby forges on, regardless. "Take this scavenger hunt list outdoors and work with a partner, someone who isn't your teaching partner and whom—you weren't with earlier in a small group. Will that work out? Yes, I think so."

———

Yoshiko and Sally find themselves together and begin to talk through the list.

"High up," says Yoshiko. "One climber, two climbers . . ."

"And 'Oh, how I like to go up in a swing,'" Sally finishes. "That's an English children's poem, Yoshiko.[8] That was easy. Next?"

"To get cool," reads Yoshiko. "There is the covered porch."

"I think that will be cool in the morning but not in the afternoon," Sally guesses. "We could make a cool place in the sand by watering it. We could make the dirt cool in the same way. I wonder how much shade there is under those trees?"

"Children can get drinks at the drinking fountain," says Yoshiko. "And we can have a wading pool full of water when it's really hot."

"That's more than three, and we've hardly started," Sally says, pleased.

They decide that children could make music by drumming with their heels on the slide, by running a stick along the chain-link fence, by banging sand tools together, and by hitting a wagon with a shovel. They can't think of five soft spaces. Although the whole sand area is soft, it seems like cheating, they decide, to divide it up into five sections. "If the wind blows, will there be leaves under the trees?" Yoshiko asks. Sally thinks so, but she asks, "It's a hard yard, isn't it?" Yoshiko agrees. That will be something for everyone to think about.

They agree that a swing is a pendulum and a slide is an inclined plane. Sally isn't sure exactly what a lever is, and Yoshiko thinks she knows in Japanese but not in English. They experiment with a pencil; and Sally wonders if a shovel could be a lever and how does the handle on a faucet work? They decide they don't have to know everything, and they move on.

They remember that Dolores has seen a squirrel, and they agree that there are lots of ways to investigate a tree. They wonder what kinds of crawly things live in the dirt and think maybe they'll water it and try digging for worms. They can't remember any place particularly beautiful and decide they'll have to go back and look. Finally on the list, Yoshiko is surprised that yelling might be considered a good idea, but Sally says that sometimes children find they have to yell—at the bad guys or at the monsters—and some places are better for doing that than others.

———

Observing what unfolds, we begin to realize that the staff can't help but learn about each other as they work through Ruby's activities. No wonder she is so persistent.

"How did that work?" Ruby asks when the group reconvenes. "Was it useful?"

"I liked it," says Marnie. "That's like analyzing cognitive concepts: What can children learn in this area or in this kind of play?" It is apparent to us that Marnie is starting to see the seriousness in all this play, even if she is still focused on the concepts that she has been trained to recognize.

"What did other people list as risks?" Bob asks. "We agreed that what's a risk for one child is old hat for another. That's partly age and partly temperament. Going down the slide is a big risk for a really little kid. But what about the kids who want to climb back up the slide, or go down it backwards? Should there be rules where risks are involved? Marnie and I started to argue about what the rules should be and then decided that was silly, we needed to know what the rules *are* in this center."

"Well, our curriculum is emergent and so are our rules," says Ruby. "We make them according to our agreed-upon comfort levels and for this year's group of children. And we don't have the same rules for all the children. We might decide that the 4s can go up the slide but the 2s can't. We might even decide that Alex can go up the slide but Sheryce can't, at least not this week, because she isn't careful about looking to see if anyone is coming down."

"I think it would be easier to have one clear set of rules and enforce them," says Marnie. "This other way, don't the children argue with adults about them?"

"Of course," Bethany says. "But we're not trying to eliminate all arguments. That would eliminate opportunities for critical thinking and for involving children as well as adults in the process of calculating risks. If I tell Sheryce she can't slide backwards because it's against the rules, period, then she can't think about how she might do it safely. But if I confront her when she turns around at the top of the slide and say, 'Sheryce, that doesn't look safe to me,' and she says, 'Yes, it is because I'm going to hold on like this and go slow, and Melanie is going to catch me at the bottom,' then I know she's really thought about it. And I might say, 'OK, and I think I'll stand right behind Melanie the first time you come down in case you need two of us to catch you.'"

"Sometimes we'll be sharing supervision of each other's children, won't we?" asks Sandra. "Don't we need to be consistent about rules?"

"I think we need to be consistent about our responsibility for keeping children safe," Bethany says. "But children can learn that different adults have different tolerance levels if adults explain it that way. If a child says to me, 'But Dolores lets me do that,' I can say, 'That's fine, and when Dolores is here you can do it. But when I'm here, you can't because it doesn't make me feel safe, and I'm the person who has to keep things safe right now.'"

"Oh, I like that," says Sandra.

"I don't think I do, but I'll try it. Do I get to argue with you all if I don't like it?" asks Marnie.

"Of course!" Sandra and Bethany say simultaneously.

"Did any more questions come out of the Scavenger Hunt?" Ruby asks.

"Yes, we had trouble with two things," says Dolores, "soft spaces . . ."

"Oh, so did we," Bethany interrupts.

". . . and places you could go to be all by yourself," says Dolores, finishing.

"How about swings and bikes?" asks Mayella.

"For soft or for being by yourself?" asks Sally.

"Being by yourself," explains Mayella. "Lots of times a new child heads for a swing. It's a place to sit by yourself and rock back and forth and watch what's going on."

"Oh, so swings belong to another category, too, don't they? Just a minute, I'll find it: 'Find 3 places that are good for watching things happening inside the yard,' " says Sandra. "Kids really do use them that way. I'm glad we've got swings."

"Swings provide a kind of softness, too. They rock you, like Mayella says," adds Ruby.

"Exactly what do you mean by softness?" asks Marnie. "I suppose it should be obvious, but . . ."

"It's worth thinking about," says Ruby. "Soft things have sensory responsiveness. When you touch water, or a sling swing, or a pillow, or a furry animal, it responds to your touch; it moves. It doesn't resist you like a hard floor or a chair.

"People design leisure environments to be soft. Think about your living room. In child care we're *living* with children."

"Leisure environment? I like that," says Bob.

"That's a really new idea for me," says Marnie slowly. "I think of preschool as being a work environment for children and for teachers. It's a place where important learning goes on. It isn't just baby sitting."

"You're right. But I like to think of it as being more like a home than like a school. Caring for young children is something that has usually

Rules That Emerge?

Beyond genuine issues of safety, rules are often arbitrary forms of social control, but they could be opportunities for responding to the democratic rights of a group. Each of the adults and children in a group has a temperament, culture, and developmental profile that can help the responsible teacher determine the appropriate rule for a particular situation. Taking into account individual and cultural differences may, at times, override the need to be universally consistent in the application of preset rules in group care and education.

Rules can also be developed "retroactively" by providing opportunities for the older preschoolers to reflect on the consequences of their actions. Jesse Goodman explains this form of power sharing at an elementary school:

> At Harmony, a conscious effort was made to keep teacher-defined, predetermined rules to a minimum . . . . Harmony had one broadly stated rule that was used as a criterion for regulating the interpersonal behavior of teachers and students. Referred to as "Harmony's Golden Rules," it stated, "Harmony is a *safe* place [free from being hurt or abused] for teachers' and students' bodies and feelings." Rather than having lists of "do's and dont's," the elementary school established most rules *retroactively* with students' partici-

pation as a result of their becoming aware of the negative consequences of specific situations. For example, specific rules governing such behavior as . . . . teasing each other, eating during meetings . . . . were decided during classroom discussions or Program or Family meetings as a result of specific instances which occurred during the school year.[9]

One of the teachers at the school referred to by Goodman expressed the following rationale for this "retroactive rule making":

> Up until now, we have consciously avoided setting up rules at the beginning of the year because we wanted the kids to understand that rules are tied to concrete situations of living. We haven't wanted students to simply 'follow rules' that they have no history in making and no idea of why they are needed in the first place. We have wanted them to help make rules that are necessary in order to live in our school.[10]

An emergent approach to rule making involves negotiation, risk taking, and a willingness to deal with complexity—and it is not always the appropriate approach to take. When safety is threatened, when children are needing the security of clear limits, or when fairness and a sense of community call for a rule evenly applied, consistency is a critical consideration. As always, the teacher acts as the intelligent decision maker.

happened in homes.[11] A good home provides softness and privacy; it's a place you can be comfortable with people who care for you," says Ruby.

"And softness helps make people comfortable," says Dolores, "and I don't think we have enough of it."

"What did you list as soft?" asks Sandra

"Sand—lots of that," says Dolores. "And water—we need to make lots of that available. We didn't think of swings as soft, so we can add those."

"Laps provide soft places for children, don't they?" asks Bethany. Realizing this, she continues, "But we won't have laps outside unless there are comfortable places for adults to sit. How about gym mats? Can we get a couple of those? And take out pillows and blankets?"

"Is there enough dirt for digging?" asks Bob.

"Why do we need dirt? There's sand," says Marnie.

"Yes, but dirt is different," says Sally. "It's harder. And it's dirtier! I think children need experience with all the different forms earth takes—rocks and gravel and sand and dirt and MUD! We certainly have some fond memories of getting dirty!"

"Don't parents object if children get dirty?" asks Marnie. "Mine spanked me."

"Yes, often," says Ruby. "We try to respect their concerns, while letting them know how important we think it is that young children have lots of sensory experience. We encourage them not to dress children too nicely. Though that's hard for some families—it can be equally important to look good when you step out into the community. So, we make sure to also keep a supply of 'work clothes' at school."

"Paint on clothes bothers parents at least as much as dirt," says Dolores. "But we're not about to give up painting. And there's another way we can add to softness outdoors, by bringing out paint and play dough and all those good things. That's a useful list, Ruby."

Ruby looks pleased. Even directors need strokes.

"Could we perhaps have a garden?" asks Yoshiko.

"Yes!" people exclaim in unison. "We do need green things, even if we can't have grass," adds Bob.

"So we've got a lot of getting-started ideas there," says Ruby. "This is such a creative group! Now, what was your other hard one? Private spaces?"

Softness

When we started thinking about softness as a dimension of programs for children, we looked at a lot of things that seemed to make a difference to children's experience in the environment. These were the indicators we decided to use in measuring the softness of a day care center, both indoors and outdoors:

- child/adult cozy furniture: rockers, couches, stuffed chairs
- large carpet or rug: half- or full-size
- grass to be on
- sand to be in: box, pit, or area
- dirt to dig in
- furry animals to hold
- sling swings
- play dough
- very messy materials: finger paint, clay, mud, water added to sand
- water as an activity
- "laps" available for children to sit on

The basic quality common to all the softness indicators is sensory responsiveness. When you touch water, or a swing, or a pillow, or a furry animal, it responds to your touch; it moves. Sensory responsiveness is a crucial quality in any leisure environment—and if full day care cannot be characterized as a leisure environment, its inhabitants, big and little, will almost invariably experience frequent tension and fatigue . . . . Introducing greater softness into an environment makes it more comfortable.

Reprinted from Dimensions of Teaching–Learning Environments: A Handbook for Teachers in Elementary Schools and Day Care Centers *(p. 15) by E. Jones & E. Prescott, 1984, Pasadena, CA: Pacific Oaks College. Copyright © 1984 by Pacific Oaks College. Used by permission.*

"Yes. Mayella says swings and bikes are places to be by yourself, and they are, I realize," says Dolores. "But they're not *private*. Everyone can still see you."

"Don't we have to be able to see children all of the time?" asks Marnie.

"Is that your requirement?" asks Yoshiko. "In Japan that is not so. Children know the rules and they take care of each other. The teacher is responsible, certainly, but she is not watching every minute."

"Don't children ever get hurt in your preschools?" asks Ruby.

"Yes, sometimes. Not often, but sometimes," says Yoshiko.

"What do the parents do?" asks Ruby.

"Usually they say they are sorry that their child has not been careful," explains Yoshiko.

"In this country, some parents are more likely to sue the school," explains Ruby in turn. "I wish our parents were more like yours. Then perhaps we could trust children more.[12]

"Even so, I don't think we necessarily have to *see* our children every minute. At home children have lots of opportunity to be out of adults' sight and make decisions about what they're going to do. That's how they develop moral judgment! It's a real loss for them in child care, I think, to be always watched. So the question for me is, how can we provide safe privacy for kids?"

A "Grassroots Curriculum"

A curriculum is grassroots in the sense that it is responsive to the "common people"—the children and teachers who frequently are not influential enough in determining what takes place in early childhood classrooms. Not only teachers and children but parents and others who [have] contact with the classroom also [make] significant contributions to the development of the grassroots curriculum. Of course, the difficulty for all who have attempted to describe curriculum is that there is no one correct way to proceed while considering the influence of these forces. A truly appropriate curriculum will not look the same from one classroom of children to the next nor from one year to the next. Because the curriculum flows from a dynamic social milieu, prescribing a curriculum that will generalize from one context to another is inconsistent with developmentally appropriate curriculum planning. Early childhood teachers can benefit, however, from the experiences of other teachers in other classrooms and the planning strategies that have proven effective in implementing appropriate practice.

Reprinted from "The Grassroots Curriculum: A Dialogue Between Children and Teachers" by D.J. Cassidy and C. Lancaster, 1993, Young Children, 47(6), p. 47. Copyright © 1993 by NAEYC.

"Privacy is sometimes being all by yourself and sometimes being alone with your friend, isn't it?" asks Sally.

"Or alone with a grown-up," adds Sandra. "That's what laps are for."

Dolores jumps in at this point. "You know, softness and privacy and feeling like a home are all important to me. Kids are always scrambling for my lap! But I also think that day care is about being in a group. Maybe it is both more, and less, than a home. Does that make sense?"[13]

There are nods of agreement interspersed with puzzled looks. Ruby seems to know that this issue will probably resurface another day; now it's lunchtime. She looks at the group, clearly pleased. "You've come up with so many useful ideas this morning," she says. "You all keep bouncing them off each other. That's how an emergent curriculum works for children, too. Nearly all of the important ideas *will* come up, over and over, if you set the stage for them. It isn't necessary to *teach* to cognitive objectives. They're simply a way to look at your environment to see if children are having significant learning opportunities."

Friday noon: Reflecting on the process

This is the end of the morning's meeting. The staff move on to eat lunch and plan in their teaching pairs. "Marnie," Ruby calls across the room, "I'll meet with you after lunch, seeing we haven't hired your partner yet."

As we observers are preparing to leave, we overhear Dolores say to Ruby, "I know I give you a hard time about some of those games you try on us, so I wanted to tell you how much I liked that relaxation activity. It really got me thinking."

"Thanks for telling me that," responds Ruby and smiles warmly. "Guided imagery is something I've never had the nerve to try before and I was anxious about it."

We catch Ruby's attention to say thanks and goodbye. Then we drive back to our college together, talking nonstop.

"Ruby's good at group leadership, isn't she?" Betty says. "She certainly had these meetings well planned, and she has a nice sense of timing—when to be flexible and when to pull things together."

John nods in agreement. "It helps to have that much leadership within the staff, too," he adds. "Bethany, Sally, and Sandra really support her and are confident teachers. This center has remarkable continuity in its staff, doesn't it? Dolores and Mayella have been here forever and they're really solid."

"How do you think Marnie will do?" Betty asks. "She seems pretty uncomfortable with this style of working together. Her lab school was undoubtedly more top-down in prescribing curriculum, and she's used to doing what she's told to."

"I don't know," says John. "Her questions will at least push the others to spell out what they see themselves doing. Besides, maybe she'll begin to understand what Piaget meant by cognitive disequilibrium!"

Betty smiles as John continues, "Bob's inexperienced, *but* he's a natural, I'd guess. And everything here is new for Yoshiko, but she obviously knows a lot and is willing to assert herself. Looks like it's going to be an interesting year."

"I do like watching webbing in action," notes Betty. "It's an open-ended, nonlinear way to plan. Teachers can go in any of the web's directions, depending on what happens, and keep adding to it and complicating it. I'll be interested to see if they use it as a way to communicate with parents."

"Or maybe the older children could use webbing as a tool for getting their ideas down on paper," continues John. "Of course, these are new ideas for most teachers; I'd guess we won't see much evidence of them this year. People make changes slowly, I keep relearning; and people want to set their own pace and make their own choices, which is what we want teachers to let children do, isn't it?"

Betty nods in agreement. "I was interested in the scavenger hunt discussion—in watching how it evolved. You could build a whole discussion around any of the items on the list, couldn't you? Do you think Ruby had an agenda she wanted to cover?"

"If she did, it wasn't obvious," replies John. "How did she start the discussion? With a real, open-ended question, I think: 'Was it useful?' And then people raised specific questions, and Ruby encouraged more, and she got to say a whole lot about why she thinks softness is important in child care."

"What if no one had brought up softness? Do you think Ruby would have?" asks Betty.

"I'm sure she'd bring it up at *some* meeting but not necessarily at this one," says John. "It looks to me as if she genuinely believes in emergent curriculum for adults as well as for children. She sets them up for learning about things she thinks are important, just like you do with children. But it looks to me as if

willing to let their questions and interests decide what happens when."

"There's such consistency between adults' and children's learning," says Betty.[14] "I'm impressed by the way Ruby uses concepts like 'softness' to help make thinking about the environment and curriculum more manageable. An experience like curling up on a lap is, of course, different from playing with sand, but making use of the idea of softness helps us focus in on the significant dimension in common."

"I'm sure they'll invent their own theories about curriculum before this year is out!" John adds and smiles.

————

This was a successful visit for us. We agree to attend the monthly staff meetings together. This is the time when we can really gain insight into how curriculum emerges. Between meetings we'll take turns observing at the center. We'll take notes and keep talking to each other about the curriculum that we see unfold over the year.

4

September Visit: Keeping a Record of Our Lives Together

The Staff Days took place at the beginning of September. Later in the month Betty visits the center to observe, being careful to avoid adding to the confusion of all the newness everyone is experiencing. Sitting in odd corners, she enjoys the 3-year-olds' pleasure in sand and water and the ease with which Sandra and Dolores seem to be teaming; she notes with delight the gradual appearance of photos and drawings on the walls. The space isn't just potential anymore, it's becoming lived-in and showing evidence of the people who live here every day.

———

Ruby, camera in hand, joins Betty at the edge of the sandbox. Here, seashells are provoking some pretty fascinating play, which Betty is trying her best to follow. "Loose parts at work?" Betty whispers to Ruby. She smiles.

"Something I really want to emphasize this year," Ruby explains between snapshots, "is keeping a record of our lives here together. I reckon the staff is more likely to take that seriously if I model it and provide real help. So I've promised myself to spend some time in every class every month—taking pictures mostly. Want to help since you're going to be visiting?"

"I'd rather write than take pictures," Betty replies hesitantly. "But I'm sure John would jump at the chance to bring his camera along. Maybe I could draw some pictures. How does that sound?"

"Sure, whatever," Ruby responds. "Photos, drawings, children's words, samples of children's work that can be saved . . . ."[1]

Sally pricks an ear. "What are you folks cooking up out here?" she asks.

"I'll make a deal with you, Sally," says Ruby. "If I take pictures of your kids doing the interesting things you've planned for them and give you the pictures, will you take responsibility for doing something with them? A bulletin board, a class book, children's individual books, communication to parents, a group activity?"

"Wow, I'd like that," says Sally eagerly. "The kids love looking at pictures of themselves and their friends. It's just hard for me to find time to take pictures. When I observe—I mean, really observe—all I can do is watch and listen, not fumble with technology. It must be hard for you to find time, too. What with all our enrollment hassles."

"Fifteen minutes of kid watching helps keep me sane," says Ruby. "It's a good trade-off. I'll leave the pictures in your box."

As Ruby goes back to the office, a small child drips water on Betty's sandaled feet. "See my shells?" the child says. "I got a daddy shell, and a mommy shell, and a teeny, teeny baby shell. They were all in the sand."

Betty writes down the child's words as she admires her shells. "I'll leave this in your box, too," Betty calls out to Sally.

On Betty's way out, she stops by the office for a word with Ruby. "Thank you for coming," Ruby says. "I can see that you're going to be a real help to me in documenting things that happen in the program—especially some of the neat things that busy teachers miss or don't have time to record. I wish I had time to do more of that."

"What do you want to accomplish with the documentation?" Betty asks. "Have you thought that through?"

"I want teachers to become sensitive kid watchers," says Ruby, "to really pay attention to children's play and language and know what they're learning. Asking teachers to keep a record of their observations helps them to pay attention, I'm convinced; certainly it's helped me as a teacher."

"Right. I watched the sand play with the seashells for a half an hour, but there was so much to follow," Betty joins in. "Your photographs and my record of children's conversation will help me better understand their play script."

Ruby nods in agreement. "You have to be a good kid watcher to plan an emergent curriculum; that's how we plan here, with some encouragement from me!

"You also have to watch kids to assess their learning.[2] We've never done a systematic job at this center of keeping portfolios for each child; I'm hoping to start on that this year. And I want to encourage staff to include more than just samples of children's work. We need to find ways to remember, and hopefully understand, how it all came about."

"It sounds as if your documentation is addressed to adults, right?" Betty asks. "For teachers to use in planning and to share with parents so they'll be informed about their children's growth and about what you're teaching the children?"

"That's certainly a big part of it, and it's the part I know most about," says Ruby. "I want

staff to be competent at that. The part I'm learning about right along with them is how children learn from adults' documentation of the children's experiences."

"I can see we're going to be learning a lot from all of you at Manzanita," Betty says enthusiastically. "Thank you again; I'm off. Both John and I will see you at the next staff meeting. I'm looking forward to it!"

Documentation: Memories for Understanding

Documentation of "what happens" in a school setting provides teachers, parents, and children with a storehouse of memories from which to research, plan, and understand. Through documentation the often missed words and actions of young children are captured and made visible, and in so doing families and the community are invited into a relationship of reciprocity with the school.

Nowhere has the process of documentation been so well understood and developed as in the preschools of Reggio Emilia, Italy. In *The Hundred Languages of Children*, Vea Vecchi, an atelierista from the Diana School, offers these insights into the process:

> Recently our interests have also shifted more and more toward analysis of the processes of learning and the interconnections between children's different ideas, activities, and representations. All of this documentation—the written descriptions, transcriptions of children's words, photographs, and now the videotapes—becomes an indispensable source of materials that we use every day to be able to "read" and reflect critically, both individually and collectively, on the experience we are living, the project we are exploring. This allows us to construct theories and hypotheses which are not arbitrary and artificially imposed on the children.
>
> Yet this method of work takes much time and is never easy. And we know that we still have much to learn. The camera, tape recorder, slide projector, typewriter, videocamera, computer, and photocopying machine are instruments absolutely indispensable for recording, understanding, debating among ourselves, and finally preparing appropriate documents of our experience.[3]

5

October Staff Meeting: Who We Are, What We Can Do— and So the Holidays Begin

In early October we join the first monthly staff meeting, held on a Monday evening right after the center closes. For many of the staff who finish up earlier than the six-o'clock closing, this is an occasion for catching up on program preparation and portfolios of each child's work, or maybe some local shopping. Meetings are the beginning of the end to a long day. Tonight we've offered to provide the food for this occasion, in appreciation of the staff's letting us sit in. Based on Betty's observations of last month, we are anxious to see if Ruby's goal of documentation has really caught hold.

We meet in the staff room, which has acquired some soft, if saggy, furniture and bright curtains. Ruby says that this year she's determined to keep a space for adults. This won't be easy; already there are overflow collage materials invading one corner. All of one wall of the room is a staff bulletin board, and we notice that since the Staff Days it has been divided into sections. Some notes have already appeared under the headings.

Ruby invites us to come and meet Gloria, Marnie's teaching partner, who missed the Staff Days in September. Gloria, casually elegant in

> ### Staff Meeting Agendas
>
> Emergent planning needs a clear structure, and it's up to the group's leader to provide it. In a program for children there are always nitty-gritty problems to be solved, and each problem is high on some staff member's priority list. Given half a chance, such problems can be counted on to take over the agenda at any staff meeting: What *shall* we do about late pickups, lack of storage, a difficult child?
>
> At meetings in which the goal is staff development and curriculum planning, such problems should *not* be given even half a chance to make their way onto the agenda. Instead, other problem-solving strategies and communication systems need to be established and made clear to all staff involved. In setting limits and retaining her authority as discussion leader while staying open to the discussion's outcomes, a director not only accomplishes her immediate goals, she also models for teachers their role in guiding emergent curriculum with children.

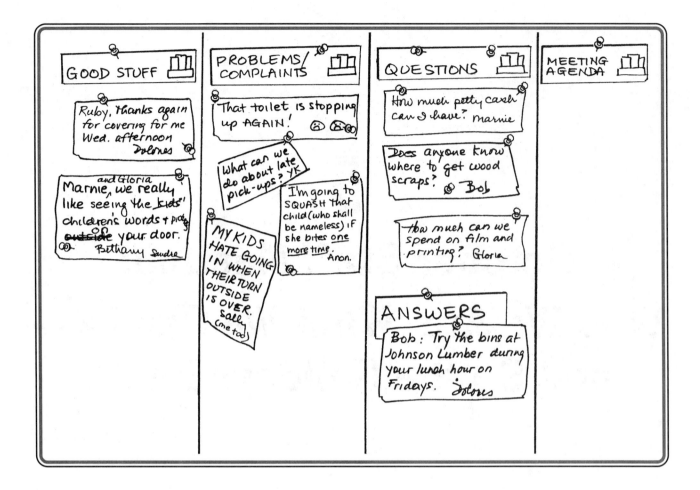

a long handwoven skirt (was she teaching in that, we wonder, or did she change?), greets us, and we chat briefly before Ruby calls the group together.

Ruby comments on the bulletin board as the meeting begins. "This worked pretty well at the old site, so let's try it again. Sometimes it's hard to catch each other face-to-face, and when we have only one whole-staff meeting a month, I don't want to use time for announcements and nitty-gritty problems. I'll check the board every day, but I expect you to, too. I'm not the only one who can answer questions, and I don't want answerable questions brought to meetings. These are program planning meetings for bouncing ideas around.

"The meetings need to be open-ended but not random, so I'm going to be a bit fierce about agendas. Anyone can list agenda items, and I'll plan from them. But if an item hasn't been listed, don't bring it up at a meeting; put it on the board in the appropriate column. I haven't worked with a staff this big before, and I'm concerned about staying focused. If you feel sat on, complain.

"No one else listed agenda items for this meeting, so here are mine:

1. What was the best thing for you that happened in this month's program?

2. What shall we do in October?"

"Best thing, first. Anyone?"
Ruby sits back and waits.

"Water play, lots and lots of it," says Sally. "We've had an ocean in the sandbox, and kids who might otherwise have had a hard time separating from their parents have found that irresistible. It's good that it's been so hot; parents have mostly seen the logic of having water available."

"I've been getting really interested in literacy development,[1] and it's so neat to have an older group this year," says Sandra. "I've been writing their names a lot on choice lists at our morning meeting. And we gave them blank books, and some are inventing writing as well as drawing. We've started to make a class book with everyone's words and pictures in it. I love the idea that children have a 'hundred languages'—that there are many, many ways in which they can represent their experiences."[2]

"This week Sandra and I made a couple of picture recipes, and we've just started trying open

32   EMERGENT CURRICULUM

snack, with kids fixing their own food. The peanut butter balls were a big hit." We could all feel Dolores's enthusiasm.

"I brought back shells from the beach," said Bob. "I got interested when we webbed seashells, Ruby. The kids have been burying them in the sand and digging them up, just like you said. Now, if I can get some wood scraps we can have those in the sand, too, for boats and surfboards and breakwaters. And I thought I might bring my board to show the kids." Clearly, Bob is off and running. We wonder if the children will keep up with him.

"A couple of my kids are into outer space, but I'm not," says Bethany. "I don't think that's appropriate curriculum for 5s; it isn't hands-on. So I told . . ."

"Hold on," interrupts Sandra. "I've found plenty of places to go with Outer Space curriculum. It's about night and engines . . . and power. Traveling to places where things happen differently. I know they don't get the astronomy—but all those wondrous questions!"

"Too much media stuff for my liking," says Bethany. "But maybe my real problem is that

---

Our Choices

Jorge — los carritos

Santos — los carritos

Elena — playhouse

Suzy — blocks

Mavis — blocks

John — blocks

Zhou — painting

Mary Ann — playdough

Ruben — playdough

Samantha — playhouse

Appropriate Curriculum: For the Group—For the Individual

Teachers' and children's interests, as sources of curriculum, always need evaluation in terms of the values held in the school and community, family, and culture as well as in terms of young children's capacity to understand a given topic and to ask useful questions about it. A thoughtful emergent curriculum does not require teachers to actively pursue all of the interests shown by children. There are a myriad of ideas initiated by children in their play, some are fleeting or momentary—exciting at the time   but not the basis for prolonged engagement; others are overly determined by the scripts and images of mass media.

Genuine questions emerge from meaningful relationships and experiences, and teachers have a responsibility to act as one important source of these experiences and, in the process, contribute their passions, values, and beliefs. In deciding what interests to plan for and actively support, teachers need to assess the potential of any interest for in-depth learning by both the individual child *and* other members of the adult–child classroom community. Teachers may consciously choose, for example, not to reinforce children's strong interest in a media drama that glorifies violence. Teachers convinced that early learning takes place through

hands-on experience may choose, if they live in the desert, to steer away from in-depth group explorations of such topics as oceans, tropical rain forests, and . . . outer space.

In any group, on the other hand, one or a few children may have unique interests unrelated to the topic chosen by the teacher to pursue with the larger group—genuine interests sparked by family members, by a book taken home from the library, or by some chance event. Teachers can take small but thoughtful steps to acknowledge and support these interests, confirming the child's disposition to *have* strong, even idiosyncratic, personal interests. Thus if one kindergarten girl is fascinated by volcanoes (her aunt had just sent a postcard from the Big Island of Hawaii), a caring teacher is well advised to find her a good volcano book or two, encourage her to show it to adult visitors as well as to any curious children, and scribe her dictated stories to bind into her own illustrated volcano book. When the child–teacher ratio in a center limits teachers' ability to support individual pursuits in these ways, it is essential to have an environment that allows children easy access to the tools, materials, space, and time they may need to independently explore their good ideas.

---

astronomy just doesn't grab me; my interests are here-and-now on earth. I like knowing that it does grab you because I know you're a good teacher, and so that stretches my thinking."

"Anyway," continues Bethany, "I told my kids that we're going to be studying space—*our space*—the new space we've just moved to. Most of the kids know each other, but they don't know this place. I want to try making a mural of our center with a map and pictures. I'm excited. You can do so much with 5-year-olds!"

"Well, what you can do with new 2s is make a safe place for them," Mayella says, "so that's what we're doing. We made three little soft areas in the room—with pillows and blankets and dolls—instead of just one place to play with dolls and get into hassles over them. So now we can steer a child to someplace nobody is if that's what's needed."

"Our room does well, I think," agrees Yoshiko. "Outdoors is harder."

"It sure is; it's *hard!*" says Mayella. "All asphalt. We gotta work on that."

"You say, I know, that right now we're supposed to be thinking about good things that have been happening," Yoshiko goes on. "But maybe I have a good idea to make the yard better: our snow fence—if we move it a little farther, to the gate, so we have a tree and dirt?"

"That sounds like an important question to add to the board," says Ruby, writing "Move snow fence?" on a card and tacking it up. "And

I promise I'll come look at the fence with you tomorrow."

Gloria picks up the mention of questions. "My question up there is about film," she says. "And that's my best thing—getting started on the bulletin boards with pictures of all of us. It's important to me that we all see our images on the walls of our rooms. When families show photos of their children at home, the children know they matter. In day care, I think it's important that children have family photos, too, so they can see those people when they want to."

We smile at each other from across the room—such a good idea, and it's been initiated, not by Ruby, but by a brand-new staff member.

"I'm interested in children's development of literacy, too, and I've been putting up their words," Marnie says. "Eric and Jun keep going back to look for their names. The other children don't seem interested, but their parents are. I thought I should follow up on the planning we did last month—that's what you said those staff days were for—and one thing we talked about was Legos. I got ours out, and when I started wishing we had more, Sally loaned me all of hers. And when children started telling me what they made, I wrote it down."

"This feels to me like a really good beginning," says Ruby. "Do you hear any themes or ideas that we should be extending—that would pick up on children's interests and go into greater depth with them?"

OUR FAMILIES

Eric built with Legos.
He built a big car.

LaVonne built with Legos.
She built a house with 2 rooms.

Jaime built with Legos.
He built a church. "Es la misa," he told Gloria.

Jun built with Legos.
He built a red and white sidewalk.

"I think several of us are doing something like, Who are we and what can we do?" Sandra says.

"And, Where are we?" adds Bethany.

"We're in water and sand and creating an ocean," says Sally. "And Bob's got ideas for more to do with that. Are you going to get fierce with me if I bring up a problem, though?"

"Try it and see," says Ruby, smiling.

"Our kids hate going in. *We* hate going in. I understand the reasons for taking turns in the yard, but in 40 minutes our kids have really just gotten started. Could we share the yard and stay out longer?"

"Well, scheduling turns was the idea you all agreed to," Ruby reminds her. "That's a question for everyone, so let's tackle it. What do the rest of you think? If you could do it any way you wanted, how would you organize the morning for your class?"

"Outdoors till 10:00," says Bethany promptly, "as long as the weather's nice; then, in for snack, group discussion, planning, and focused indoor activities."

"I'd rather start inside," says Sandra, "and then give children outdoor/indoor choice from about 10:00 until we have to put the cots down; then I'd like them all out." Dolores nods agreement.

"I like Sandra's plan," says Marnie, "but I assume we can't both have that."

"Don't assume anything," says Ruby, writing it down on the chart she's just invented. "We're brainstorming! Gloria?"

"I haven't been here long enough," says Gloria. "I'll go along with whatever Marnie wants, for now."

"Sally?" Sally and Bob have been whispering together.

"Oh dear," says Sally. "I think we're going to mess it up. Right now we'd like indoor/outdoor choice all morning, mostly outdoors."

"Hang in there," says Ruby. "Yoshiko and Mayella, do you want access to the big yard, or shall we see what we can do with your little one?"

"Little, please," says Yoshiko.

"OK," says Ruby, calculating on her chart. "If we were enrolled to capacity and no one was absent, we'd have anywhere from 20 to 50 kids outside on that schedule. Is that manageable?"

"I don't think we'd ever have more than about 35," Sally guesses, "not if kids can choose to go in and if some of them have already been out for a long time. And when I say outdoors, I'm thinking about the porch, too. That's where it's shady later in the morning and where we can set up table activities. Our problem would be staffing, with our littlies. With only two of us, if four of our kids wanted to be indoors and six were on the porch and the rest were in the sand, how could we supervise closely enough?"

"My bigger kids are such competent players, they don't need me breathing down their necks," says Bethany. "And several of them would love taking care of your littlies. Could we share responsibility for each other's kids? We didn't have separate groups at our old center, and I liked that. We were smaller then, of course. Still, I'm really missing team teaching, and younger kids, when I'm all by myself with 5s."

"Oh yes," says Gloria earnestly, "that would be more like a family. Children need to learn to care for each other. Being in day care sometimes keeps them from learning that if they're separated by age."

"That might get some bigger kids into my ocean stuff," says Bob eagerly. "There's so much I'd like to do, and these little kids just want to puddle about. Sally's been telling me I talk at them too much, but what do I do with my *ideas?*" We note that Ruby doesn't respond to Bob's plea.

There is an anxious moment until Bethany breaks the silence. "Speaking of ideas, Marnie, I've just had a truly wild one. About your Legos. One September in Seattle I took my kids to Bumbershoot—their arts festival—and there were absolutely millions of Legos on the stone wall all around the huge fountain at Seattle Center. And *everybody* was building with them, adults as well as children. What if we *all* loaned Marnie our

Legos and she put them all out on the porch to see what would happen?"

Bethany is looking nervous, but Marnie brightens. She *likes* the idea and adds to it. "I think I'd put out paper and markers and tape, too. And builders who want to save what they make, at least overnight, can make signs to put on their constructions."

"Such good ideas," responds Ruby, beaming. "And I have a confession to make. When Sally brought up scheduling, I was worried about my agenda; scheduling sounded like another way to sidetrack curriculum planning and go back to endless discussion of nitty-gritty problems. I decided to chance it—and here you've taken it right back to curriculum. Bless you! Mixed-age grouping will have important implications for our curriculum, and you've already started reinventing it. It sounds like a go. Shall we try the new schedule next week?"

No one objects. "Good, let's! Please try to speak to each other about the glitches—I guarantee there will be some—and get them up on the board under 'Problems' if they need further attention. Yoshiko, I'll come spend some time in your yard, and we'll see what we can do with it.

"Now, will all of this keep you going, or do we need to do more planning for October?"

"Wow, that's Halloween!" says Bob eagerly. "Can we have pumpkins and a parade?"

"And so the holidays begin," mutters Bethany. "I hate holiday curriculum."

"I love it," says Gloria. "Holidays were so special for me as a child. They were something to look forward to when all the family was there. It was exciting."

"Can we talk about that for a while?" asks Ruby. "What are your childhood memories of Halloween?"

"Halloween?" asks Yoshiko. "Is that when you have those . . . bones?"

"Oh, skeletons," says Dolores. "*Día de los Muertos* was very important in my family. We went to the graves and pulled the weeds, and we brought flowers—*cempasúchil*, marigolds; I can still smell them—to honor the dead. We made an *ofrenda* in our house—an offering to *los muertos*. It was like a fiesta, with good food and all of us together.[4] Tio Fernando talked about *la abuelita*, his mother—my little grandmother."

"My brother had a skeleton costume when I was 2 or 3, and I was terrified!" remembers Bethany.

"My mother wouldn't let me go trick-or-treating with the rest of the kids," says Marnie. "She said it was begging, and our family didn't do that sort of thing. I was humiliated. The kids came to our house, and my mother told them to go away.

Why Holidays?

Louise Derman-Sparks and the A.B.C. Task Force provide this perspective on holidays as curriculum.

> In many early childhood programs, holidays are a mainstay of the curriculum: Columbus Day, Halloween, Thanksgiving, Christmas, Valentine's Day, and so on become the focal point for themes and activities. Curriculum guides and educational supply companies make teaching holidays convenient by packaging sets of activities and materials. Curriculum courses frequently suggest using holiday units to teachers-in-training. Why this has happened seems to be an educational mystery, for there are no meaningful developmental reasons for such an abundant emphasis on holiday activities. In fact, the overuse of holiday units interferes with a developmental approach to curriculum as too many prepared, "canned" activities take the place of activities tailored to meet the needs of specific groups of children.[6]

Critical discussion of holiday curriculum is likely to arouse strong emotions in teachers and parents. Some people love the rhythm of the year as defined by holidays and, if they are teachers, have all their planning boxes organized by holiday themes. Other people see extended holiday celebrations as an arbitrary interruption of more developmentally appropriate activities.

In one view, holidays serve to connect children with patriotic, religious, and cultural traditions. In the contrary view, many of these holidays take one tradition for granted while ignoring others, and some of them promote racist and sexist stereotypes.

Some families have religious prohibitions against the celebration of holidays with pagan roots (including traditional religious holidays). But, ask other people, don't we need shared celebrations in order to create an adult–child community?

What can we do about these formidable differences among us? Talk about them. Agree to disagree. Downplay specific holiday-identified celebrations and look instead for the universally shared meanings underlying the holiday traditions of different cultures. Share ideas and questions with parents. Respect decisions made by individual staff, while continuing to challenge them with genuine questions: Why . . . ?

They soaped our windows. And *I* had to clean the windows. I hate Halloween."

"And Bob loves it," says Ruby. "Pumpkins and a parade, you said, Bob. What's Halloween *about?* What's *Día de los Muertos* about?

"It's about the dead, isn't it?" asks Sandra. "About remembering them, or being scared of them, or dressing up to scare them. Ghosts. Skeletons. Jack-o'-lanterns. But what do pumpkins have to do with all of it?"

"I suppose they were available—it's harvest time," sounds out Bethany. "And someone thought they would be good for carving scary faces in. Is Halloween just American? I think pumpkins are."

"It's about evil, I think. Witches dancing, ghosts haunting," says Dolores.

"But evil witches are a sexist invention," says Gloria. "Witches are women of power; they were healers. And men resented women having power."[7]

"We've got a lot going on here," Ruby says. "What have we said that sounds like interesting curriculum for young children?"

Día de los Muertos

Carmichael and Sayer describe the meaning of the celebration.

> That a festival to do with the dead should be a joyous occasion perhaps strikes those of us from other cultures with our different perceptions as something hard to come to terms with. The Day of the Dead is just that: a festival of welcome for the souls of the dead which the living prepare and delight in. The souls return each year to enjoy for a few brief hours the pleasures they once knew in life . . . . It is a time of family reunion not only for the living but also the dead who, for a few brief hours each year, return to be with their relatives in this world.[8]

What can we learn from the celebrations of each other's cultures? For many *norteamericanos*, death is a taboo subject, hidden not celebrated. Children, and adults as well, are left without opportunities to talk about and act out their feelings and to make connections with those they have lost. The Mexican Day of the Dead, celebrated by many people in the United States as well as in Mexico, offers rich imagery and shared events to make the strange and fearful more familiar.

Teachers of young children can broaden their perspective on potential curriculum by examining the images, messages, and meaning of any holiday significant within the school's community (see chart shown on p. 52, "Images, Messages, and Meaning").

"Not much!" Sally says. "Being scared, death and evil, and witches. Not good stuff for little kids. But how can we ignore it? The older kids will bring it to school, whether we do it or not. And parents will ask us about costumes."

"Just to remind you, we have two Jehovah's Witness families in the center," says Ruby. "They've asked me to let them know if we do holidays, so they can make other arrangements for their children that day."

"Oh dear," says Bethany. "That doesn't seem fair, to do things we can't all share. I'm wondering; could we choose some of the things connected with Halloween that we think really *are* appropriate curriculum for children, to be begun this month and carried on beyond it? I'm the one who said I hate holiday curriculum. But I don't think we can just ignore it, given families' expectations, and children's. We need to be able to explain what we're doing and why."

Ruby moves to the board, where she writes the headings:

Halloween/Día de los Muertos

Good stuff

Bad stuff

"I don't want to lose *Día de los Muertos*," she explains. "It's important to Dolores and to some of our families. So let's think about that and Halloween. What's the good stuff in them for children? What's the bad stuff—the things that don't reflect our values?"

"Isn't it interesting that we have some of the same things on both sides?" comments Ruby. "Take skeletons. They're bad if they scare you. They're good because you can eat sugar skulls during *Día de los Muertos* and because you can dress up as a skeleton and pretend to scare other people."

"And because they hold your body together," says Bethany. "Now *that*, I think, *is* appropriate curriculum for 4s and 5s: What's inside me?"

"And who's behind the mask?" murmurs Gloria.

"Oh! All this is about people inventing ways to deal with the unknown, isn't it?" says Sandra. "Death—that's the big unknown. It makes people sad, and scared. Getting sick can be scary, too, because sometimes when people get sick, they die. So healers and their magical powers are really important. And knowing how your body works and how to take care of it is important."

"What can children—and adults—do with their fears?" says Bethany, thinking aloud. "Talk about them. Learn more about them. Play them out! These holidays are all about playing out fears, aren't they? Now *there's* a real issue for young children."

"Are any of you getting ideas about what you might want to do?" Ruby asks, just as we were wondering when she would shift the conversation back to actual plans for the coming weeks. Ruby clearly understands the need for good curriculum to be grounded in the teachers' own grasp of what makes a theme meaningful for a particular group of children—and adults.

"I can give up the parade but not the pumpkins," says Bob. "Can we go find a pumpkin patch and get *lots* of pumpkins? We'll web from pumpkins if you like, Ruby."

"If you get pumpkins and *don't* make jack-o'-lanterns of them, I don't think that will be a problem for our Witness families," says Ruby. "Mrs. Stone explained to me that their family takes joy in the natural world and they're happy to have creations of God at the school. It's fine for children to talk about those and make pictures of them. Pumpkins, trees, and eggs are all good things. It's

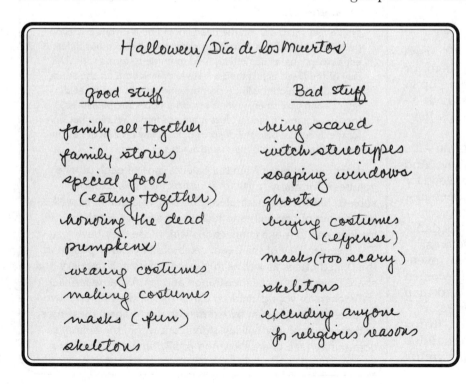

Halloween/Día de los Muertos

Good stuff

family all together
family stories
special food
(eating together)
honoring the dead
pumpkins
wearing costumes
making costumes
masks (fun)
skeletons

Bad stuff

being scared
witch stereotypes
soaping windows
ghosts
buying costumes
(expense)
masks (too scary)
skeletons
excluding anyone
for religious reasons

when they're decorated that they become unacceptable to her."[9]

"That's fine with me," says Sally. "Little kids can't cut pumpkins anyway; they just have to watch while an adult does it. Let's get some other kinds of squash, too, and look at all the different shapes and colors. And then cook the squash and roast the seeds and investigate them as *food*—which is why they're important to people. Would that be OK with everyone?" She looks around to general agreement.

"Dolores, can we work on *Día de los Muertos?*" asks Sandra. "My parents wanted us to be Americans, and they ignored the holiday. But *their* parents told us stories about celebrating it in Mexico. As a kid I only did Halloween, but I'd like to go further back.

"I wonder if I could get my grandma to come to our class? That would really surprise the kids, wouldn't it, to discover that their teacher has *una abuelita?* And we could talk about grandparents and families and about missing the people who have died."

"I guess we can't take them to the graveyard, but we could go to the *mercado*," says Dolores. "They'll hear everyone speaking Spanish; and the flowers and *dulces* and *calaveras* will be there, and we can get some to bring back to school."

"Can we go with you?" asks Bethany. "It would really help me if I can learn about it with you. And it would introduce Spanish. I want to use Spanish in our class whenever we can, both for the children whose language it is and for those who take English for granted. In this community it seems to me that everyone should grow up bilingual."

"Really?" says Marnie, surprised. "But this is America. I've always thought . . ." She stops abruptly, aware of the evident reactions of several other group members. "No, that's not what I was going to talk about. I've been listening to you all, and it sounds as if it might be OK if we just skipped Halloween in our class? Right? I mean, the kids will talk about it, but we don't have to make it official, do we? I really don't have good memories of Halloween." Nervously, she looks around, but no one seems to have any objection. Marnie thinks some more. "Or . . . I wouldn't mind doing pumpkins. Can we share that with you, maybe?" Bob and Sally nod.

"We, too," says Yoshiko. "Our children don't need to go to buy pumpkins, but they will like to visit yours."

"I've got another idea," says Bethany enthusiastically. "I want to start a Bodies curriculum

with the 5s. I have this sort of grand plan of a From the Outside In curriculum, in which we keep mapping and drawing and writing about things. We've begun with Our Space here at the center, and now I want to start looking at Our Bodies: What's on the Outside? and tracing everyone and getting them to paint their clothes on the paper bodies. And then asking, What's on the inside? and next asking them to draw what they think is inside them."

Sandra breaks in. "Why," she asks, "is what's inside your body? any more hands-on than what's in outer space? Just to continue that argument."

"Oh dear," says Bethany. "I think you've caught me. But I do like inside the body better, as you can tell. It keeps making other connections for me—like, with luck, we could get to skeletons by Halloween and look for a lifesize cardboard one at the *mercado* to hang up in our room. That would make it look as if we were doing Halloween like all the other kindergartens in the neighborhood, instead of human anatomy!

"Oh, and we might even get into, How can you hide your body so no one will know it's you? And think about masks and costumes and why you might want to hide, sometimes. And . . ."

"Whoa!" calls Ruby. "You're inventing your whole year's curriculum. That's great, but you don't need to do it all tonight. It's getting late. Besides, we need to find out where the children are going to take all this first. They may have some things in store that we haven't even dreamed of."

"No doubt!" agrees Sally. There are scattered smiles and nods from this tired bunch.

"This is certainly a productive group," says Ruby. "There's just one more thing I want to say, about my current thinking. I've talked with several of you about it. I think it's important that the center be full of *representations* of things the children do or say, for them and their families, and for all of us to see and talk about. I'm thinking of photos, and sketches, and children's words written down, and children's paintings and drawings—whatever you can think of to help us create a visible history of our lives together."

Sally suddenly remembers something. "Oh, those photos you took and the words that Betty wrote down about the shell play, they've just been sitting on my shelf."

"Well, actually I'd been thinking of making a kind of . . . story, about the ocean and what we've been doing," says Bob. "Maybe on the bulletin board that the parents can see. Do you think it's too late?"

"Not at all," smiles Ruby. "Children need help from us to revisit old experiences. Who knows what new adventures might begin? So, Gloria, in answer to your earlier question, yes, we did budget for film. I wanted this resource to be a high priority, so don't be surprised if I have to say 'no' to some of your other requests.

"I'll be giving you the photos I take, and I'm sure you'll come up with creative ways to use them. And as time goes on we'll give some of them to families for their portfolio of their

child's time here. Some of you might want to make books for the children. And not just photos, remember. For instance, Marnie has her Lego stories and the web they made up on her door. See what *you* can think of."

Re-presenting Children's Activities

An important task for the teacher of young children is taking notes and making other representations of children's spontaneous activity. In the role of *scribe* for the group, the teacher becomes its keeper of memories.

A scribed record helps adults remember what happened and suggests ideas for planning curriculum, but that's not all. Re-told to children, it helps them remember what happened, too, and demonstrates the strategies people use for remembering. Re-telling may be oral and pictorial—and written, as well, as children begin to discover that their words and actions make print. Many children are eager to "read" and re-tell in their turn. *The Play's the Thing* describes what happens: "When adults draw or write, they are models for children, who can try drawing or writing too. Children are most likely to understand representation when it mirrors their own actions." And further

> Scribed representations of children's play can stimulate a debriefing process in which children and adults encounter each other on the shared turf of mutual curiosity. What happened? Let's remember it, and look at it, and talk about it.[10]

This was an exhausting meeting and both of us are amazed at the commitment of these teachers to their curriculum process. And it is clear that this really is *their* process, and that Ruby has been essential in making this happen.

"Ruby is really patient," begins John. "There were times in that meeting when I just wanted to jump in and speed things up or straighten things out—like when Bob was whining about what to do with all his

THERE'S AN OCEAN IN OUR SANDBOX

See my shells. I got a daddy shell
and a mommy shell
and a tiny baby shell! Ronda

We had water. Ann

Bob brought back shells from the beach. We've been burying them and digging them up.

I digged and I digged and I found a snail. Wanda

My feet was wet and sandy. Willy

This is me and Bobby digging. Pauly

My red bucket. Lots of water. Luanne

EMERGENT CURRICULUM

great ideas. His stuff about surfboards seemed like taking over the play to me. But Ruby just let him stew for the moment."

"Of course," says Betty. "She's giving him the chance to figure this all out. Besides, the discussion nicely moved into the ways in which the staff could work with other age groups than their own. Maybe Bob will find his strength is with the older ones."

John smiles hopefully. "There's a fine line to walk between bringing your interests as a teacher into the curriculum and simply taking over. Teachers are more powerful to begin with, so there's a built-in risk."

"Sure," agrees Betty. "Like Bethany and the way she changed Outer Space to Our Space. I'm not so sure about that, but then teachers have to be invested in what they're doing. Ruby really trusts (and expects) her staff to be competent and think things through. That's one of her strengths."

"Certainly her hopes about documentation are slowly taking root. Again, she's patient," says John. "I'm just anxious to see where it all has led by the time I come to observe."

6
October Visit:
Pumpkin Patch, Lego Land, and Looking at Each Other

We were curious to see what people would do with last month's Halloween discussion since Ruby gave the teachers plenty of room to "emerge curriculum"—curriculum that they could get excited about.

John arrives for his October visit, and his first glance makes it clear that pumpkins are making an impact. A dozen of them, in varied sizes, are piled around one of the trees; the pumpkin-patch trip must have taken place. Someone has posted a "Pumpkins" curriculum web, using orange pumpkin shapes for all the items. Sandra is taking dictation from a couple of children; she has photos of each child at the pumpkin patch and has invited them to talk about their photos. "It's going to be a class book," she tells John when he asks.

Later, in the 3s' room, John finds that the teachers really are prepared to pool their resources. Marnie has indeed become the recipient of everyone's Legos. Her children are carrying tubs and tubs of Legos out onto the porch, where Marnie and Gloria are spreading out blankets to define work spaces. "Let's put three tubs on each blanket," Marnie calls out. "And remember our rule: Legos stay on the blanket. They don't go anywhere else in the yard." John is impressed by the risk she is taking by having manipulatives outside and by her clarity in limit setting.

Under a big sign, Lego Land, some of the children settle down to build. Others run off to the

---

WE WENT TO THE PUMPKIN PATCH

There was lots and lots and LOTS and LOTS of pumpkins! (Jody)

Big ones and little ones, all over the ground. That's me holding a big one. (Patty)

Yo vi calabasas de color de naranjas. ¡Pero son mas grandes que naranjas! (Luisa)

I sat on a pumpkin and it didn't break. I sat careful, though! (Mark)

We bringed all the pumpkins home. (Jeremy)

Looking at Each Other

Our project "Looking at Each Other" developed from the children's (ages 2 and 3) growing interest in peer relations . . . . The provocative event which introduced the project to the children involved face masks prepared from a 5 x 7 color photograph of each child's face, cut out, laminated and mounted on a stick (adapted from Forman and Hill, 1984). These "face puppets" were very exciting to the children and allowed them to compare one another indirectly and then interact in non-threatening ways. On this and subsequent days they traded face masks with each other, drew on them, and used them as props in dramatic play. Unusual and unexpected uses of photography provided a central means to carry this project theme forward.

Laminated photographs of the children were on different occasions hidden in the sand table and in the play dough, taped to doll heads, etc. We used photographs to make books about each other. Photocopied photographs of the children were made and given to the children to use in different coloring and collage activities over several weeks.

Reprinted from "Connections: Using the Project Approach with 2- and 3-Year-Olds in a University Laboratory School" (pp. 259–60) by D. LeeKeenan and J. Nimmo, in C. Edwards, L. Gandini, and G. Forman, eds., The Hundred Languages of Children: The Reggio Emilia Approach to Early Childhood Education, *1993, Norwood, NJ: Ablex. Copyright © 1993 by Ablex Publishing Corporation. Used by permission.*

See also Notes to Chapter 6, no. 4.

---

slide, the sand, and the easels under the trees. We notice that Marnie has taped up the Legos web she made at the inservice, and next to it is another web with "Classification" in the middle. "I like planning from cognitive objectives," she explains to John. "That helps me to remember what I want the children to learn from an activity. So I chose classification because Legos have so many attributes to be classified: shape, size, color, and number. And before we brought them outside, we introduced them at small-group time and played classification games with them."

John watches for a while. Raul is building a tall stack against the wall; then he builds another to match and tries to add a bridge between them. Marnie admires it. "This side is the same as that side, isn't it?" she says. "Let's see how many Legos there are on this side. Can you count them? One, two, three . . . ." Raul is busy driving one of the small vehicles under the bridge. "There's bad guys, *arriba*. I have to be careful.

Soy la policía—RRRRRrrrrrrrRRRRRRR"—and the police car turns on its siren and scoots under the bridge. Its driver shoots at the bad guys. Then he shoots at John. John reacts by getting down on the floor and starting to drive a car, too— looks like it's time to add an ambulance to the script. Soon, it's time for John to move on.

Pumpkins and Legos are ideas we were in on at the beginning. In the 2s' room, on the other hand, something is happening that we hadn't heard about before.

John learns about new happenings for the 2s as soon as he enters their room, where he sits on the floor so his presence won't be too obvious. There are squeals from the playhouse corner, and several somethings—looking like enormous lollipops—are waving in the air. What *do* the children have? John scoots closer to see.

Mayella, noticing John, moves in his direction. "You didn't see them before, did you?" she chuckles. "Yoshiko calls them *kao*. I think that's Japanese for faces. There was a coupon special at Rocky's—the photo place, you know—and Yoshiko took the kids' pictures and got them enlarged there. And then she photocopied a whole bunch, and cut them out, and laminated them to do different things with. Those got sticks attached, and the kids are calling them babies and putting them to bed. There's some other little ones stuck on the blocks. It gets real noisy when the kids find their pictures."

After watching delightedly for a while, John asks Yoshiko where she got the idea. "Some of the big children, they make masks," she explains. "They like to hide and surprise each other. I want the little children to *find* each other, get to know each other. I read American books to see what teachers do in this country. This idea came from a book. I like it."

As the children begin to gather for snack, John leaves the room, remembering something Yoshiko said, "Some of the big children, they make masks." That sounds like Halloween. Nobody discussed masks at the staff meeting and John wonders where they came from.

He finds them among the 5s, whose teacher "hates holiday curriculum." "Hey, Bethany, what

Defining the Boundaries of Peer Culture

It can be useful for teachers to pay attention to the shared peer culture[1] that their children invent and participate in and to notice to what extent these activities and rituals overlap with the curriculum sanctioned and supported by the teacher.

Much of peer culture (the social curriculum of young children) lies outside the limits that teachers impose for their classrooms—spitting, swearing, fighting, and maybe Barbies and war toys. These behaviors can also include creative attempts at risk taking or opportunities to build group solidarity and a sense of identity. Teachers must make choices about when to outlaw, ignore, covertly encourage, or seek to reframe these as part of the classroom curriculum. In making decisions about emergent curriculum, teachers need to be clear about the values and ideas they hold, in deciding how they will use the resources and power available to them.

What Makes a Project Topic?

A project topic . . . should be something concrete, close to children's personal experience, interesting and important to the children, and "dense" in potential meanings (emotional and intellectual), so that it is rich in possibilities for varied activity during different parts of the day and for sustaining long-term interest.

Reprinted from "Connections: Using the Project Approach with 2- and 3-Year-Olds in a University Laboratory School" (p. 255) by D. LeeKeenan and J. Nimmo, in C. Edwards, L. Gandini, and G. Forman, eds., The Hundred Languages of Children: The Reggio Emilia Approach to Early Childhood Education, *1993, Norwood, NJ: Ablex. Copyright © 1993 by Ablex Publishing Corporation. Used by permission.*

happened to you?" John asks. Bethany is busily stapling cloth tape to paper plates; the plates have eyeholes and a variety of fierce expressions, child-created. "I thought you were going to do bones, not Halloween."

"Right. But that was *my* idea." Bethany grins ruefully. "I console myself that it's still anatomy; we're just beginning with the head. And with hiding your body; I did have that idea, too. We haven't taken our trip to the *mercado* yet. We can collect *Día de los Muertos* skeletons there, and that should get the kids into bones."

John had admired the pumpkins in the yard, but there's no evidence of pumpkins in this room. "Are you boycotting pumpkins?" he asks.

"No, but my kids are," says Bethany. "I read them "Peter Peter Pumpkin Eater" and they thought it was dumb. Some of the girls were particularly outspoken about the mere idea of 'keeping a wife'; who did Peter Peter think he was, anyway? On the other end of women's liberation, however, are my girls who were enchanted by the idea of pumpkins as houses. Whenever they get a chance, they're out there arranging pumpkins into a village with acorn-lined paths in between—for their Barbies. Barbies are *their* curriculum, not mine.[2]

"And remember the idea I started the fall with, how we were going to map 'Our Space' and study the people in our school? Ha! Reality is too tame for this group. You know those medieval maps with fabulous creatures drawn around the edges, warning sailors of the unknown? 'Here be dragons'—this place is full of fabulous creatures and buried treasure. First, the kids discovered the shells in the sand and decided they were gold pieces. Now, they're inventing treasure hunts, burying treasure for each other to find. Then they took the dinosaurs out to bury in the sand. Dinosaurs are *their* curriculum, not mine.

"I'm sneaky, though," Bethany continues. "You know that neat book, *Bones, Bones, Dinosaur Bones?*[3] We've been reading that. And I sent home a note to parents asking if they had any chicken bones or ribs they could send to day care for us to boil, and use for our archeological dig. I figure if we start with prehistory, we may yet get to 'Our Bones.'

"After *Día de los Muertos* I think I'll try storytelling with a skeleton: Bones, Bones, Your Bones, My Bones. I can teach them 'Dry Bones'; do you know that song? 'The foot bone connected to the ankle bone . . .' We'll trace their bodies for bones first, and do clothes later."

———

Emergent curriculum—John muses as he leaves the center—is an endless series of connections. What, he wonders, will be the next pieces to be connected, by teacher and by children, to this unique and growing kindergarten curriculum?

7

November Staff Meeting: Hiding and Finding and Who's Thankful for What?

During the drive to the staff meeting, John fills Betty in on his recent visit to the children's center. He's delighted that the idea Yoshiko got "from an American book" is one he has written about. Yoshiko hasn't made the connection, however, and he's not about to mention it since she has made the idea her own. "Those ideas didn't just come from Debbie [LeeKeenan] and me,"[1] John says with a smile. "Creative teaching involves adapting old ideas to new contexts. You can't teach in a collegial vacuum. What's that saying? Give someone a dollar and you still have a dollar. Give someone an idea and you'll have two."

Pumpkins are still in evidence around the center as we walk in. "When you don't cut them, they don't rot," Betty remarks. "How nice to be able to keep them for a while."

"Time for show-and-tell again," says Ruby, as the staff settles down. "And that reminds me, if any of you are into show-and-tell with kids, I encourage you to do it the way we're doing it here—with stories about what's happening at school rather than 'Look what my mommy bought me at the mall.' Asking a whole group of children to listen while someone shows off his new shoes or her Barney™ is too much like TV commercials for me, and kids get enough of those. Kids do need to show their stuff to each other and to us, but let's keep it informal and not turn it into meeting agenda. I'd rather we acknowledge kids' creations than their possessions. Those are *my* values—just thought I'd make my pitch.

"Anyway, what's the best thing that happened for you in this last month's program? And where do you want to go with it?"

"Pumpkins," says Dolores. "I brought the web because I thought we might want to talk about it if we're going to be planning for this month. I think we've just gotten started on some of these ideas, especially on eating and cooking and other kinds of vegetables. We should be doing something with healthy foods, shouldn't we? Here's our chance." She tapes the web on the bulletin board.

"OK, great! Let's get back to that," says Ruby. "Who's next?"

Yoshiko explains her face puppets; Bethany, her treasure hunts; and then Bob takes a turn. "This doesn't really feel like a 'best' thing, but I learned a lot about kids and curriculum plans.

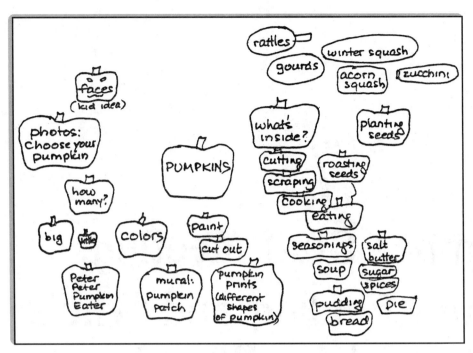

The following text contains labels from the web diagram: rattles, gourds, winter squash, acorn squash, zucchini, faces (kid idea), photos: choose your pumpkin, PUMPKINS, what's inside?, planting seeds, how many?, cutting, scraping, roasting seeds, cooking, eating, big, little, colors, paint, cut out, seasonings, salt, butter, sugar, spices, soup, Peter Peter Pumpkin Eater, mural: pumpkin patch, pumpkin prints (different shapes of pumpkin), pudding, bread, pie

because I know you like webs, Ruby—and I've been trying to guide their play, but they keep ignoring me. With the kids in my own class, I can follow up in our small groups, but the other kids are heavy into Batmobiles. Is that OK with you if they're just playing and not learning anything?"

Bethany gulps audibly, smothers it in a hasty cough, and is clearly thinking hard before she says anything. She apparently decides to begin with personal experience, not theory. "That sounds like my treasure hunters," she says. "I was all set to teach them about mapping, and then about bones. They're busy teaching themselves about hiding and finding. Wow! Buried treasure and masks are both about hiding and finding, aren't they? And so are archeology and anatomy. Oh boy, I think they're better planners than I am!" She stops abruptly, enchanted with her aha!

I did bring my surfboard. I told the kids I like to float on it in the ocean. And then we made an ocean; I dug a hole in the sand and put a plastic liner in it. And I put the wood scraps I got (thanks, Dolores, for the lumberyard info) into a tub by the sand to see if any of the kids would connect them with the surfboard. I wanted to really talk up the idea of surfboards, but Sally wouldn't let me."

"Little kids learn by doing, not by listening," Sally defends herself. "And besides, there's no surf in the sandbox."

"So what happened?" asks Gloria.

"No surf," says Bob, ruefully. "They just wanted to throw things in the water, and the wood scraps were great for that. They tossed in some shells, too. And the wood floated, and the shells sank; and I thought, great, we can do sink-and-float, but that turned out to be a talkabout, too. The kids weren't into science principles, just throwing.

"A few days later they got into boats, and gluing wood. They made some great wood structures, and I guess the science lesson they learned is that top-heavy boats tip over and white glue stops sticking when you put it in water. How's that for emergent something-or-other?"

They sympathize. "That's something like what's happening to me," says Marnie. "You know all those Legos? There are lots of kids using them, and I thought it was a great opportunity to emphasize concepts like classification and seriation. So I wrote up my plan—I webbed it

Negotiating the Curriculum

Curriculum is *negotiated* between teachers and children, even in the most teacher-directed classroom. Where the only choice is to do or not-do what the teacher presents, there will always be a few children who choose the not-do option.[2] Others will try to do, and fail; while others—the majority, if the teacher has planned appropriately—will succeed.

Where negotiating the curriculum is part of teachers' conscious agenda,[3] there are likely to be planned discussions between teacher and children: What do you already know about this? What do you want to learn? With younger children, however, negotiation often appropriately takes the form of action rather than discussion. The teacher provides ideas and materials, but the children ignore them to pursue their own ideas. Deciding when to insist, when to try it another way, and when to let go of one's plans altogether is a never-ending challenge for the teacher of young children.

EMERGENT CURRICULUM

Ruby picks up the theme. "Where does curriculum come from?" she asks, partly as if to remind herself. "It comes from our good ideas, and children's good ideas, and concepts we want them to learn, and unexpected events, and what's already there in the environment . . . . So we plan, but we can't predict what will happen to our plans; the kids are busy planning, too. Bob and Bethany and Marnie, you're all getting a chance to practice letting go and honoring the children's good ideas. Your good ideas will come 'round again, later, when children are ready for them, and you invent an effective way to introduce them."

"This still sounds irresponsible to me," says Marnie, not getting it. "We're *teachers*. We're responsible for what children learn."

"I agree," says Ruby. "What are the children learning as you watch them inventing with Legos? Let go of your agenda for a minute and try identifying theirs. All of you, what have you noticed?"

A fast-paced discussion generates lots of examples from casual observations of the children at play with Legos. The result is a long list of what individual children were saying and doing and, in the process, learning.

"What do you mean by *script*?" asks Gloria, when Sandra offers Police Script as one idea of what children are learning.

"Oh, it's all the things police do," Sandra explains. "Like driving a police car, making the siren noise, giving tickets to other drivers, catching bad guys—you know."

Interrupting Play to Teach Concepts

It may be tempting, for a teacher who has honored children's initiative in defining their own play, to try to seize the initiative back again in order to teach. Cognitive curricula encourage teachers to do just that. However, *The Play's the Thing* suggests

> If teachers care about sustaining play, they must tailor their interventions to conform to the script the children are playing. [Sometimes] the interruption of play happens in the name of cognitive stimulation; the teacher intervenes to teach vocabulary and concepts. Adults who have learned that play should be taken seriously sometimes try to adapt it to their own ideas of what's serious.[4]

Children know better; what's serious is the integrity of the story, the script that is being played out. Teachers *can* introduce vocabulary and concepts so long as they fit the logic of the children's script.[5]

"So there can be a script for anybody, and children can play it if they want to be that person?" asks Marnie. "Is there a Batman script?"

"Yes, indeed. Someone gets paid for writing that one," says Ruby, adding it to the list. "More?"

More ideas come right along, and the list turns out to be a mixture of play scripts, physical skills, interpersonal skills, concepts and dispositions—all the different sorts of things children learn as they play. "Oh," says Marnie. "They are learning, aren't they?"

Ruby apparently decides the point has been well made; she moves on. "OK, folks, we have most of November ahead of us. What shall we plan to do—even as we recognize that the children will, of course, have their own ideas?"

"Let's see—Thanksgiving. Any problems with celebrating that?" asks Bob. "Can we have a harvest feast?"

"I have seen a good idea in a book," Yoshiko volunteers. "Children make handprints with their five fingers out, so . . . and you have the turkey feathers. That is what this holiday is, yes?"

"Well, I do have problems," says Gloria, "because this holiday is only partly about turkeys and celebrating harvest together. It's also about Native Americans helping white settlers—some of whom later did their best to wipe out the

---

Lego Learnings

fitting pieces together	police script
fine motor skills	Batman script
building buildings	construction script
making roofs	city building
making bridges	conflict resolution
mathematical relationships	using your words
comparative sizes (will the car fit under the bridge?)	taking turns
	sharing
	asking adults for help
shapes	staying within spatial limits
colors	
problem solving	testing limits

peoples who were here before. So I don't celebrate Thanksgiving. For my people it's a day of sad memories."

"Are you Indian—Native American?" asks Bob in surprise. "I thought you spoke Spanish."

"I do. I am *mestiza*—that means mixed—like most Latinas," says Gloria. I'm brown, not white. Thanksgiving is a white holiday."

Bob is silent. So is Gloria. After a moment, Sandra asks, tentatively, "Could we go back to the pumpkin web? And to my cooking web from September, which Ruby has up over there? Lots of cultures have harvest festivals. How could we celebrate harvest, and eating good food together, and being grateful for good food, and families coming together?"

"We could build a *sukkah*," says Sally.

"A *what?*" asks Mayella.

"A *sukkah*. *Sukkot* is the Jewish harvest festival celebrated early in the fall, and you build a little booth and cover it with leaves. I think the children would like that; little houses really appeal to them. And I'd like that; it has special meaning for me. We could build it under the tree, where the pumpkins are, and put the pumpkins in it."

"What happens then?" asks Mayella.

"We could have snack in the *sukkah*," says Sally. "That's what people do, have parties in it. And there's a bundle of branches, the *lulav*, to shake; that's done with prayers, which we wouldn't do, but maybe we could sing and children could dance with little branches. It's a harvest festival, with thanks for rain and

Who's Thankful?

Native Americans have more than one thing *not* to be thankful for on Thanksgiving. Pilgrim Day, and its antecedent feast, Halloween, represent the annual twin peaks of Indian stereotyping. From early October through the end of November, "cute little Indians" abound on greeting cards, advertising posters, in costumes and school projects . . . . Virtually none of the standard fare surrounding either Halloween or Thanksgiving contains an ounce of authenticity, historical accuracy or cross-cultural perception.

Can Schools Build Community?

Demographic and structural changes in North American society have created the need for extra-familial contexts in which children's feelings of belonging and connection are nurtured and sustained, that is, communities . . . . Many years ago John Dewey issued a call to build community in schools; yet the problem of defining the meaning of community and its place in school settings remains. Certainly, school settings do offer important prerequisites for building community—a shared time and space under the guidance of adult community members. Could a sense of community be nurtured within a school setting and then radiate outwards to touch and strengthen children's lives within family and neighborhood?

thanks for food. All kinds of food—you hang them on the sukkah."

"I'd like that," says Bethany, and there are nods from others.

"So we need to go to the store with the children," says Sandra. "Last month someone had the idea of looking for other kinds of squash, besides pumpkins, but we haven't done it yet. And then we can start cooking them. What are all the ways you can cook pumpkin? Some people just eat it as a vegetable."

"I'll bring you my one-hundred-ways-to-cook-zucchini recipes, from my home gardening days," chuckles Bethany.

"I've been wanting to work with clay, with the children," says Gloria. "Think about all the kinds of vegetables children could make out of clay. To make something, you really have to pay attention to what it looks like, and feels like. I think it's important to encourage children to pay attention."

"All the colors and shapes of vegetables could be a real stimulus to children's work in different art media, couldn't they?" says Bethany. "Paint, and markers—we could make a group mural—colored paper. Colored play dough—that's different from clay. I think this sounds exciting."

"Could we have a parade?" asks Bob. "I didn't get my Halloween parade. How about a harvest parade, with singing and each child carrying something to the table? 'Come, ye thankful people come, raise the song of harvest home.' Maybe procession would be a better word than parade."

"We haven't had an open house for families yet, and we should," says Ruby. "Would you all be up for a harvest feast? We could cook with the children, and ask parents to bring food too."

After further discussion they agree to have a small committee from each of the three older groups of children, to involve the children in planning, and to document the whole process.

———

The meeting ends, and we drive home, talking nonstop as we usually do . . .

"They're really coming up against the risks of an emergent curriculum, aren't they?" says Betty. "What do you do when you have a teaching plan and the children have other good ideas? Marnie has the traditional answer: 'We're teachers; we're supposed to teach them.' But, in practice that often means pretending to teach them even if they're not paying attention. That happens all the time in schools."

"It was happening to Marnie when I visited," John recalls. "She was diligently teaching one-to-one correspondence to Raul, who had been building a Lego bridge. It was nice timing, except that Raul was busy shooting bad guys and ignoring her. She didn't seem to know how to let go of her agenda and acknowledge his."

"I admired Bethany's restraint when Marnie made that remark about children just playing and not learning," says Betty.

"I think Marnie wants her children to be able to concentrate and see something through, but

There Are Always More Good Ideas

Adults accustomed to thinking open endedly will come up with far more ideas than they can ever use in their teaching. It's useful to discover this and to practice letting go of good ideas in the faith that there will always be more—and that many of them will come from the children.

Before a project is begun with children at Reggio Emilia, as B. Rankin writes, "the adults involved meet to discuss various possibilities, hypotheses, and potential directions that the project might take." She quotes *pedagogista* Carlina Rinaldi, who explains how important this discussion stage is:

> If adults have thought of 1,000 hypotheses, then it is easy to accept the fact that there can be 1,001 or 2,000 hypotheses. The unknown is easier to accept and adults are more open to new ideas when they have generated many potentialities themselves. The problem comes from having only one hypothesis which then draws all the attention to the adult.[6]

Isolating a teacher in a classroom and giving her or him a prescribed curriculum that presents only one hypothesis at a time is the opposite approach to ensuring quality in education. It assumes the possibility of "teacher-proof" canned curriculum rather than reliance on teachers' continuing growth as the source of quality.

Clay As a Medium for Exploration and Representation

Clay is invaluable in teaching three-dimensional thinking, and thinking-in-the-round, in the architectural and global sense. We present drawing, painting and collage to our preschoolers, but clay is often excluded. This leaves the atmosphere for full art expression ungrounded, unbalanced. Clay presents an opportunity for children to put their whole being into safe physical connection with the earth, and to gradually learn a sense of inner power from working with the material . . . .

As I introduce clay I say that clay comes in all colors, as many different colors as there are colors of earth . . . . I talk about clay being safe, that flowers and vegetables come from the ground, too. I talk about volcanic changes, how

the earth a long time ago made soft clay and how, when clay is cooked (fired), it becomes hard. As I talk, I play with the clay . . . .

[As children develop skills in the use of clay] universal themes appear. There are families (animals and humans), homes (rooms, furniture), space, school, city life (buses, cars, street lights), natural phenomena (flowers, volcanoes, caves, tunnels), friends and pets, and food (cookies, pizzas), and wonderful amalgamations.

———
Reprinted from "The Care and Feeding of Clay" (pp. 4–5, 8) by K. Neubert, Pacific Oaks College Occasional Paper, 1991, Pasadena, CA: Pacific Oaks College. Copyright © 1991 by the author. Used by permission.

she doesn't pay enough attention to whether the curriculum is important to them," John suggests. "Sure, children often need support in sustaining their focus; so do I! but it needs to be a genuine question for them, or it just becomes another imposition.

"On the other hand, Bethany has really been thinking about planning and when to let go," John continues. "When I was in her room, we talked about it, and she kept saying, 'That's their curriculum (the kids'), not my curriculum.' She was picking up some of their ideas and temporarily shelving some of her own, and having such a good time in the process. She's a relaxed sort of teacher, isn't she?"

"She never intended to become a teacher, she told me," says Betty. "Bethany fell into teaching when her own kids were in preschool. Having the kindergarten now is making her a little anxious, but mostly it's clear how much she likes watching kids to see what they'll do next. I can identify with that."

We drive for a bit in silence. Then John says, "They're ambitious, aren't they, planning a feast? I'm impressed. That's the sort of event that does so much to create community in a child care center. Shall we go?"

"I wouldn't miss it," says Betty. "What shall we bring?"

Images, Messages, and Meaning

We find that most teachers have not really examined the religious or historical origins and perspectives that most holidays represent. To provide awareness . . . of specific holidays, we ask them to work in small groups to fill out the chart [see our filled-in examples] below. With four people in each group, they can each choose a holiday for the group to discuss and make notations on the chart. When this is completed a whole group debriefing can be held.

During the debriefing we ask if anyone has holes in their chart, things no one in the group knew about the holiday. In that case we solicit information the rest of the group may have. We then see which holidays have been considered and with each, consider what various groups may have put on their charts. Each box [heading] on the chart gets to the heart of the discussion we want to have with teachers as they plan holiday curriculum.

Holiday: Pesach (Passover)

Images: matzoh, wine, family around the table
"Why is this night different from all other nights?"

Prevailing messages*:
remembers an important historic event
celebrates freedom
courage under oppression
religious — but celebrated by non-religious people too
not commercialized

Why celebrated?
To be together as family
To remember the endurance and liberation of our people

Does it reflect cultures of children enrolled?
yes, some Jewish families - religious and non-religious

How is cultural awareness and sensitivity increased?
spring holiday which isn't Easter
Jewish children's identity is acknowl.
Communication with their families

*Consider historical origins, religious values, commercial of economic interests

Holiday: St. Patrick's Day

Images: shamrocks   parade
leprechauns   GREEN

Prevailing messages*:
patron saint of Ireland
religious holiday: [we're not sure]
heavy economic interests:
teaching and party materials

Why celebrated?
in U.S., an immigrant groups special day together
[Is this an Irish holiday or only Irish-American?]

Does it reflect cultures of children enrolled?
not as far as we know

How is cultural awareness and sensitivity increased?
stereotypes rather than cultural sensitivity

*Consider historical origins, religious values, commercial of economic interests

---

Reprinted from Training Teachers: A Harvest of Theory and Practice *(pp. 144–45) by M. Carter and D. Curtis, 1994, St. Paul, MN: Redleaf. Copyright © 1994 by the authors. Used by permission.*

8

November Visit: Burying Dinosaurs and Planning a Harvest Feast

Betty decides to visit Manzanita just after the children's trip to the *mercado* to see what's happened. There are *calaveras* in several rooms. Bethany got her skeleton, and she has several body tracings under way, with children's efforts to draw what's inside them. Right now, though, her children's action is in the sand as usual, where dinosaurs are still being buried. And the children who were making pumpkin Barbie houses last month have invented a new creative focus—they're making elaborate graves for the dinosaurs. They've found paper flowers somewhere, and they're busy adding leaves and seed pods fallen from the tree. Bob's wood scraps have been converted into tombstones, and several children are happily writing on them with markers. "Can you write *stegosaurus* on here?" one of them asks Betty as she comes near.

"We should have a funeral," a small boy says solemnly. "My grandpa had a funeral. And the dinosaurs died, too."

The funeral theme is also evident in Sandra's room. A visiting student took notes on Monday's block play, Sandra tells Betty, and left a copy of her notes for Sandra to put up on the wall. "I've been trying to explain to parents that children *play* with the difficult ideas they're trying to understand. They don't understand dying—how could they?—so they play it. I'm hoping this observation might spark some more parent questions—about this, and probably about all the doctor play that's been happening, too."

Ruby comes by as Betty is reading about the coffin play. "Oh, I saw part of that," Ruby says. "So I had a chance to ask the girls about their coffin bed. It turned out that they had just seen Snow White on video. That's what they were playing; Snow White lies in her glass coffin, but she isn't really dead."

Sandra reappears. "And then the prince comes and wakes her up, and they live happily ever after," she says, with annoyance. "That may be reassuring, but it's certainly misleading—both about death and about relationships. I really don't like those Disney fairy tales, but the kids love them."

"Can't you do what I've seen you do with some other media fantasy—keep asking questions?" asks Ruby.[1] "At 4, the children aren't going to

Observation: 11/8, 3:30 to 4 p.m.
Center: Manzanita, block area
Age group: 4s
Observer: F. Morrison

Patty and Margo start talking about coffins.

Patty: Let's make a coffin. (They start building with the large cardboard blocks.) We are going to make a coffin bed.

Margo: We are not going to die, right?

Patty: Right. We are going to just sleep.

They work together, making a coffin with blocks on the outside and a mat in the middle. Luisa joins them and starts making her own coffin.

Patty: We are making a big coffin.

Margo goes to get some blankets and sheets. Patty helps her spread them in the coffin; it's time to lie down. Patty lies on the side Margo wanted to lie on, and Margo gets upset.

Margo: This is my blanket.

Patty: No, this is my blanket.

Margo: No, it's not.

Patty: I'll put some blankets and blocks here.

Margo: Take my blanket, OK?

Patty: Let's share. You have that one, and I'll take this side. Look at our bed (to the adult). It has pillows and blankets and blocks on top of a mat. It's our coffin bed.

Patty goes to get a snack.

Margo: I'll wait on you, Pat, OK?

Ten minutes later, Patty returns to the coffin. She lies down and covers herself, saying to Margo: "It's time to go to sleep."

get very far with the big questions, but at least you don't have to leave them with pat answers."

"I'm trying to do that," Sandra says. "It's hard to know what to ask, though—what the children's real issue is. I did say to Patty, 'Is that really a coffin?' She said, 'Yes, it's Snow White's coffin, and I'm Snow White.' And so I decided not to ask my next question, which was 'When people are in coffins do they always wake up?' I guess I'm nervous about bringing up death if that's not really what they're playing."

"Do you ever retell children's play stories to them, or to the whole group?" Betty asks. "Do the girls know you've put their story up on the wall?"[2]

"Oh yes, I read it to them when I put it up," Sandra says. "They were pleased. They found all the places where their names were, and Margo said she's going to make a picture of the coffin beds and Snow White so we can put that up, too. But I don't want to get into Snow White. As Bethany says all the time, 'That's *their* curriculum, that's not my curriculum.'"

"What if you were to read their story to a group at storytime?" Betty persists. "It doesn't say anything about Snow White. And Margo and Patty aren't wanting to talk about dying, but some of the other kids might. You could try asking them your question if a discussion of 'tender topics' is what you'd like to stimulate."[3]

"Read the Room"

"Whose name can you see in our room?" a teacher might ask a group of 4- or 5-year-olds. "Where do you see it? Do you need the pointer to show us?"

"Why is Jun's name there? Do you remember? You're right; those are Jun's words about our trip to the *mercado*. Do you remember what he said? Let's read them."

In a classroom where emergent literacy is consciously implemented as a goal of the emergent curriculum, children's names and their words and their pictures and original artwork can be found in many places. Frequent invitations to re-read and re-tell the history thus displayed embed literacy learning squarely in children's collective experience. Revisiting past events weaves them into the emerging present and generates ideas for the future, creating meaningful connections over time as the group creates its life together.

"I'll think about that," Sandra says. "Oh oh, I think I'm needed over there . . . "

———

"Thanks," Ruby says to Betty. "Sandra's a risk taker; she'll probably try that once she's thought it through. I've been encouraging her, but I hadn't thought of that idea.

"Speaking of good ideas, have you seen our planning board for the harvest feast? Stop by the teachers' room if you have time. You'll be impressed."

Betty is impressed. The board in the teachers' room is covered with planning notes. A book collection has begun on the table; she notices *Bread, Bread, Bread, The Carrot Seed, The Little Red Hen,*[4] and several holiday stories. Some song words and explanations of four festivals are already up on the wall; it's evident that staff have been doing their homework. "Are you going to celebrate all of them?" Betty asks.

"No, it's going to be a generic sort of festival," Ruby says. "We've agreed to call it a Harvest–Home celebration and not say much about Thanksgiving. Carrying the harvest home is an idea children can

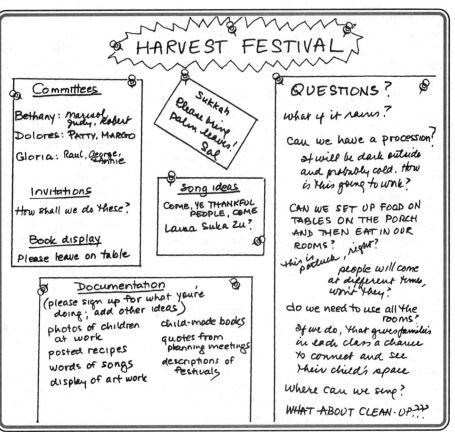

HARVEST FESTIVAL

Committees

Bethany: Marisol, Judy, Robert
Dolores: PATTY, MARGO
Gloria: Raul, George, Annie

Invitations
How shall we do these?

Book display
Please leave on table

Sukkah
Please bring
palm leaves!
Sal

Song ideas
Come, ye THANKFUL PEOPLE, COME
Lama Suka Zu?

Documentation
(please sign up for what you're doing; add other ideas)
photos of children at work
posted recipes
words of songs
display of art work
child-made books
quotes from planning meetings
descriptions of festivals

QUESTIONS?
what if it rains?
Can we have a procession? It will be dark outside and probably cold. How is this going to work?
CAN WE SET UP FOOD ON TABLES ON THE PORCH AND THEN EAT IN OUR ROOMS? right?
this is potluck, people will come at different times, won't they?
do we need to use all the rooms? If we do, that gives families in each class a chance to connect and see their child's space
Where can we sing?
WHAT ABOUT CLEAN·UP...

Harvest Home

North American Thanksgiving has its roots in the Harvest–Home celebrations of Europe, which marked the end of seasonal tasks and expressed gratitude for the bounties of nature. Churches were decorated with the fruits and vegetables and grains of harvest, and the first bread loaves made from the harvest wheat were blessed. The service, with its hymns and its liturgy, was one of the joyous festivals of the church year.

In many countries in the fields outside the church, the last sheaf of grain was dressed as a woman and paraded through the fields. In the British Isles it was variously called the Harvest Doll, the Kern (Corn) Baby, and the Maiden. In parts of Eastern Europe, it was dressed as an old woman, the Baba or Boba, and borne in triumphal procession to the farmer's house. On the way it might be drenched with water to ensure plenty of rain for next year's crop.[5]

Hounen-Odori

In Japan the harvest festival, Hounen-Odori, takes place on the 15th day of the harvest moon. It is a time of rejoicing. A large platform may be constructed in the village center and decorated with fruits and vegetables, sheaves of rice, green leaves, and garlands of flowers. People dress in traditional kimono, and each region has its special costume, song, and dance. There is music, dancing, and feasting. Each family contributes good things to be eaten with thanksgiving in the light of the full harvest moon.[6]

At child care centers, children and teachers go to the fields and dig up sweet potatoes or onions. Sometimes they cook them at school, or sometimes they take them home.

understand, we think. We brought pumpkins from the pumpkin patch to our school. Our families bring food home from the store. We didn't have a garden with a real harvest, but I hope that can happen next year.

"Yoshiko says she really doesn't know much about Hounen-Odori; it happens mostly in the countryside. But Sally is excited about building the *sukkah*—the little booth—at school; she has wonderful memories of the *Sukkot* celebration from her trip to Israel. Did you see where they've begun?"

Betty hasn't noticed any little booth. "Well, it doesn't look like much yet," Ruby goes on. "But they've been collecting palm leaves, and Sally is singing a Hebrew song the children like to dance to.

"Bethany surveyed her families and found that two of them celebrate *Kwanzaa*. It comes later in the calendar year, but it's a harvest festival. Families have been willing to lend her some things for a display—real treasures; their children were in her class last year, too, and there's been time to build trust. I do think continuity is important," Ruby comments further.

"Some parents have begun bringing produce, too," continues Ruby, "as they notice what's going on. A few people have late produce from gardens of their own; others pick up sale items at the store. Our snacks this week have been wonderful, with lots of conversation about foods of all sorts."

"Remember the old 'horn-of-plenty' image?" says Betty. "I think you're tapping one here.

Sukkot

Thousands of years ago, most Jews were farmers. Fall was a busy time of year. It was a time to bring in the foods they grew on their farms.

The grapes burst with juice on the vines. The olives hung ripe on the trees. The grain stood tall in the fields. Everything was ready to be picked.

It all had to be gathered quickly. If not, a rain storm or cold spell could ruin it.

The farmers worked long and hard every day. They cut the harvest and gathered it. They started when the sun came up and did not stop until the first star came out. They built little booths, so they could sleep out in the fields . . . . *Sukkot* is the Hebrew word for "booths."

So, every fall, as the leaves begin to change color, we build a *sukkah* outdoors—a little house, just like the farmers built in ancient Israel. We cover the roof of the *sukkah* with leaves and branches. We leave spaces between them so we can see the sky above our heads. We hang fruits and vegetables on our little *sukkah*. Apples, pears, and shiny green peppers. Long ears of Indian corn and funny-shaped gourds. There is so much to choose from!

We eat in the *sukkah* all week and have parties in it . . . . We thank God for all that He gives us.

Reprinted from Sukkot and Simhat Torah *(n.p.) by Miriam Schlein, 1983, New Jersey: Behrman House. Copyright © 1983 by Behrman House, Inc. Used by permission.*

Kwanzaa

Kwanzaa is an African American cultural celebration whose name is derived from the Kiswahili phrase *matunda ya kwanzaa,* meaning "first fruits." It reflects the thanksgiving celebrations for successful harvests by agricultural peoples in Africa. The seven principles of the *Kwanzaa* celebration are intended as guidelines for living, as well. They are

Umoja (unity)

Kujichagulia (self-determination)

Ujima (collective work and responsibility)

Ujamaa (cooperative economics)

Nia (purpose)

Kuumba (creativity)

Imani (faith)

The *Kwanzaa* ceremonial table, covered by a straw mat, holds the candleholder for the seven candles, the unity cup, ears of corn (one for each child), and many kinds of food.

ReGena Booze describes how she celebrates *Kwanzaa* with the children she teaches:

Because Kwanzaa is a harvest celebration there should be plenty of fruits, vegetables, nuts placed in baskets. I set out dates, coconuts, peanuts, bananas, oranges, pineapples, yams, almonds, and raisins. After we light the candle of the day and discuss the principle, the children help themselves to the finger foods set on the mkeka.[7]

You've talked a lot with John about community building, haven't you, and helping adults care for each other in the context of caring for their children? I think you're teaching us all about how it can be done, with both staff and parents."[8]

"Well, I don't know if I'm teaching, but I'm certainly learning," says Ruby. "You know, last year I was starting to feel burned out and was thinking maybe I'd been in this job too long. But I'm feeling reenergized. I like having the practical and theoretical challenges all mixed up together—figuring out how to organize new space and how to build community in child care, both at the same time.

"My sister told me I was fooling myself, thinking I could write my thesis the same year we moved the center. She's probably right, but having to analyze what we're doing, in between doing it, has really kept me focused. You know, I think I see something like that happening for teachers, too, in our meetings."

"That's what I've always believed. It's so reassuring to have you say it!" exclaims Betty. "I think schools lose so much creative energy by failing to treat teachers as thinkers, as people with ideas who should be talking to each other all the time. The same thing happens for kids in classrooms where they're expected to be quiet and do what they're told and not talk to each other. Schools often 'dumb people down.'"[9]

"Does that mean we're 'smarting them up'?" Ruby adds with a grin.

Betty grins back, nodding vigorously. She's due at work and should be on her way, but she pauses to finish reading the Harvest–Home description on the wall. "Did you see this part about 'drenching the Baba'?" she chuckles. "How's that for part of the celebration—a water fight?"

"Shhh!" says Ruby firmly. "*Don't* bring up that idea for a late-fall evening event. We'll save it for Midsummer's Day."

Celebrations: Meaningful or Trivial?

It is important to honor the cultural traditions of the families in any early childhood program and to incorporate some of the richness of these traditions into celebrations and documentations at the center. How can this be done without trivializing symbolic meanings, on the one hand, or offending persons with different beliefs, on the other?

As staff at Manzanita Center plan their harvest feast, for example, they are recognizing that many cultural traditions celebrate harvest and that religious and historical symbols and stories are central to these celebrations. How to proceed presents the staff with a dilemma. If the embedded meanings of these traditions are omitted (because a child from a nonreligious home shouldn't be asked to sing "God, our Maker" at a school event; and, besides, young children don't yet understand history and symbol), will they run the risk of being left with mere superficialities? There are no easy answers. Dialogue is essential, and the answers it generates will, of necessity, be thoughtful compromises.

9

December Staff Meeting: Lights in the Darkness

We reminisce about last month's Harvest-Home Feast on our way to the staff meeting.

"I'm so glad it didn't rain," Betty says. "The weather bureau was making dire predictions, and staff would have scratched the parade if it had poured rain—and the parade was really important to everyone."

"Celebrations build community," says John with certainty. "My guess is that's what they've always been for, to bring people together and reaffirm the values they share and the tasks they've accomplished. Having a procession with singing was wonderful. Even the youngest ones can *feel* connected to the community when they share in that kind of joy."

"All the displays of children's work helped give teachers and parents something to start talking about, I noticed," says Betty, "and *children* something to show their family members. 'Look, here's my name.' 'Look, here's the skeleton at the *mercado*.' 'See my painting? This is a Tyrannosaurus rex!' I like the way paintings are staying at school for display instead of just going straight home. In a way, they create a kind of historical record of teachers' and children's time together."

———

The staff, as we greet them, seem tired but cheerful. They respond quickly when Ruby asks, "What was best for you at the feast? What wouldn't you do again?" It's a good way for teachers to unwind, to acknowledge how much work it was, and to affirm why it was worth it.

"It's nice to have a festival when the days are getting gloomy," says Sandra. "I don't like winter; I miss the light. And when it gets dark so early, it's really hard for kids in child care. 'When is my daddy coming?' they keep asking. 'Where's my mommy?' They want to go home. I want to go home, too, and build a fire and make popcorn."

"We *could* make popcorn," Gloria suggests. "I suppose it might spoil their dinners, but maybe we could just call it first course. It sure would smell welcoming when parents arrived."

"Has anyone talked with their kids about the dark?" asks Sally. "I'm on the morning shift, but the shrinking days are an issue then, too. Some kids are getting up in the dark. Adrianna even noticed I had the lights on in the room when she arrived today. I hadn't thought about it until you brought it up, but there's a real solid curriculum idea—light and dark. Why is it dark, and what do people do

Coping with Feelings

"[At Reggio Emilia] teachers actually plan activities and experiences knowing that they may worry or frighten some children . . . . When asked why they would purposefully provide such an experience, the explanation, simply enough, was that children need opportunities, within the safety of the group setting, to understand and learn how to cope with their own and others' feelings. The American preoccupation with protecting young children from experiencing negative emotions is in marked contrast to this practice," describes Rebecca New.[1]

Darkness is among the many experiences about which some adults may have negative feelings that they pass on to children. Inventing provocations invites adults as well as children to reexamine their automatic, first reactions to a variety of phenomena. What's interesting and beautiful about darkness (or about snakes, or insects, or a foreign language, or old people)? If we pay attention, what can we find out?

about it? There's science and social studies, rolled into one."

"Festivals of light—now there's a thought," says Bethany. "I've been wondering what we'd decide to do about December holidays. People in lots of cultures have festivals of light, don't they?"

"Are you thinking of starting with festivals or with the dark?" asks Ruby.

"We've just *had* our festival," says Mayella, looking tired.

"I think I'd rather start with the dark since that's what the kids are thinking about," says Sandra. "I'm 'festivaled' out, too. And I like your idea, Sally. I'm going to try it tomorrow afternoon—call a group time and sit close in a circle, turn out the lights and talk about what's been happening. Why is it dark? How could we make light? Could we turn on the sun? I think I want to tape-record what they say, and that might give us more ideas about what children understand and what their questions are."

"I know how hard it is for folks to find time to record and then listen to and transcribe kids' words, the way they do in *The Hundred Languages of Children,*[2] but that sounds like a conversation worth catching to me," says Ruby, in support.

"Actually, I've found the morning commute to be a time that I can at least listen to some tapes,"

says Sandra. "But just taking the time to place that tape recorder on the table seems to help me focus on what the kids are *really* saying."

Dolores is looking doubtful, and Ruby notices. "What's bothering you?" she asks Dolores.

"I'm thinking about the dark," says Dolores. "I'll be on my way home by then, but I think a couple of the kids will be scared."

"Luisa, probably, and maybe Jasper," says Sandra. "But maybe I could get them to sit by me, and if they're scared, I'll give them a hug. And I could turn the light back on if they want it on."

"I think it may be all right if they're scared," says Yoshiko. "Being scared is an important feeling."

"Sure! Children need chances to name it and talk about it," adds Bob.

"And you can help them think about what you can do when you're scared," suggests Yoshiko.

"If it's dark, you can turn the lights on, or turn on a flashlight, or light a candle," says Sally. "Could you light a candle in the middle of your circle and have a Candle-Time story? Stories around campfires are one of my best memories. Our kids may be too little to chance using candles, but yours can be careful about fire when it's really important."

"Day care children see less of the basic things like fire than they would at home," says Ruby. "It's hard to practice fire safety if fire is only a word or a picture. We provide all sorts of experiences with earth and air and water; weren't those and fire the four basic elements in the European Middle Ages or whenever?"

"So can we try Candle Time? Can we have a menorah, too?" asks Sally. "I'd like that."

"And here we are at the winter holidays, says Bethany. "How do people feel about that?"

"With all this talk about lights and fires, I've been thinking about Solstice," says Gloria. "That's the darkest night of the year, and so you light bonfires to be sure of the sun-return. Can children this young understand why days get shorter and then longer again? I'm not sure I *really* understand it myself, even though I can say the words. But I like to celebrate Solstice."

"I suppose *Las Posadas* is too religious?" asks Dolores.

"What about the Christmas tree?" asks Marnie. "Of course we'll have that, won't we?"

"See what you think of this idea," says Ruby. "Suppose we begin with the dark, and lights in the darkness, and maybe some other ways people comfort each other in the darkness—singing, and eating together, and caring for each other. Can we draw on those parts of the traditions that have meaning for any of us, without getting into the religious stories that underlie them? Those stories are for home, not for a school with people in it from many different religious backgrounds."

"So we could have candles," asks Sally, "with different kinds of candleholders—the menorah is the kind of candleholder in my home and it's important to me? And maybe we could make *latkes* for snack? But not talk about the Maccabees? I'm not sure if that feels OK, it seems hollowed out. Still, I understand what you're saying, Ruby. Let me sleep on it."

"Then maybe we shouldn't sing "*Vamos a Belén*" or do the procession, but we could make *luminarias* as candleholders," says Dolores.

"What about making candleholders out of clay?" asks Bob.

"I'd like to make both candleholders and candles," says Bethany, "if I could do it with a small group. Hot wax is another risk, but I think 5-year-olds are ready for activities like this that require care and patience."

"I got ignored when I asked about the Christmas tree," says Marnie. "What does that mean, that we aren't going to have one?"

"We aren't going to have a school tree," says Ruby. "People are making choices about what to have in their own classrooms, and we can decide what we want to share. Most of the children in Christian families and even many families who aren't religious will have a tree at home. Christian symbols dominate everyone's experience, at the mall in particular. They've become commercialized and taken for granted, but they don't reflect everyone's beliefs. I'd like our school to be a place where less-dominant symbols get more attention to provide some balance. And as people were saying, we've had our festival. Can we keep December low-key at school? It won't be anywhere else."

"If you think about lights and foods from your own background, Marnie," continues Ruby, "what would you want to share with the children?"

Marnie persists. "But it's the presents under the tree that are really exciting to children at Christmas. How can we just ignore that?"

"Children will be getting presents at home," says Dolores. "At school we could talk about *giving* gifts, instead."

No Traditional Holidays?

Consider, for a moment, the possibility that a child care program is an inappropriate place to celebrate holidays—period . . . . Children love anticipation and planning and all the excitement that goes with festivity, and I love sharing all this with them. [BUT] . . .

1. It's extremely difficult to give holidays meaning that is developmentally appropriate for very young children. Most holidays are based on abstract concepts that are beyond their comprehension.

2. It's difficult to be inclusive. Are we going to celebrate holidays based in cultures represented in our program? What if there is little diversity? What if there is a great deal? What if some parents object to all holidays? Do we have the time and resources to do justice to them all? How much of our curriculum do we want to devote to holidays? What important activities are being displaced?

3. Many holidays are overdone anyway. Children see signs of the major commercialized holidays everywhere, so they'll be asking questions and their families will be making choices . . . . If families are celebrating, why do we need to celebrate too? . . .

When we make choices about what to celebrate, let us be very conscious of who we are doing it for. . . . If we are doing it for the families, we must choose carefully what to celebrate so that we are inclusive. If we are doing it for the children, let us be conscious of all the subtle messages inherent in what we do and choose things to celebrate that are meaningful, developmentally appropriate, and healthy for them.

Reprinted from "Going One Step Further—No Traditional Holidays" by B. Neugebauer, 1990, Child Care Information Exchange, 74 (August), p. 42. Copyright © 1990 by Exchange Press, Inc., P.O. Box 2890, Redmond, WA 98073. Used by permission.

"We already have gifts," says Gloria cheerfully. "All the things the children have been making out of clay. And Bob wants to make candleholders, and maybe the 5s will make candles. Everyone can make wrapping paper and cards and write notes."

"A couple of our kids will really get into that; I can just see it," says Bethany. "Can I volunteer them to help make cards for some of the little ones?"

We notice Ruby is beginning to look exasperated. Dolores notices, too. "What is it, Ruby?" she asks.

"You're certainly not behaving like people who are willing to go easy on the holidays," says Ruby. "Shall I just give up? This happens every year as I remember. I think I'm swimming against the tide."

"I've gotten sucked in, too, haven't I?" Bethany chuckles. "Me, who doesn't like holidays. I'd like to go back to what you said before, Ruby—what was it, about lights in the darkness and people caring for each other? Could we keep a lid on our enthusiasms by saying that's what we're doing and that we respect different families' holiday celebrations and won't be trying to duplicate them at school?"

A couple of people nod enthusiastically. Others are silent. Bob looks uncertain; Marnie looks miffed.

"I don't think we're going to get consensus," decides Ruby, "so I'm going to make a directorial decision to enable us to be somewhat consistent in responding to parents' questions. In December some of us will be looking for lights in the darkness. We'll be singing and eating together as we always do. Some of us will be creating gifts for people we care about. Different teachers and children will be doing different things as they always do. We will not be celebrating any particular holidays at school; children will be part of family celebrations at home, and for young children we'd like school to be a place of calm rather than overstimulation.

"I trust you'll do your own thing, as usual. I may ask questions if it looks to me as if what you're doing isn't reasonably consistent with what I just said. I'll try to stay open to good answers to my questions. And you can argue with each other, for which you hardly need my permission. If we didn't argue, how would we ever learn anything new?"

That, for the moment, seems to be that. People are silent for several moments. Then Sandra says very tentatively, "Would you all bite me if I asked you to help me web *lights in the darkness?*"

"More webbing? I think I might bite," Sally replies with a grin.

"You can't do that. It's a bad example for the kids," says Mayella unexpectedly. "Sure, I'll help you. Why not?"

———

"Downplaying holidays is such a challenge," John comments afterwards. "Somehow holidays have become *the* curriculum in schools, and hardly anyone wants to give them up."

"It's what you were saying earlier, isn't it? Celebrations build community, and celebrating

---

Religious Holidays in a Diverse Classroom

Although Christmas is celebrated as a national holiday, it really reflects a specific religious belief system. For children who are not Christian—be they Jewish, Buddhist, Muslim, atheist—Christmas can be a problem. How do teachers handle the dual reality of Christmas, as a Christian holiday and a national holiday, in a way that is supportive and fair to all? Here are some solutions other teachers have used.

Alternative 1: *Integrate December holidays from several cultural groups . . .* identify common themes and observations . . . .

Alternative 2: *Do December holidays other than Christmas . . .* to expose Christian children to other important December traditions and to support the children who do not celebrate Christmas . . . .

Alternative 3: *Don't do December holidays at all in the classroom.* When children return from Christmas break, they can share what they did. Encourage children to identify the similarities and differences in the way they spent their time . . . .

Reprinted from Anti-Bias Curriculum: Tools for Empowering Young Children *(pp. 91–93) by L. Derman-Sparks and the A.B.C. Task Force, 1989, Washington, DC: NAEYC. Copyright © 1989 by L. Derman-Sparks. Used by permission.*

Teacher–Teacher Relations

Planning together, teachers don't necessarily agree. But continuing dialogue is a significant source of mutual learning. This idea is strongly emphasized in the child care centers of Reggio Emilia, Italy, which are characterized by in-depth emergent curriculum. As their founder, Loris Malaguzzi, explained,

> Collegial work represents for us a deliberate break from the traditional professional and cultural solitude and isolation of teachers. This isolation has been rationalized in the name of academic freedom, yet wrongly understood. Its result, certainly, has been to impoverish and desiccate teachers' potential and resources and make it difficult or impossible for them to achieve quality.[3]

Rebecca New stresses that

> The Reggio Emilia conception of adults as lifelong learners has vast implications for the ways in which adults in the school setting work together. . . .Through the use of a constructivist framework to guide staff development goals and activities, teachers. . .actively seek out multiple perspectives, exchanging points of view with each other and with parents as well. . . . The view. . . of adults as learners enables teachers to acknowledge their uncertainties as they construct for themselves an understanding of children's development. Furthermore, this attitude includes a tolerance for debate that far exceeds American notions of productive conversation. When commenting on the satisfaction of working together for more than 17 years in the same school, two Reggio Emilia teachers begrudgingly acknowledge that familiarity brought its own problems: "We don't argue as much anymore."[4]

makes people feel good. And they're breaks in the routine; child care can get awfully routine," says Betty.

"I guess the question isn't whether to celebrate, but *what* to celebrate," says John. "That's something that staff in any program need to decide for themselves, but they won't necessarily agree."

"And speaking of agreement, did you hear any dissenting voices during the

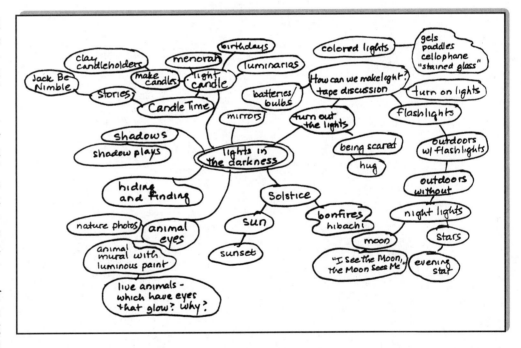

discussion of dark as scary?" Betty asks. "They all got into how you can make light in the darkness, but no one suggested that darkness might be friendly rather than threatening."

"I know. That bothered me," says John. "This observer role is hard; I don't get to speak up when I'd like to. I guess we'll just have to wait and see what they do with the children."

10
December Visit: Candle Time

John arrives at Manzanita in the late afternoon as the cool breeze and impending dark hasten the children inside. With their numbers dwindling, Gloria's remaining children have joined Sandra's 4s for the final hour of a long day. For John, there is the opportunity to find out what Candle Time is really like. Dolores (who has to leave early), has asked him to help document the event with his camera and low-light film. With candles in use, Sandra and Gloria will be plenty busy maintaining safety and calming any fears.

John discovers that Candle Time has quickly become something of a ritual. There's a list of candlelighters—the children—posted on the wall and a collection of different shapes and sizes and colors of candles and candleholders displayed on a table. "We're adding to this," Gloria explains. "Several parents have offered to bring in candleholders. And as children make their own candleholders, they'll go on the table for a few days, until they're ready to be wrapped for gifts. Dolores went to the *mercado* to do her Christmas shopping and couldn't resist the *candelaria*—the candle shop. That's where the pierced-tin

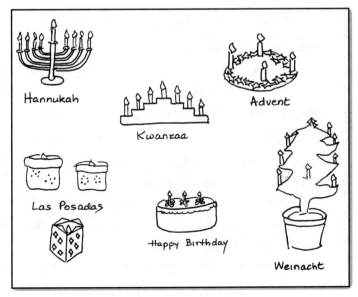

CANDLELIGHTERS

~~Jan~~
~~Mark~~
~~Rachel~~
Lucy
Jeremy
Patty
Margo
Jody

candleholders come from and the scented *candelas*."

"If it's your turn to light the candle," Gloria continues, "you get to choose your candle and your candleholder (and discover which ones fit together and which don't)."

Today it's Lucy's turn. She finds her name on the list and carefully crosses it off before moving to the table, where she sniffs candles one by one and finally chooses a strawberry-scented red one. It will fit in a pierced-tin holder, she discovers; she's pleased about that. Carefully, she carries it over to place it on the metal tray that Gloria puts down in the middle of the rug. "Candle Time," Gloria and Lucy call out together.

As children come to sit around the edge of the rug, Gloria turns off the lights. Then she hands Lucy a long, thin taper; she lights it for her and walks with her to her red candle. Lucy lights it carefully. She doesn't want to blow out the taper, so Gloria does. Then they join the group on the rug.

"This little light of mine," Sandra starts singing softly. "I'm gonna let it shine." "Let it shine,

let it shine, let it shine." These are words the children learned on first hearing, and they're enthusiastically singing them now. The song goes rapidly from soft to loud. It would be a good dancing song, but there isn't room to dance safely at Candle Time. So the adults calm the children down, and Sandra holds up one of several pictures she's found in nature-photography magazines. "Know what this is?" she asks the children.

"Dog!" "No, fox!" "No, wolf!" Whoever it is, its eyes are glowing in the dark. "Its little lights are shining," exclaims Lucy, to Sandra's delight. There's a glowing-eyed raccoon in the next picture, a bobcat in the third.

"Why do their eyes shine in the dark?" asks Sandra. There are lots of guesses; Gloria has the tape recorder on to catch them for use in continuing discussions.

The adults don't provide right answers; Sandra isn't sure, in fact, what the right answer is, though she knows both she and the children will find out before this project is over. "You have lots of good ideas," she says. "Here's some homework for you. When you go home, ask the people in your family what they think about why animals' eyes glow in the dark. We'll talk about it again tomorrow," Sandra concludes.

"Now do you know what we're going to do?" says Sandra, opening a new topic.

WHY DO THEIR EYES SHINE IN THE DARK?

Margo: They turn them on at night.

Patty: The headlights.
The headlights shine them.

Jeremy: So they can see to run.
Coyotes run after little mice.
They eats them.

Sandra: Do the mice's eyes shine too?

Jeremy: I don't know. I don't think so.

Mark: Yes they do. My mouse's eyes are pink and shiny. And I don't let no coyotes eat him.

Jody: Magic Mouse shines in the dark! Do Magic Mouse!

EMERGENT CURRICULUM

"Magic Mouse!" exclaims a child. "Do Magic Mouse again!"

"Not today. We can do Magic Mouse tomorrow," Sandra assures him. "But I don't want to get out the flashlight today, because today we're going outside without flashlights."

"No, flashlights!" several children chorus.

"*No* flashlights" says Sandra firmly. "See if you can guess why not when we go outside. Hold a friend's hand, please. We're going to line up at the door so we can all go outside together."

Outside, they cluster on the porch, where Gloria has turned off the outdoor lights. "We didn't bring any lights," says Sandra. "But do you see any lights here waiting for us?" A child points to a streetlight, and Sandra nods. "There's one. Let's go out a little further and look up at the sky. Do you think there are any lights in the sky?"

"There's the moon!" Lucy points excitedly. "The moon, the moon!"

"I see the moon," says Sandra. "Lucy sees the moon. Mark, do you see the moon? Who sees the moon?"

"Me!" "Me!" "Moon, moon!"

"Let's sing it," says Sandra. "'I see the moon, the moon sees me, the moon sees somebody I want to see.'"

"Who do you want to see, Mark?"

Homework

One teacher, Georgina Villarino, recounts, "I said to the children, 'This is your homework. Ask your parents where butterflies go when it rains.' When children answer questions in the group, they say what their friend said. When they bring answers from home, they're all different."[2]

Homework used to be only for big kids in schools, but now it begins in kindergarten. In our view, homework for young children is appropriate not as an extension of conventional school work but only if it is designed to generate genuine family discussion of topics being explored at school.

What ideas do the people in your family have? What experiences have they had? Go home and ask them; come back and tell us what they said. Asking questions, children can build bridges between home and school.

Several parents have arrived and are waiting at the edge of the group.

"My daddy!" shouts Mark.

"And here he is!" shouts Mark's daddy, hugging him.

11

January Staff Meeting: Playing Birthday and Telling Our Stories

"I can't believe it!" says Sandra. "The day of the storm, when the lights went out, I was scared; but the kids acted as if it was the emergency we'd been preparing for all along. Jun ran to get the flashlights, and Rachel said, "Where did you put the candles? Can we use the menorah so we'll have lots of candles?"

"Talk about serendipity," says Ruby. "It had never occurred to me that lights in the darkness would turn out to be emergency preparation. That's pretty exciting."

"Lots of things about lights have been exciting," says Dolores. "I think we'll be going on and on with them. We tried turning the pinhole candleholders around and around to see if they'd make little lights moving on the wall, and that has gotten us into shadows; now we're going to practice a shadow play behind a sheet. We'll invite you all to come and see it when we get it worked out."

"We're making an animal mural, and when it's done, I'm going to add eyes with luminous paint as a surprise for the children," says Sandra. "The other day when we'd been talking about animal eyes glowing in the dark, Jun suddenly asked, 'Do our eyes shine in the dark, too?' We didn't know, so we turned off the lights to see."

"Do they?" asks Marnie, uncertain.

"No," says Sandra. "So now we're wondering which animals' eyes do and which don't. And can we bring animals to school and turn off the lights to see if their eyes shine?"

"It's really fun because we don't know a lot of the answers either," says Dolores. "So when we ask questions, they're real questions. We're not just playing teacher; we're curious, too."

"Can I ask a question, even though I'm supposed to be an observer?" John asks, his and Betty's presence at staff meetings now customary. "When I was last visiting, the kids wanted to play Magic Mouse. What's Magic Mouse?"

Sandra's face lights up. "When I was little, my papa and I used to play Magic Mouse at bedtime," she explains. "The grown-up has a flashlight and shines it around the walls. Children can try to catch the light, in which case the play gets real rowdy. Or they can just guess where the light's going to appear next.

"We've been discovering that you can do it with a mirror, too. Even outside in the daytime."

"But mostly, outside in the daytime, everyone's playing birthday," adds Dolores. "The children do that all the time every year, of course. We're not celebrating birthdays as a class. We've decided we're more interested in whole-group rituals than in that kind of focus on individual children. But birthday is a spontaneous play theme. The children asked if they could have candles for their cakes—a reasonable request—and we said no. They were making pretend cakes, and pretend cakes need pretend candles; and how many kinds of pretend candles could they think of? They've been very imaginative."

"I don't understand something you said, Dolores," says Marnie. "That you don't want to focus on individual children? Aren't we trying to build self-concept and self-esteem? I've always thought of birthdays as one way to do that."

"So have I," says Sandra. "I used to put up the little train with all the kids' birthdays and have a crown for the birthday child and all that. But when I learned that Mark's family are Witnesses, I talked to his mother about what they believe and how we could be respectful of that. Their family has baby showers, she says, and weddings; and they celebrate anniversaries of things like weddings. But not birthdays because the day you were born isn't a choice you made—it's just part of the natural order of things.[1] I thought that was interesting. I started wondering how we could celebrate the things we accomplish as individuals, and the discoveries we make as a group. Could we create our own rituals as we go along, that belong to us and aren't something that gets commercialized? I love the way that's happened with Candle Time. And we're thinking about ways to share special paintings children make, or particularly interesting words they use so that children will all have turns to be recognized for what they contribute to our life together."

"I like that," says Bob. Marnie is silent.

"So do I," says Bethany. "I really like how clearly you've thought it through. We should have a celebration of that!"

"Let's have a toast," says Bob. "That's a good adult ritual. Cups up, everybody."

———

"It's January," says Ruby. "What does anyone have planned?"

"It's Dr. King's birthday," says Mayella. "We'll be celebrating that."

"But we've just been talking about not celebrating birthdays," says Marnie, surprised.

"Girl, you didn't hear me talking about not celebrating Dr. King's birthday," says Mayella. "This is my holiday, and we gonna do it. We're respecting what's important to each other, right? I marched in Selma, and you better believe this is important to me."

"I'm with you there," says Ruby.[2] "Whether or not the children need heroes—and I think they do—I know I do. That's part of my history I want to share with families here."

"That's important, isn't it?" says Bethany. "We don't really know each other without our histories. And our teaching reflects what we value, so we'd better be

---

BIRTHDAY CANDLES

Jeremy and Rachel were making birthday cakes out of sand.

They were pretend cakes.

Jeremy and Rachel wanted candles for their birthday cakes.

"Dolores," they said, "Can we have candles for our birthday cakes?"

"You have pretend cakes," Dolores said.

"You need pretend candles.

How can you make pretend candles?"

Luisa had a good idea.

She made pretend candles out of little sticks.

Jeremy had a good idea.

He made pretend candles out of dry grass.

Rachel had a good idea.

She made pretend candles out of eucalyptus leaves.

HAPPY PRETEND BIRTHDAY!

Telling Our Stories

Human beings are the animal that tells stories. Every family, every culture, every religion has its own central stories, which are told and retold to remind us of our collective meanings and our personal place in them. People don't just endure life or live it unreflectively; they attribute meaning to it. Families save treasured possessions and take pictures and tell stories to make connections with loved people who aren't here but to whom we belong. Each culture has its myths, its history; these are its central truths, passed on to each generation. They provide the context within which we understand and remember our experience.

What does this have to do with the lives of young children? The majority of young children in this country are spending their days in groups of strangers—people with no continuing connection with them. If child care is to provide a meaningful, connected growing place for both children and adults, it must consciously build a shared culture. Cultures are built around significant images, shared rituals, and collective stories told and retold.

clear about that. I've heard Mayella's freedom march story for two years now, and I want to hear it again. And I want to see again Ruby's pictures of Martin Luther King with her daddy. And I'll tell my kids about Rosa Parks on the bus. Children need to hear adults talk about important things like the civil rights movement.

"The thing that bothers me about heroes' birthdays in schools is that they seem to justify coloring books to teachers. We make such a point of creative art the rest of the time, so can we please not give the children pictures of Dr. King to color? Surely we can think of better hands-on activities than that?"

"Have you ever role-played Rosa Parks on the bus?" Gloria asks Bethany. "The 5-year-olds did that at my other center."

"Actually, a teacher at my daughter's school did a dreadful attempt at that role play. I was annoyed, and I told her so. She approached it like any old game, not something that is really important to people," says Bethany. "But with your help, Gloria, I might like to try it for myself. Could you tell me later about how they did it?"[4]

Gloria nods. Then she takes her turn in the group discussion, saying, "You know what I've been wanting to do? I really like those skin-color paints you can buy now. Several children in our class have made comments about color. 'She's ugly,' one girl said about the darkest-skinned child in a multiracial poster on our wall. And the other day a child suddenly looked at my hand and said, 'Didn't you wash your hands?' I explained, 'My hands are brown. The color doesn't wash off.' The child didn't say any more. But it's time that we all look at skin color together; and I'd like to do handprints if we can get those paints."

"We've got some," says Ruby. "I've been saving them until someone asked."

"Oh, good," says Gloria gratefully. "And, see what you think about this idea: I'd like to make a friendship quilt with all our handprints. If we have squares of paper in different background colors, and let children choose their background color and match their skin color for their handprints, then they can put their names on their squares and their squares up on the wall under a We Are Friends sign. I'd like that."

"Do we really want to talk about differences like that?" asks Bob.

"I've been wondering that," says Marnie. "I try to teach children that we're all alike and that color really doesn't matter."

"Maybe you all think it doesn't matter to you, but it sure mattered to those folks in Selma," says Mayella firmly. "It matters to a whole lot of folks here and now. You don't think my

Are You Color-Blind?

Some teachers are proud of being "color-blind," but in the article, "Meeting the Challenge of Diversity," the limitations of this view are described:

Originally a progressive argument against racial bigotry, it [color denial] implicitly establishes the dominant (Euro-American) culture experience as the norm and ends up equating "we are all the same" with "we are all White." Moreover, "colorblindness" ignores what we know about children's development of identity and attitudes as well as the realities of racism in the daily lives of people of color.[3]

grandkids have it different than you do? Pay attention to what's out there."[5]

On the drive home after the staff meeting, Betty asks, "Were you surprised at Bob's color-blind comment?"

"A little," says John, "but then this setting brings up issues of diversity that he probably hasn't confronted before. Mayella certainly made her point clearly, though I expect she's tired of being the person who speaks up. Do you think Bob and Marnie got it?"

"Marnie does keep putting her foot in it," Betty remarks. "She's amazingly persistent, though. She has a solid early childhood background, and it's given her confidence in what she knows. But she certainly isn't used to questioning what she knows or confronting different points of view. Do you think she'll last here?"

"She showed me her engagement ring when I asked if she'd gotten home for the holidays," says John. "I think she and her fiancé are planning to get married this summer. He's in graduate school in her hometown, she said. It will probably be a relief to her to get back there."

"She's really a good teacher in many ways," Betty says. "She's doing a lovely job of scribing children's words and of keeping her classroom an interesting place visually. She really enjoys children, too, and they enjoy her. It's the diversity issues that are new to her, and I don't get the sense that she wants to learn more about them. She's not a risk taker."

"And here she is in a hotbed of risk takers," John adds. "Plus people who aren't particularly, but who have a history at this center of helping to shape some of its values.

"Wasn't the birthday discussion great?" John goes on. "Children's birthdays have become *their* curriculum, not teachers' curriculum. But Dr. King's birthday is emphatically teachers' curriculum. It's a commemoration of their history and their values, and they're not about to deprive children of the chance to be a part of those things. That's how community building happens, when adults talk about their values and create rituals to share with children and with each other."

"I wonder how they're going to involve the parents?" says Betty.

12

January Visit:
Dear Martin Luther King,
We Love You

It's the end of the morning, and the two older groups of children are gathered together in the 4s' room to listen to Mayella's and Ruby's stories about the civil rights movement. Having watched these lively children in group gatherings before, Betty is awed by how subdued they are today. It's evident that, regardless of how much they do or don't understand about the issues, they do understand that this is a very important story for the adults who care for them. Several have noticed the tears that appear on Sandra's face as she listens. And many children join the adults in wholehearted singing, "We Shall Not Be Moved." Sometimes they feel those feelings, too, in the struggles of their own young lives.

Betty stays for lunch, at Bethany's invitation, in order to sit in on the kindergarten's afternoon meeting. "Do you have anything you'd like to say about

Martin Luther King?" Bethany begins by asking the children. "I thought I'd write down our words since it's his birthday and we're remembering him." As they talk, she writes.

"I have a big question!" says Freddy, who has been frantically waving his hand. "How can he have a birthday? He died. You can't have a birthday if you died."

Now Althea's hand is waving. "I know," she says. "When people get borned they get birthdays. When people get died they get funerals. We need to have a funeral for Dr. King and put flowers on his grave, so he'll know we're sorry he got shot."

MARTIN LUTHER KING

Danny said, "I saw Martin Luther King on TV."

Althea said, "God loved Martin Luther King."

Kyle said, "Martin Luther King got shot."

Jorge said, "He changed the rules."

Paulina said, "Ruby's daddy helped Martin Luther King."

Robbie said, "And Mayella marched with him."

Taking Children's Word for It

Teachers writing down young children's words are well advised to act as scribes, not editors. A teacher accustomed to respecting children's grammar-as-spoken has established a precedent for respecting content-as-spoken as well, and thus he sets the stage for acknowledging diversity of language and belief without necessarily lending his own authority to it.

A child who says *borned* instead of *born* is confirmed in her independent construction of grammar—a more advanced stage than simple imitation—by the teacher's acknowledgment of her language as spoken. A child in a diverse classroom who states her family's religious beliefs is confirmed in her identity by the teacher's recording of her words. This is quite different from a teacher's statement of his *own* religious beliefs in a school without religious affiliation and enrolling families with many different views because the teacher's words, unlike the child's, have authority in the group.

"We need a big gravestone for him," explains Jorge. "Because he was very important. When people are important they get big, big stones in the graveyard."

"You're right," says Bethany. "And people who loved them put writing on the stones. What do you think we should write on Dr. King's stone?"

"Dear Martin Luther King. We love you. God loves you," says Althea.

"And we can sign all our names," says Robbie.

Dear
MARTIN LUTHER KING

We love you.
God loves you.

ЯOИIᴱ
ALTHEA
ᴎ Jorge
Ⱪyle
Pᴀᴜᴧᴀ

13

February Staff Meeting: Funerals, Quilts, and Families

"I think it's amazing how curriculum keeps getting connected," comments Bethany as the meeting begins. "Who could have guessed that *Día de los Muertos* would lead to a funeral for Martin Luther King? Children's logic is all their own, but it makes sense. If someone is dead, you don't have a birthday, you have a funeral. They took it very seriously; clearly, they needed to do something for themselves, after listening to grown-ups being serious.

"And several children are still making tombstones—miniature ones, now—and decorating graves. I suggested that they needed to move them out of the sandbox, where children play, and into a protected area by the fence. So they're struggling to make a little fence of popsicle sticks and figure out how to make it stand up to protect the graves. They want a sign saying Cemetery—there's lots of writing going on in our class. And they've begun decorating the big fence; chain link is just right for weaving."

"A few parents have questioned the graveyard play, wondering if it's healthy for children," Ruby mentions. "I've explained that children need to practice dealing with death. So do adults. Learning the culture's rituals for doing that is helpful to children. I also told one insistent father whose son spends a lot of time

shooting people in his play that I think it's important for children to learn that when people are shot, they don't come back. They're dead. Shooting isn't a game to me, though I understand children's need to play it."

"What did he say?" asks Bob.

"Not much," says Ruby. "Just looked at his watch and went off. But maybe he'll think about it. His wife has been wanting to limit the shoot-'em-ups on TV, but *he* likes to watch them."

———

"Our group is still big on lights and shadows," says Sandra. "We've been showing children how to make animal silhouettes with their hands. And we've found out that nighttime animals (several children love the word *nocturnal*) have eyes that glow. They reflect any light, so the animal can see better in the dark. We've been making charts of nighttime animals and daytime animals—I had to look up the word for that, it's *diurnal*—and counting how many of each we have on our mural. And adding more. And turning off the lights so we can get excited about the glowing eyes. That luminous paint really works. I've been tempted to use it to paint some stars on our ceiling as another surprise."

"If the kids like making animals with their hands, do you think they might like to learn some signing—American Sign Language?" asks Bob. "It seems like a natural follow-up."

"I don't know any Sign," says Sandra.

"I do," says Bob. "A little. Want me to teach them?"

"Yes!" says Sandra. "Let's talk about it tomorrow. Oh, and does anyone know about the differences between shadows in winter and shadows in summer? Do they get longer or shorter? At noon, are shadows longer in winter?"

"I think so," says Marnie.

"Isn't it the other way around?" says Sally. "No, wait . . . bother, now I'm mixed up. I _know_ they're shorter at noon, whenever in the year. I even think I know why . . . maybe."

"And how can we all find out?" sings out Bethany, cheerfully. "I foresee lots of chalk tracings on the asphalt, which _is_ a good use for asphalt. Let's! You know, I've developed a wonderful collection of shadow activities over the years. This might be a good opportunity to dust all of them off and bring them out."

"Oh, please not any 'canned' curriculum from those glossy books you see at the teachers' conferences," pleads Sally.

Bethany smiles. "Well, some of the ideas came from 'glossy' books, but I've managed to make them mine over the years."

"I just get annoyed by books that tell me what I _should_ do with _my_ kids," stresses Sally. "The ones on self-esteem really press my buttons. How can they possibly know how to work with kids they've never even met. It's so standardized."

"Agreed," says Bethany, "but sometimes the right opportunity emerges and books and other collected ideas can be just what you need. I always watch to see how my kids are responding and adjust accordingly."

"Besides," adds Dolores, "we can't be always coming up with new ideas—who has the time? I'm with Bethany. We can make smart choices from the ideas in books if we've spent plenty of time getting to know our kids."

Sally looks unsure, but for now she simply rests her case.

Curriculum: Canned, Embalmed, Accidental/Unidentified, or Emergent?

Canned curriculum comes from the district, the state, the textbooks, workbooks, and tests. It is the expert-designed compilation of What All Children Need to Know. It may be consciously intended to be "teacher-proof," effective no matter what the teacher's skills. It will always fit some children and not others, children being as they are, but it isn't supposed to be changed to fit either children or teacher.

Embalmed curriculum originates a little closer to home—with the teacher and all her years of experience. She started out with enthusiasm—writing her lesson plans, collecting her resource materials, working every night and all weekend. She can't work like that every year—so for every set of fresh faces, she brings it all out and dusts it off and is ready to roll. It is, after all, new to *them*; they're not being shortchanged by her shortcuts. That she may be shortchanging herself only occasionally crosses her mind as she wonders where her energy has gone and remembers how challenging teaching used to be before she was so good at it.

Accidental/unidentified curriculum just happens, and no one names it or follows up on it. It's full of starting points for an emergent curriculum, but the teaching staff isn't about to put in extra time and energy for wages so unworthy, and planning takes time and energy. They're content just to hang out with kids.

Emergent curriculum is more work. It's also more fun.

Why bother? It's a value choice: What are we modeling for children? A preplanned, rational curriculum routinizes teaching and can't work because there are too many variables involved. Children in school are a captive audience, for years and years; school shouldn't be a deadening experience. In a speech given to NAEYC and published by the Association, Margaret Mead described it as "the transcendent boredom—to be shut up in a room, away from anything that moves or breathes or grows, in a controlled temperature, hour after hour after hour—means that we are taking away from them any kind of chance of responsiveness."[1] When this occurs, it is a problem shared by teachers and children alike. Teachers shouldn't model giving in; they should model intelligent problem solving.

"I'd like to do more with quilting," says Gloria. "I like the way our handprints turned out. Children keep climbing on chairs to match their hands to their handprints now that we've put them all together up on the wall. Is anyone else interested? I was wondering if we could go from paper to cloth and do real sewing. And involve families."

"Say more," says Ruby, noticing interest on several faces.

"I went to a women's history workshop last year. And there was a session on quilts, as a craft that is specially women's and which tells their stories," Gloria says. "A family can have a quilt, and a community's quilts tell a lot about it. We're trying to be a caring community, and one way we could tell our history is in quilts. And we could work together."

"When I was a child every church had a quilting frame," says Mayella. "And the women got together and sewed and talked. I bet a lot of important things got said in those talks.[2]

"You know, the other day one of our kids came to school wrapped in her special blanket. She needed it that day, but some of the bigger kids were teasing her, calling her a baby with her 'blankie.' I didn't think that was fair, and I said to them, 'I have a blanket too.' 'You *do?*' they said. 'Yes, I do,' I said. And I told them my story about how tiny I was when I was born, and that I had a special blanket my grandma wrapped me in. I still have a quilt my grandma and my aunties made, and it has pieces from my favorite red-flowered dress, and from our baby's blue overalls, and from the tablecloth we used for company dinners. The kids wanted to see it, but I haven't brought it in. I could, though."

"I've been wanting to start talking about all of our families and who's in them," says Sally. "I thought we could ask children who's in their family, encourage them to make pictures of their families, and write the names of everyone on their pictures. Bob wants to take photos of all the families and put them on our wall, but

The Memory Quilt

"Memory is made as a quilt is made. From the whole cloth of time, frayed scraps of sensation are pulled apart and pieced together in a pattern that has a name . . . " relates Stafford in characterizing memory development.[3]

A teacher whose class of 5-year-olds created a Memory Quilt describes what happened:

Originally conceived of as a Back to School Night icebreaker, to be made of paper and taped together, the Memory Quilt grew into a 5' x 6' patchwork quilt, pieced together and sewn of calico and white cotton. It drew the whole year together . . . . It was the visual reminder, the concrete evidence of the memories that parents had been sharing and that we had been talking about together.

I sent home 7" squares of white cotton fabric with an explanatory letter . . . . I asked the parents to "think of the key words or images that pop out at you from your childhood. Something worth passing on to your children." I gave each family two squares of fabric and suggested that they could draw, print, sew, applique, or whatever on the square as long as they left a 1/2" border for stitching together. (Although quilting began as a women's art, fathers' memories were represented by eleven squares and six men created their own.) . . . .

As the squares were returned, I took them home and sewed a 4" calico border (some red, some blue) around the edge on the machine.

These pieces were then layered and pinned together with batting and lining and brought back to school for the children to quilt. It's rare that a quilt is made without a few bloodstains, and our quilt was no exception. The children worked hard, mastering the threading of needles and the running stitch that gave dimension to the quilt squares. As the squares were completed we pinned them to the wall, alternating the colors to give a preview of how it would look when it was all sewn together. As rows were completed, I would take them home, stitch them together on the machine and bring them back. The excitement built. The children dragged every teacher and staff member into the classroom to see the quilt, show *their* square and tell *their* story . . . .

It was a project that documented and validated the looking back experience. It had a beginning, middle and end that children could see and touch and talk about. It said "my family is special . . . it is not exactly like yours, it may not be perfect, but this is who we are." The quilt gave substance to their memories, made them tangible. The children watched their parents decorate their family square(s). They helped stitch the quilt together. They could see it and touch it. The memories were the glue that held the quilt together. It expanded their memory circle and became a springboard for diving into other family experiences.[4]

we weren't sure how to do that. Can we ask people to send family photos? I'm worried that we might not take good enough care of them. But that's another issue. What I'm thinking now is that it would be easy to use paper all the same size for family drawings and then join the pieces together like a quilt. This doesn't get past paper, Gloria, but I think that's all we can handle in our group."

"With the 5s I think I want to concentrate on making books," says Bethany, thinking aloud and comfortable in a ski sweater, jeans, and boots, with her feet up. "Literacy grows out of children's interest in the important words in their lives—like their names and the names in their families.[5] If I were to send home a note to ask parents, 'Who's in your family?' I think that would get family stories going. And counting and classifying, too."

Ruby is looking pleased. "Would everyone like to do something on families during the next few months?" she asks. "It will be time for another celebration in May or June. I thought we might have a family picnic, and we could have a display of children's family projects. What do you think?"

"Yes, I have an idea," says Yoshiko. "I don't tell about it yet. You will see." She grins at the group. After five months at Manzanita, Yoshiko has become a more playful and comfortable member of the staff. And more casual about her appearance—she's wearing jeans tonight, too, though hers are newer than Bethany's.

———

There seems to be general agreement—families is a big enough theme to go on and on, and it's one that includes everybody. Not everyone has an idea yet, but they're good at ideas. We are aware of the assumptions that some teachers might make about what "family" means to children, but we figure that Ruby will raise the issue at a more appropriate time. We'll wait and see what happens.

_____

"I love the way you're emerging a whole-community theme, with *families*," Betty says to Ruby as the meeting breaks up.

"I do, too," says Ruby. "I've been hoping something like this would happen. Working with staff is a lot like working with children, in my experience. You seize the teachable moment, and take advantage of their energy to promote your goals."

Ruby pauses. "Does that sound patronizing?" she asks. "I don't mean that I think of teachers as children. I do think of both children and teachers as active learners, constructing knowledge out of their own questions and interests. I do the same thing myself."

"I heard the word *goals*," John says. "What *are* your goals? Do you have them written down anywhere, or are they in your head?"

"We've got broad program goals written out in the parent handbook," Ruby says. "But those are the developmental outcomes you'd expect, the things we early childhood folk take for granted.

For staff development I've got some personal goals in my head. (I guess I need to get them written down to include in my thesis, don't I?)"

"Like what?" John persists.

"Like getting a really concrete sense of how curriculum emerges when we're paying attention to children and to each other. And finding themes with potential for involving parents as well as teachers and children and getting beyond superficial and trivial stuff—there's so much of that in schools. And being accountable to parents for their children's learning," says Ruby, thinking as she talks.

"How's it going, do you think?" asks Betty.

"I'm really happy with the emerging curriculum. I don't think we've done enough with community building; some opportunities for connecting with parents, like Martin's birthday, didn't get followed through. Right now I'm wondering how much we can rely on evidence of developing literacy as our accountability to parents.[6] That's pretty new stuff for me, but Bethany and Sandra and Marnie are all really into it, and I'm grateful to them."

"Did I hear my name?" asks Bethany, passing by.

"Yes, I was appreciating all your literacy stuff," says Ruby, giving her a quick hug. "I know you had doubts about tackling kindergarten, but I think you're doing a great job. I keep learning from you."

_____

John and Betty keep right on talking as they leave the center.

"I thought of another question during the discussion of shadows," says John. "None of the staff seem to be sure about how shadows change with the seasons. Does that matter? When do teachers need to know more than the children do?"

"Most of the time, teachers do know more than children, and they should," says Betty. "But I think maybe sometimes it's a good thing if they can be genuinely curious with the children. That gives them practice in asking questions instead of giving answers.

"They certainly need to know more than children do about *how you can find out* what you don't know. They need to be good at asking questions. But the worst thing about a lot of schooling is that teachers just give answers out of a book or ask questions to which they already know the answer. Real learning

_____

Dear Parents,

The children in our class will be making My Family books to honor their own family and to learn about and appreciate the differences among our families.

Who's in your family? Could you write down the names of family members for your child to have as a reference for our book making at school? You might like to ask your child what names s/he wants.

If you'll print, not too small, the names will be easier for your child to copy.

If you have other ideas for our books, please let your child or me know.

Many thanks,

Bethany

An Organic Model for Curriculum Planning

An organic or emergent model of planning and implementing curriculum . . . is different from the typical thematic approach used in many preschools which is often predetermined and laid out by the teacher months in advance. In that case, the use of themes may be merely a kind of external "decorating" in the classroom where materials and props are often superimposed on children and the classroom to help give some structure and order to the curriculum, such as a fall theme with leaves, pumpkins and apples. The length of the theme is preset by the calendar or teacher even before the project starts. As a contrast, in the . . . [organic model] . . . there are no time con-

straints. The projects evolve on their own organic time table, creating a sense of adventure for both children and adults. The end result of these joint ventures is rarely clear from the start . . . . The teacher starts with careful observation of children's interests and questions, which are then developed into concrete learning experiences.

Reprinted from "Connections: Using the Project Approach with 2- and 3-Year-Olds in a University Laboratory School" by D. LeeKeenan and J. Nimmo (pp. 252–53) in C. Edwards, L. Gandini, & G. Forman, eds., The Hundred Languages of Children: The Reggio Emilia Approach to Early Childhood Education, *1993, Norwood, NJ: Ablex. Copyright © 1993 by the Ablex Publishing Corporation. Used by permission.*

isn't about memorizing facts; it's about inquiry. Adults need to model *learning how to learn* for children."

"I'm not sure I agree, as you well know," responds John with a smile. "Surely, reinventing every wheel isn't necessary; sometimes a teacher can offer an answer, a fact, a technique that allows the child to get on with the *really* engaging questions."

"Certainly for social knowledge—this is green, that's a wombat—but scientific "fact" is mostly

someone's theory, our best guess so far, and as such is open to change," replies Betty.

"So, what if the child asks you?" persists John. "Aren't we a useful resource for children as long as we're not imposing our facts on them when they're invested in finding their own?"

"I just want to make sure that teachers are able to stay open to the child's process of constructing her answer," says Betty. "Adults might learn something if they paid attention to children's magical theories."

14
February Visit:
Shadows and Sign Language

It's cold today, but the sun is bright when John arrives at the center in midmorning to find three of the 5-year-olds crouched on the asphalt drawing with chalk. Paulina, always alert to visitors, calls to John as he shuts the gate:

"Come see what we're doing."

"What are you doing?" he asks, crouching down with the children to see.

"We're drawing the fence's shadow," Paulina explains with enthusiasm, "so we have a fence on the ground to match that one up there."

"And when we weave the real fence, that fills up the hole in our shadow fence, too," says Althea. "Kyle put a cloth through this hole right here, so I can color it in." She points to a square of light on the asphalt. Kyle obligingly takes a strip of cloth from the basket by the fence and starts to weave it into the fence. "*No, not there,*" Althea yells at him. "*Here!* Right here, where I'm pointing." She points to the shadow. Willing but puzzled, Kyle tries to figure out how to match it on the fence. Both girls move to help him.

Bethany comes from her room to say hello. She's carrying a box of colored chalk, and she pauses to watch as Althea fills in the newly shadowed square with white chalk. "What color cloth did you weave with this time, Kyle?" she asks.

"Pink," he says. "See! It's this piece right here. I put it in here, and then under here, and then over here . . ."

"I see that your weaving on the fence is all different colors," Bethany comments, "but your shadow weaving on the ground is all white. Would you like to make them match? I found some colored chalk."

Althea pounces on it, grabs the pink chalk and redoes her new square. Then she tries to figure out which other new shadows go with it. Paulina is enchanted with all the new chalk colors; ignoring the shadows, she starts a new drawing of a flower garden on the asphalt. Two other girls look down from their perch on the climber, see the colors, and quickly arrive; they're into rainbows. Kyle is nearby busy weaving, with strip after strip of cloth. Bethany, pleased with the varied responses to her new idea, goes back into the room.

And John goes into Sandra's room to find a group meeting in progress. Bob is there with Sandra, but Dolores isn't; she's helping Sally so as to free Bob to be a sign-language resource for the 4s. Sandra has just sat down in the circle; she has a stuffed gorilla on her lap.

"This is my friend Amy," she says to the group.

"Hi, Amy," says a child.

"She can't hear you," Sandra explains.

"HI, AMY!" says another child, louder.

"She still can't hear you," says Sandra. "She can see your mouths moving and she's very curious about that. But her ears can't hear."

"Aw, she's just stuffed," suggests a preschool realist.

"Well, yes," Sandra agrees. "But in this story about my friend Amy, that's not why she can't hear you. Amy can't hear anything. No matter how loud you yell, she can't hear. She's deaf."

"She's got ears," says a child. "Big ears. Why can't she hear?"

"She's got nice ears," Sandra agrees. "She can even wiggle them—see? But they don't work on the inside, which is the part of your ears that hears."

"Why not?" someone asks.

"I don't know exactly why not," says Sandra. "But when she was born, her ears didn't work. Sometimes things like that happen. She can see you smile at her, though. And you know what else she can do? She can read sign language."

"What's sign language?" asks a child.

"I know!" bursts out one of the boys. "My grandpa took me to a show where a lady was singing, and another woman was telling the song with her hands. And she said it was sign language and showed us how to do it, too. And this is how you say I love you." He shows us.

Shadowiness

There are very few things, I think, as rich in fascination and mystery for a child as shadows. A shadow is at the same time both *real* and *unreal*; it is something which is objective but which does not however show certain characteristics which belong to other objects of the physical world . . . . A shadow is there in front of their eyes with a form which can easily be out-lined and with its homogeneous standard dark color. They cannot move it or put it where they would like to put it but instead it goes just where it itself seems to want obstinately to go. It also seems to come out of things just as if it had been hidden inside them until the very moment when something per-suaded it to come out and show itself, to spread itself on the table or on the floor.

But when they try to catch hold of the shadow their hands grasp nothing at all and if they try to imprison it the shadow escapes through the mesh of the net or melts through the ropes. And then, suddenly, it may disap-pear, swallowed up by a larger shadow or just dissolving into the air like mist or smoke. What happens with shadows is what happens with dreams and the people a child meets in dreams, who seem to be there in front of him and can make him happy or scared but who nonetheless disappear entirely when he wakes up . . . .

Shadows, therefore, offer us extraordinary educational opportunities. Not only do they rouse a spontaneous curiosity in a child by stimulating his or her imagination and exercis-ing their emerging intellectual abilities, but they are also to be found everywhere (even more than stones, sand, water or pencils and paper, because you only need some sun or even a candle to make them). Given the ease with which the variables which effect their formation and transformation can be manipulated, shadows can be used more easily and more effectively than virtually anything else to satisfy and stimulate the need to do and to experiment which is present in every child.

Reprinted from "Shadowiness" (pp. 72–73, 76) by G. Petter in The Hundred Languages of Children *[I Centro Linguaggi Dei Bambini] Italian/English ed., 1987, City of Reggio Emilia, Italy: Department of Education, Region of Reggio Emilia Romagna. Copyright © 1987 by Comune di Reggio Romagna Assessorato all'istruzione. Used by permission.*

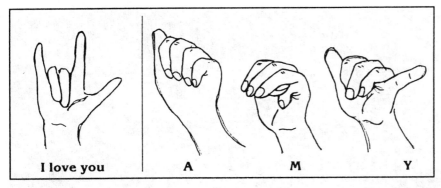

I love you | A | M | Y

"Try saying that to Amy," says Bob happily, "and see what she does."

He does, and Amy responds with a big bounce on Sandra's lap. "Me, too!" several other children chorus, and everyone tries saying I love you in sign. Amy tries, too; she has nice long arms, and it's easy for her to do signs that don't need precise finger movements. Bob teaches the children a bit of finger spelling, though; he teaches them how to sign *Amy*. Amy is delighted by their efforts. So are Bob and Sandra. When John gets a chance to talk for a few minutes as the children go outside, he shares Bob and Sandra's delight, and asks, "Wherever did you get the idea of a deaf gorilla?"

Sandra smiles. "I was impressed by the *persona-doll* idea in the *Anti-Bias Curriculum* book,"[1] she explains, "but we don't have enough dolls to pull one out and keep it just for storytelling. This is my own gorilla, and her name really is Amy. I decided she probably gets lonesome at home when I'm at school, and it would be nice to bring her along. Her being deaf is new, though; that's so Bob can teach us all to sign, and so we can help the children become more aware of differing abilities. I think that's important."[2]

"So, had some of the children been mentioning sign language?" asks John.

"Now that would have been helpful," Bob adds with a grin. "And we might have waited for that moment to come round, but Sandra had Amy, and I just couldn't wait anymore to share Sign with the kids!"

"And judging by today, the children will be anxiously awaiting Amy's return!" affirms John.

"Other times we've talked about physical difference when it's something the kids have noticed," adds Sandra. "Remember the discussion about your friend who had lost his hair from chemotherapy? It was hard to explain, but the questions were important to them."

Bob nods in acknowledgment.

John has a story, too. He tells it: "One center I know had a month's curriculum about wheelchairs that evolved from the occasion when a visitor had to be lifted up the entrance stairway. The kids were really mad about that. They were soon inviting in parents who were architects to help plan a ramp. Some of the kids got into blueprints and drawing; others seemed to really get the idea that bodies work differently."

"It's great when questions come from the children," says Sandra, "and I used to think I had to wait for that to happen. But now I take more initiative. When Bob offered to teach Sign, that was too good a resource to pass up. Since there aren't any hearing-impaired or deaf folks in the center this year, I brought Amy. She lives at my house, and so she's part of our community, too."

Persona Dolls

Kay Taus, who created the idea of persona dolls, has written:

> Good stories capture the heart, mind, and imagination and are an important way to transmit values. However, too few children's books depict people from diverse backgrounds respecting each other and living in a mutually beneficial way. Moreover, even good books do not always deal with the specific events that occur in children's daily lives. So I began to write and tell my own stories. I found that using dolls enhanced young children's connection to the stories and their participation in solving the problems that arose in the dolls' "lives."
>
> Each doll has his or her own life story. Stories reflect the composition of the class and offer a vehicle for introducing differences that do not exist within one classroom.[3]

Laurie Read, who in real life created Amy, was developing disability-awareness curriculum in her classroom. She adapted the persona-doll idea in her own playful way of interacting with children, thus avoiding the risk of treating a serious subject with the didactic formality some adults fall into on such occasions. (While young children may respond to serious adults with serious attention, they may refrain from the active questioning and open-ended exploration through which they learn best.) It takes an imaginative teacher to breathe joyous life into a hearing-impaired stuffed gorilla, but that was Laurie's gift.

EMERGENT CURRICULUM

15
March Staff Meeting: Who's in Your Family?

"Everyone has been coming up with such good ideas around the Families theme that I've asked them all to bring something to share," Ruby explains to us before the meeting begins. "This is the kind of show-and-tell that makes sense to me; it's all about 'See what good ideas we've been having.'[1] As I've said before, I think that's what children should be showing—and telling, too."

Ruby goes on. "It also gives me a chance to be clear about how much I value *different* ideas. Theme planning worries me, sometimes, when people all try to do the same thing. I still remember visiting a large child care program and finding every room doing penguins in January."

"Why penguins?" Betty asks.

"Because it was winter, I guess," says Ruby. "But this was in Arizona where penguins really aren't part of children's experience, or teachers' either! And so all of their penguins looked pretty much alike. Families, on the other hand, are basic to everyone's experience, and so that's a theme children and staff can really innovate with. Just wait 'till you see."

Displays are being propped up all around the room, except by Yoshiko, who has a pile of something on her lap and a pleased smile. "Yoshiko,

since people haven't seen your idea yet, could you tell us about it?" Ruby asks, to begin.

Yoshiko holds up two of the somethings. They're photographs of faces, mounted on sticks, like those she created in the fall (see p. 44). But now, instead of children's pictures, they're children's parents. "We have only a few of these now," she explains. "We will get more when parents come. Little children often miss their parents. I didn't think of this idea at the beginning of the year when it could be nice for sad children. But now children can play, and we can talk: 'I see a mommy picture. Whose mommy is this?' I think they will like to do that."

The pictures are passed around and admired. When it's Sally's turn, she points to the taped-together drawings she has hung on the wall. Pastel squares of construction paper serve as background for children's drawings and dictated words: "Me. I'm big." "My name is Natalie." "This is my kitty." Some of the drawings are easily recognizable; others look more like scribbles, but the words clarify the artist's intent.

"This isn't done yet," Sally explains. "We'd like every child to do one eventually, but for now we're just putting out the paper and markers as a regular choice and inviting children to make a picture when they aren't busy with something else. Some children may have made several; they help us choose the one to put in our quilt, and we're keeping the others in a folder we've started for each child. You asked us to think about a developmental portfolio, Ruby, so we're trying. I wish we hadn't sent home all the drawings they made early in the year, though. We don't have evidence of the growth that has taken place in some children's drawing."

"We've begun a quilt, too," says Gloria. "I wanted to try it on cloth, and I've cut squares in two colors: light blue for the children's squares and a little darker blue for a square to be taken home. I'm telling children they can draw whatever they want to on their square—something they really like. And I'm sending a note home to parents with *their* square.[2]

Dear Parents,

We're making a Families quilt. Could you make a picture for your family on this square and bring it back to the center? You could draw with permanent marker or crayon, or glue on pieces of cloth, or sew. We hope you'll talk with your child about what she or he thinks your family's picture should be.

"And then I'd like to sew it together and make it really nice. Maybe some parents would like to help. Do you think any of our bigger kids might be able to sew, too? If we show them how?"

"I'll volunteer you some helpers," Bethany says. "I really want 5-year-olds to take some responsibility for helping us be a community. They're the biggest kids here. It's good for them to get recognition for that and to practice skills that are really useful in our life together."

"We have two projects in our class," says Marnie. "Gloria wanted to do the quilt so I'm working on a bulletin board—We Live in a House. I've put up a house outline for everyone and I'm interviewing each child with these questions:

> My name is . . .
> I live in a . . . (color) house.
> Who else lives in your house?

And then I write down their answers, like

> My mommy lives in our house.
> My daddy lives in our house.
> My sister lives in our house.

And finally,

> (number) people live in our house.

Developmental Portfolios

A developmental portfolio should be more than a random collection of all the products a child happens to make. Ideally, it is the outcome of a process in which teacher, child, and parent are all involved in contributing to, selecting, and reviewing its contents for the purpose of documenting both developmental milestones and this child's unique ways of representing his or her experiences.

A "literacy album" in which evidence of a child's independent explorations of representational drawing, construction, and writing is collected is one among several possible focuses for a portfolio. In it are saved name-writing attempts, drawings with dictated stories, photographs of play constructions with child comments, special scribble messages (such as invitations, signs, letters, and lists), lists of favorite books, and so on.

Roskos and Neuman have written "Of Scribbles, Schemas, and Storybooks," asking

How can adults assess early literacy status and progress in a way that respects young children's ways of knowing and preserves their self-confidence? . . . . Unlike more traditional forms of assessment (such as inventories and scales), albums have the capability to accommodate the great variability in young children's literacy learning, as well as their diverse and often concrete ways of expressing what they know . . . .

Albums stimulate collaboration between children, their teachers, and other adults in the child care environment. Because choosing which items to include is at the heart of developing a literacy album, this activity inherently calls for interaction and dialogue between children and adults. Through their efforts at communication in the process of choice making, caregivers and children share important meanings and understandings about literacy. As a result, adults learn more about children's literacy conceptions, and children respond to new information that adults provide.[3]

Engaging Teachers' Minds

If teachers are to ask children genuine questions and sustain their own motivation for the effort of in-depth collaborative projects, the choice of thematic content should engage adults' serious interest as well as children's. Skills, crafts, and investigations that adults have traditionally carried on whether or not children are present—such as gardening, cooking, quilting, sewing, working with clay, and caring for animals—enrich the significance of an early childhood curriculum by enabling children to become involved as apprentices in work and knowledge significant to adults. In contrast, topics chosen only because "children like them" (possible examples include Disney versions of traditional tales, teddy bears, leprechauns, shapes and colors, circuses, snowmen, Easter bunnies, penguins, and dinosaurs) limit the potential for serious mutual involvement by both children and adults. (Any of these topics *could* be the focus of genuine passion and investigation by an adult, but that is rarely the reason for their inclusion in curriculum.)

"And then the child gets that number of gummed dots to stick inside the house, and I put her words in the house, too, after I print them nicely. So it's a math and language experience all in one."

———

As Marnie shares her activity, our fears about "family" and "house" curriculum are taking shape before our eyes. We glance at Ruby, wondering if she's going to comment, but she doesn't. Bethany, though, is taking a deep breath.

———

"I guess ours is sort of a 3-D version of that one," says Sandra. "Where's the box, Dolores? Oh, here it is." And she brings out two glued-wood constructions, each with a row of figures on a board base. "My uncle is a cabinetmaker, and I asked him to save interesting wood scraps for me. Last week I had dinner with his family and he gave me a whole box of these. I can't imagine what the red ones were for, but aren't they lovely? So we've started a small-group activity, asking children if they'd like to use these pieces to make everyone in their family, all in a row. We're writing the names they tell us on the base. Some of them get a little carried away, as you can see (Dolores has brought out more and put them on the table, and some of the "families" are quite a lot larger than in real life). It's such fun. I made my family, too.

"And I've brought a member of my family to school," continues Sandra. "Her name is Amy, and she's deaf, and Bob is helping us learn sign language so that we can talk to her. Would you like to meet her?" And so Amy is introduced, and more explanation follows.

———

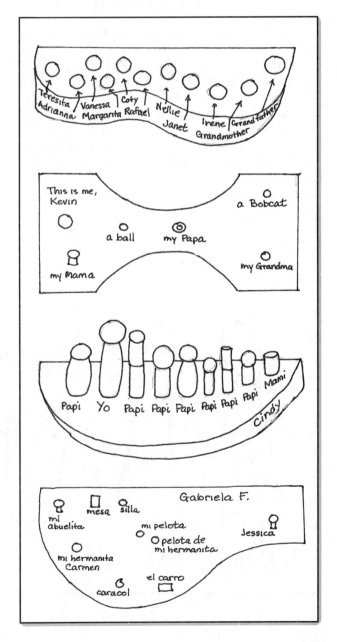

We're finding it interesting as we sit in regularly on these staff meetings to watch for the subtle cues to staff members' differences. People don't always think their colleagues' ideas are good ones. Here, Sandra's playful assumption that a stuffed toy can be a family member, and hearing impaired to boot, has raised an eyebrow or two in the group; "*I certainly wouldn't do that,*" is the implication. But they've learned to think before they speak, though often they do speak up eventually.

Bethany is doing that now. We'd noticed her drawing a breath during Marnie's description of her House activity and then settling back again; it was, after all, Marnie's turn. On her own turn, however, she can raise questions less critically. She begins by making connections.

———

"I'm glad you mentioned portfolios, Sally, because that's a real issue for me with the 5s," says Bethany. "They'll be going off to school next year, and some of the parents are really wanting to know how their kids are doing. Marnie's thinking about math and language experiences, and so am I, and so, I'm relieved to see, are the kids. We're graphing everything these days and making class books and individual books; I do some of the writing for them, but many of them do their own writing.

"Families are a major topic in these activities. And every time I think I have a sensible idea, some child complicates it. Haven't you encountered the problem, Marnie, that comes up right away for us—What if you live in two houses, Dad's house and Mom's house, or maybe no house at all? I started with How many people are in your family? instead of How many people are in your house? and that got Greta saying 'There's me and Mama and Papa and Tante and Sven and our baby'; and I said, surprised, 'I didn't think your baby was born yet,' and she said, 'It isn't. It's inside my mama,' and drew a picture to show me. She insisted that there are six people in her family, and who am I to argue? Of course, ultrasound pictures soon arrived from home, and off we went again.

"My version of your gummed dots, Marnie," continues Bethany, "was a paper doll—the kind you fold and cut. I cut them in advance, to simplify the task, I thought. But I made them all the same size, and Greta said firmly, 'My papa is BIG; I need a big one.' Derek tried cutting one for her but got frustrated, so I ended up teaching them how to cut paper dolls. Several are making whole doll families now and ignoring my idea that they should just make their own family portrait. Children are so inventive."

"Aren't they? And so are you all," says Ruby. "It sounds as if you have plenty of ideas to follow up. Will this keep everyone busy? Are there any other plans hatching?"

"There's a birds' nest being built in the big tree, but nobody's hatching yet," says Bob. "We'll keep watching and let you know, though."

"Isn't it time to plant a garden?" Dolores asks. "Someone—wasn't it you, Yoshiko?—mentioned a garden way back at the beginning of the year, but we haven't done anything about it."

"We had a harvest festival," says Sally.

"But it wasn't our harvest," says Dolores. "What does that teach children about how things grow? We need our own garden. Does anyone else want to help?"

There are several volunteers, including Ruby, who asks, "Do you suppose we could raise enough vegetables to serve a salad at our picnic?"

A lively discussion begins, but it doesn't include everyone—it's clear that not all the staff are enthusiastic gardeners—and it's nearly time to go home. So Ruby breaks in: "It looks to me as if we need a gardening committee. Who's on it? Dolores? Yoshiko? Gloria? OK!— and me. Let's meet tomorrow during naptime and make a plan.

"Now go home, all of you. Morning comes early."

———

"Can you two stay for a few minutes?" Ruby adds an aside to us as we prepare to go. "I need to talk something through with you."

We stay. Ruby says goodbye to people as they leave; then she settles down with a final cup of coffee. "Were you as bothered by Marnie's We Live in a House activity as I was?" she asks. "I decided not to say anything in the group because Marnie always seems to be getting publicly dumped on for something or other. But there she is, promoting stereotypes again. She just doesn't think beyond her own limited experience."

"Yes, I was," says John. "Frankly, I was surprised that you just let it go."

"In your place I think I would have done the same thing," says Betty. "And I happened to be watching Bethany, who reacted the same way you did, Ruby. I was impressed that she waited for her turn and then simply asked Marnie if she hadn't come up against family diversity in trying to do her activity. That was unusually tactful, for Bethany."

"Agreed," nods John. "I especially appreciated her reference to children who might be homeless.[4] I know your community has seen an increase of families in transition since the cutbacks of the '80s."

"She didn't bring up the issue that is really going to challenge Marnie, though," says Ruby. "One of the children in Marnie's class has two mommies—her mother has a lesbian partner— and Sara, the child, talks casually about both her mommies. I've established a lot of trust over this past year, and her parents really want to be open in this community. What will Marnie do when she gets to making Sara's House?[5]

"Gloria knows the family well; Sara went to the child care center Gloria worked at last year. It was actually Sara's mom's idea that Gloria apply for this job. Gloria will certainly be alert if Marnie gets upset or tries to cover up. But I can't just leave that to Gloria. I have to talk to Marnie, don't I?"

"You do," we agree.

"OK, I will," says Ruby. "And I knew that; I just wanted the chance to say it out loud. But I'm glad I didn't bring it up in the meeting. I was afraid I was being cowardly, but I think I was being considerate, too. Teachers need continual challenge to examine their biases, but it needn't happen in front of an audience. For Marnie, it's better that it doesn't. I think she'll have trouble acknowledging nontraditional family structures, but I can count on her to care about children's self-esteem. She wouldn't want to do anything to undermine Sara, or any other child. So that's where our values converge, and I can help support her in those values."

Kien

That's Kien getting Apple. Baby in the house in the window. That Kien and a Flower.

Eduardo

A kid is playing something. Toys outside. Eduardo is the kid.

I am riding my bicycle very fast in front of my house. I stop with the tree and went back home to play with my new toys

Leslie

Esta es una gallina que fue a la nieve. Y hizo una pelota y se derritió porque estaba caliente.

Erick

Estos son monstruos que quieren llevar a la gallina

My family playing football   Santos

Dad   David   Rubin   me   mom

Christian

The sun is coming out and is making color to the rainbow and is getting bigger and bigger and turn the page and is BIG.

Windy

I made two apple tree and my biggest brother and me. I made a little plant outside. And my house.

This is the car next to the house.

Window   Door   Flowers

Sophia

This is English writing

My brother outside

Quilt Art

16

March Visit:
Animals and Gardens

A garden has been staked out at one end of the yard, and when Betty arrives, Dolores and Yoshiko are digging in it along with half a dozen children. Two of Yoshiko's children, released from their small yard into the big one, are holding their stick faces as they sit on a bench by a table, watching the big kids dig.

On the table Sandra has put a pile of wildlife magazines, scissors, paper and glue to see if they'll interest anyone. Jody, a 4-year-old, is looking through a magazine for animal pictures when she notices the 2s' stick faces. She pokes her friend Pat excitedly. "Look," she says. "They've got people puppets. Let's make animal puppets. I've got a wolf. Want a buffalo?"

"No," says Pat. "I want this mountain lion. This is my lion." "Rrrrrr!" roars the lion as it is cut out. Lion and wolf have a friendly fight before they're glued onto colored paper.

"Sandra!" Jody calls as she runs into the room where Sandra is supervising wood gluing. "Look at my good idea. Can we have sticks to put them on, like the little kids'?"

"Wow, you do have a good idea," says Sandra admiringly. "I don't know if we have any sticks. Let me check the cupboard." She rummages, but without success. "I wonder if Yoshiko has some she'd let you use. Want to ask her?"

They do. "Yes," says Yoshiko. "I have many sticks. We can share. But now I am busy digging. Can you wait?"

Emergent Gardens

Why gardens? Because Gardens is one of many open-ended themes that can serve as a starting point for emergent curriculum involving children and adults as learners together. Even grown-up gardeners have many questions. If we plant a carrot seed, a potato eye, a kernel of corn, what will happen? Will something come up? Will nothing come up? How much water do plants need when it's hot? How much water play do *children* need when it's hot? Will our garden be good to eat—for aphids, snails, and us? How can we tell the vegetables from the weeds? Will young children be interested in a garden, or will they ignore it? Will it generate language? Drawing? Dramatic play?

Reprinted from "Observation Notes: Play and Language Development" (v. 5) (n.p.) by E. Jones, Pacific Oaks Occasional Paper, 1993, Pasadena, CA: Pacific Oaks College. Copyright © 1993 by the author.)

It's clear to Betty, watching Jody's face, that waiting will be very hard. Good ideas have great energy; they itch to happen *now*. Sometimes an observer can be useful. "Yoshiko, if I take Jody and Pat to your room, could we find the sticks, perhaps?" Betty asks.

"Yes, thank you," says Yoshiko. "They are in the big cupboard on the top shelf. Mayella knows, if you don't find."

The sticks are easy to find on neatly organized shelves. We take six and go back to the table, where the two girls glue their animals onto two sticks. But when Jody holds up her wolf, it flops over. She's unhappy. A floppy wolf isn't properly fierce.

"What could we do?" Betty asks her.

"I know," says Pat. "We need cardboard. It doesn't flop like that dumb paper. There's some on our art shelves. I'll go get it."

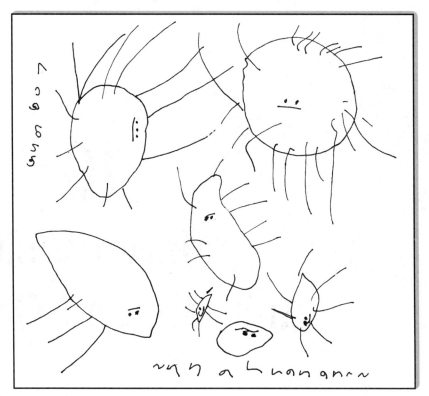

―――――

"Here's a bug. Stomp him!" is heard from the garden. Yoshiko moves quickly to the bug's rescue, but it's too late. "Let me see. Did you find a bug in our garden? Oh, how sad. The bug is dead.

"We need ladybugs in our garden. Can you find more and keep them alive? They help us."

Individuals As Resources

Every child and adult in a classroom is a source of curriculum. For this reason, early childhood teachers in a private school in rural Massachusetts recognize the importance of getting to know each other well:

> Each child (and adult) has expertise that he or she brings to and develops within the [classroom] community. This expertise is acknowledged within a wide definition of valuable skills. There exists mutual community knowledge of each member's profile of both strengths and weaknesses. As such, individuals are encouraged to act as "resources" to the learning of other community members. The community brings together a complementary array of individual differences that cements interdependence between autonomous actors.[1]

"I stomp bugs. I'm He–Man," Jeremy defends himself. But his friends are looking for more bugs, which, happily, they find on a tall weed.

"Yoshiko, see! We found them."

"There's spiders, too," adds Paco. "*Arañas.*"

"Good," Yoshiko says. "You looked very well." She turns over a leaf, and then another. "Ah, see," she says. "And here are the little bugs the ladybugs eat. They are called . . ." She pauses. "Dolores, how do you call these little green ones?"

"Oh dear! Aphids," says Dolores. "They'll like our garden."

"But the ladybugs like them," says Yoshiko. "So we will have many ladybugs. Arnie, can you go in your classroom and find some magnifiers? Ask Sandra, if you need help. With magnifiers we can see little things better."

"Dolores, I found something!" calls a digging 5-year-old excitedly. "Come look!" He is holding a small, white, dirt-encrusted object.

"Is it a rock?" Dolores asks.

"I don't think so," he says. "It has holes in it. "Maybe it's a dinosaur bone."

"It's *very* small for a dinosaur bone," says Dolores doubtfully. "I don't know much about bones."

"Why don't we go show Bethany?" suggests another child. "She likes bones."

"Good idea," agrees Dolores. "I'll put your shovels right here till you come back."

17
April Staff Meeting: Finding Hidden Things

"We're back to bones!" says Bethany delightedly as the meeting begins. "When I tried to do bones in the fall it kind of petered out. They liked the *calaveras,* but they didn't want to *study* skeletons; they were into funerals and fantasy play. But now that they've found the mouse, there's lots of interest in what's inside of animals, including us."

"Mouse? What mouse?" asks Mayella. "We got mice in this place?"

"Oh, I guess I haven't told everyone," says Bethany. "One of my kids was digging in the garden and found a little skull, almost intact. It's a beauty! We brushed the dirt off, very carefully, and talked about what it might be, and looked in some books, and decided it was probably a mouse. Actually, I think it's a meadow vole, not a house mouse, but *mouse* is a good enough word for 5-year-olds. And for most adults.

"So I've been to the museum and borrowed a frog skeleton and a snake skeleton and a couple of comparative anatomy charts, and several of the kids are really interested in how you can tell one animal from another when they don't have their outsides on. And when I suggested tracing their own bodies so they can draw their bones in them, there was a lot of interest. I had

Fantasy Play

In early childhood, pretend seems to come before real. For 3- to 5-year-olds, Paley indicates that "Fantasy play is their ever dependable pathway to knowledge and certainty. I pretend, therefore I am. I pretend, therefore I know. I pretend, therefore I am not afraid."[1]

In a review of Paley's book on growing up in school, Maria Piers, founding director of the Erikson Institute comments: "There are certain phases in human development that seem characterized by a greater need for free play and daydream or fantasy. Adolescence is one, and preschool age is the other."[2]

Five- and six-year-olds who have had ample opportunity to pretend begin to move toward the "serious play" of the primary classroom.[3] *The Play's the Thing* offers this thinking:

> Developmentally appropriate curriculum in primary schools engages children's minds by challenging them to think critically about the *investigations* they undertake both in their spontaneous activity and in their action and interaction as serious players at teacher-planned, open-ended activities.[4]

the idea last fall, but they were too busy with other ideas. Kids are amazing; they know what they're ready for if we listen to them. I did have a good idea after all; it was just my timing that was off."

"So you're all doing bones?" Bob asks.

"Oh no, we don't *all* do anything, really," Bethany explains. "I try ideas on the whole group, in the same way that I read a story to the whole group. But it's always a smaller number of kids for whom an idea or a story really connects, and so I try to build on that for them while other kids just go on with their day-to-day activities. I'll find special projects for the others later when an idea grabs *them*."

"But it is necessary that all the children learn the important ideas. Do you not teach them?" Yoshiko asks.

"Well, I've tried teaching concepts or skills to the whole class, but that doesn't mean everyone learns what I think I've taught," says Bethany. "Kids don't only have different interests, they have different readiness. If I think everyone should learn to cut, which I do, we could all have cutting practice; but I don't think it's good use of kids' time to do it all together. Some kids already cut beautifully. A few others are still struggling, and those kids need more practice without feeling they're failures.

"Oh, but you've given me an idea," continues Bethany. "I'm always looking for ways to motivate the strugglers, and two of those kids are

---

Serendipity: Unexpected Events—A Source of Emergent Curriculum

When the unexpected happens in the classroom, the community, or the natural world, teachers have choices. They can try to ignore it. They can join it briefly. Or they can invent ways of incorporating it into their short-term or long-term plans. It's important for teachers to become skilled in on-the-spot decision making and to be prepared to take the risk of shifting the focus of the curriculum. Birds nesting, street repairs, windstorms, and a child's medical emergency are among the many examples of potential curriculum that must be responded to when they happen—or not at all. The engagement potential of a serendipitous event can so easily be lost forever.

---

really into bones. Maybe I could draw outlines of some basic human bones—child-sized, on white paper—and ask the kids to cut out bones. They could glue them on their body tracings instead of drawing bones. And if the scissors slip and any bones get 'broken,' we can set the break with tape. And kids who love cutting will have to do body tracings if they want some place to put their bones. That's something I see happening a lot: a few kids pick up an idea, and other kids notice and want to do it, too, and pretty soon just about everyone is into it. And that feels different to me than *my* telling them this is what we're all going to do.

"I think I've used up my turn," concludes Bethany. "How's the garden going, apart from digging up bones?"

"It goes well," says Yoshiko. "The radishes and peas begin to come up."

"But there's no sign of anything else we planted, yet," says Dolores. "Plants are pretty slow for young children. Fortunately, some of them have been happily discovering the crawly things that live in the garden and around the yard, and that gives them more action."

"Oh, I love the way things happen over and over," Sandra comments enthusiastically. "*Finding hidden things* is something that's been happening off and on all year. Finding treasure, and hiding behind masks, and discovering bones, and now looking for bugs. I've noticed kids turning over bricks, and leaves, to see if anything lives under them. Lots of pill bugs—and they're so satisfying when they roll themselves up to hide and then unroll again and walk off."

"I've been watching what children do with holidays when we don't emphasize them," says Ruby. "A delegation of kids came to ask me why we weren't having an Easter-egg hunt. They said their teacher told them to ask me, 'cause I was the *boss*."

"I didn't say you were the boss," protests Marnie. "That's their word. But when they asked me, I didn't know what to say, because I *wanted* to do Easter and you wouldn't let me. So I told them to go talk to you because you make the rules around here. I'm sorry."

"No, that's fine," says Ruby. "I think that's a really appropriate thing to do. We had a great conversation. I asked why they wanted to hunt eggs, and they said, 'Cause it's Easter'; and I asked why they couldn't hunt eggs, and they said, 'Cause their teacher didn't have no eggs'; and I said, 'Well, you're good pretenders. What do you think you could use for eggs?' That set

Individualized Instruction

In our program we begin the individualization of learning by offering choices among interesting materials and activities. Then we stand back and watch. Observation becomes the driving force behind our curriculum development.

Each day we note a child's approach to tasks and his first choice of activity. A lot can be learned about a child's interests and areas of confidence from both the things he chooses and the things he never chooses. Sometimes I use the record of children's choices to select a group of children, or an individual, for a special activity.

For many weeks I noticed that Adrian never chose to work with scissors, crayons, or markers. The drawings in his journal were slightly marked, random crayonings. It was becoming clear to me that Adrian needed to practice doing some of the things he steered clear of. Since Rosa Linda, the instructional aide, and I

agreed that Adrian needed to be taught to cut, she sat with him one morning, and without passing judgment because he couldn't use scissors, she showed him how. After that he practiced whenever he chose to; I never singled him out again for "cutting" . . . .

When Adrian came to school, he didn't know how to cut; now he can. That's important learning. Teachers need to be accountable for children's learning—for making sure it happens and knowing when it does. Important learning is specific to the individual learner's needs; Maria could cut beautifully before we even met her; and Marco hasn't got the knack of it yet.

Reprinted from "It's All Academic" (p. 96) by J. Meade-Roberts in E. Jones, ed., Reading, Writing and Talking with Four, Five and Six Year Olds, *1988, Pasadena, CA: Pacific Oaks College. Copyright © 1988 by Pacific Oaks College. Used by permission.*

off a lively discussion. And eventually they decided they could use round rocks, or make eggs out of clay, and paint them and hide them and find them. Has any of that been happening?"

"Has it ever!" says Bethany. "My kids got involved because the little kids needed someone to hide their eggs. And because my kids couldn't resist making eggs, too. How's that for 3-year-olds generating 5-year-olds' curriculum?"

Yoshiko suddenly giggles. "We had eggs," she says. "We really had eggs. Mayella, tell!"

Mayella is caught off guard. "They don't want to hear *that*," she says.

"Yes they do," Yoshiko insists. "Tell."

"Well, I was doing Humpty-Dumpty," Mayella begins, chuckling. Sometimes I say those old rhymes to the kids, when they come into my head. My teacher taught them to us, way back, so I guess that's why I do it. Anyway, I got to 'All the king's horses and all the king's men'—you know—and Ella, she's a sharp little one, says Why?

"'Why what?'" I said.

"'Why they couldn't put Humpity together again?' she said.

"'Because,' I started to say, and then I got stuck. Yoshiko was listening, and she said to me, 'We could let them find out.'

"'How?' I said.

"'I will bring eggs tomorrow,' she said.

"I didn't even want to think about what was going to happen. 'Ella, baby,' I said, 'you just hang onto that question. We'll talk about it again tomorrow.'

"Sure enough, that Yoshiko, she brought a whole carton of eggs, and she scrubbed out the dish tubs we use for water play. I took some of the kids to wash their hands. Then Yoshiko gave each of those kids an egg and said to them, 'Open your egg. Put it in a tub to open it.'"

Sandra winces, just thinking about it. "So they did?" she asks.

"They did," nods Mayella. "Well, a few decided to just watch. But it was a sight. Some of them hated having egg on their hands and some of them loved it. So, that went on for a little while, and then Yoshiko said, 'OK, now put your egg back together.' That was just hysterical. Some kids really tried to, and some were just confused. And then Yoshiko asked, 'Shall we call all the king's horses and all the king's men?' and that caused more confusion. But Ella got it and squealed, 'No, 'cuz they can't put him together again!'"

"Humpty Dumpty is an egg. I think the children do not understand," Yoshiko adds. "So perhaps my idea is not so good. Except for Ella, who had the question."

"But it was OK," Mayella reassures her. "Cracking eggs is something they'll remember.

The Challenge of Creativity

In a resource room for 5- to 7-year-olds, as Lisa Meckel describes, "The structure for the day supporting choice time was, 'From 10 different activities choose one option. After thirty minutes have passed you may represent what you have done in a different medium.'"[5]

Shelley, age 6, chose to work with the scissors, paste, and a collection of cutting scraps from other projects to make a snowman in paper mosaic. Then she chose to represent him in a different medium—at the paint easel. (She could have chosen clay, wood, blocks, words. Later she did use words, telling a story of her snowman.) In completing this process,

> Shelley processed through the entire cycle of "intellectual exercises." Indeed she performed perhaps the highest creative act by inventing/ creating her own problem to solve. She then broke down the problem into solvable parts, and recreated it into an expressive form to complete her original vision. At all times she was motivated by the self-fulfilling process of intrinsic reward, the completion of an act to her satisfaction and the pleasure in sharing it with others as well as herself.[6]

Playing with Food?

Many early childhood programs make use of foodstuffs as play materials: macaroni for necklaces, beans of different colors for collage, pudding for fingerpaint, flour and salt to make play dough, rice or cornmeal in the substance table. In other programs this practice raises a moral question: When some people go hungry, should others be wasting food?

In a society that wastes great quantities of food, children's programs may or may not decide to take on this issue. Yet, young children need rich and varied sensory experiences, and raw foodstuffs are among the materials that offer such experiences.

Among programs that take the question seriously, various compromises are made. The substance table may be filled with birdseed, which feeds birds; but not rice, which feeds people. Food play may be permitted for toddlers who put everything in their mouths and thus need edible sensory materials, but not for 4s, who are more discriminating. Foods may be used only in their preedible form (raw grains, for example), which isn't so clearly *food,* from the child's vantage point; and thus not contradictory even as adults communicate to children their concern that the food we eat should not be wasted. With some creativity there are other options that affirm conservation as a value, for instance, using spent coffee grounds as a sensory material.

Like all such moral issues with implications for curriculum, this one is worth discussing at length by the staff and parents of an early childhood program.[7]

And when we got out the eggbeaters, a few kids really got jazzed by that."

"Does our center have a policy about using food as a play material?" asks Gloria. "At my other center, we decided not to do that."

"That's an issue we haven't discussed this year," responds Ruby. "It's an important one, but at this point I'd rather not get into . . . ."

"Oh, but you haven't heard it all," Mayella continues. "We added some water, so the eggs would go all frothy. Just perfect for Bob's famous cheese omelettes. It was a mess, and a little shelly, too. Kids like mess, though—and cheese omelette for snack."

"And we all scrub clean before starting," adds Yoshiko. "Is this wrong for Gloria's food policy?"

"No, you were following up your good idea," Ruby answers. "We do need to come up with a policy though—maybe you and Gloria could talk about it, for starters. But for this year I figured it'd be teacher choice. Like many other things.

"Little children need many kinds of sensory experiences, and this was certainly sensory! And Ella got her question answered. That's on-the-spot, responsive curriculum; I'm glad you told us about it.

"I had a question," Ruby continues, "when Bethany was describing how the big kids were hiding eggs for the little kids. Didn't I see some mapmaking while that was going on?"

"Oh yes, that's come round, too," says Bethany. "This time it happened when the kids were consulting on where to hide eggs, and I asked, 'Will you remember where you've hidden them? What if the little kids don't find some of the eggs, and you want to help them?' Arnie said of course he'd remember; he doesn't forget important things like that, but a couple of the others weren't so confident. And then someone said, 'We need a map,' and started arguing about how to make one.

"Map making, they discovered, is hard—so I got to start teaching mapping skills, which is something else I wanted to do in fall only they weren't ready. I'm just about to try doing a map of the yard with the whole group. See, I *do* do some whole-group teaching when the time seems ripe."

"Oh, mapping reminds me of something I asked the kids," says Sandra. "It came out of the quilt, which Gloria will tell you about, I think. She was laying quilt squares out on the table to start planning how to put them together, and a couple of my kids noticed and asked her about it and then came to me to ask, How come they've got a quilt and we don't? And I said well, we've been busy doing other things; but then I added, mostly to get them off my back, 'If you want a quilt, why don't you paint one?' They ran off, and I wasn't sure whether I'd just been a good teacher or a bad teacher

because I didn't hear anything from them for a long time until they burst into the room to announce, 'Come see what we did!'

"Here's what they did," exclaims Sandra holding it up. It's a recognizable painting of a quilt in bright and light blue, with four squares in one direction and three squares in the other, and some squiggles in other colors on some of the squares. She continues, "Gloria had pinned together just this many squares, and they counted and got it right; and they even mixed white and blue paint to make light blue. They started trying to add pictures on the squares before the paint was dry, and got unhappy when the paint ran . . ."

"And complained to me," Gloria says. "And I said, 'Try waiting until the paint is dry, and come help me while you wait.' They did; and we talked about sewing the quilt, and they want to help with that. I had thought maybe just the 5s would do that, but they're so interested . . ."

"Actually both those girls were 5 last month, and they're really careful workers, as you saw," says Sandra. "I think they'll do fine."

Sandra goes on. "I didn't bring Amy tonight because she's on a home visit. The kids have maintained their interest in learning to sign, and since some of the parents started asking about it, I decided we could build connections between home and school by letting Amy go home with kids to stay overnight. (That took some letting go for me; she's *my* gorilla. It's scary to let your little kid go stay over at someone else's house!) The kids get to take a special part of our room activity home to share with their family (a kind of security blanket in reverse). And they've been insisting that their parents learn to sign in order to communicate with Amy. We have a 'travel diary' in which we record her adventures; and as we read her diary out loud, we all get some insights into each other's home lives."[8]

"A little earlier, when we seemed to be into bones and bugs, I was about to ask what's happened to Families as a theme," Ruby says. "But maybe I don't need to ask."

The Content of Teacher–Child Relationships

Individuals cannot just relate to each other: They have to relate to each other about something . . . . [In] early childhood settings all over the U.S . . . the content of teacher–child relationships seems . . . focused on the routines and rules of classroom life . . . information about the child's conduct and level of performance. Thus it seems that the content of relationships . . , when not focused on mundane routines, is about the children themselves.

My impression of Reggio Emilia practices is, in contrast, that to a large extent the content of teacher–child relationships is focused on the work itself . . . . Adults' and children's minds meet on matters of interest to both of them. Both the children and the teachers seem to be equally involved in the progress of the work, the ideas being explored, the techniques and materials to be used, and the progress of the projects themselves. The children's roles in the relationships were more as apprentices than as the targets of instruction or objects of praise.

Such relationships have several benefits. The first is that the children's minds are engaged in challenging work which includes making decisions about what to represent, how to represent it, how to coordinate the efforts and resolve conflicting views of the various contributors to the project, and so forth. Second, because the teachers' and children's minds meet on matters of real interest to both of them, teachers' minds are also engaged.

Reprinted from "What Can We Learn from Reggio Emilia?" (pp. 28–29) by L. Katz in C. Edwards, L. Gandini, & G. Forman, eds., The Hundred Languages of Children: The Reggio Emilia Approach to Early Childhood Education, 1993, Norwood, NJ: Ablex. Copyright © 1993 by Ablex Publishing Corporation. Used by permission.

"Oh, we're doing Families," says Sally. "Only they aren't all people families. We have a litter of puppies visiting tomorrow."

"And you know that nest in the big tree?" adds Bob. "There's a family in it now. The parent birds are very busy feeding them. We can't see the babies, but we've got some books with baby-bird pictures. And there's lots of baby-bird feeding in the house play corner. Whatever kids are trying to understand, they play, don't they?"

————

Before leaving, we manage to catch Ruby's attention for a quick chat. Having been a part of this staff's planning process for almost 10 months, it is getting easier to talk more openly about concerns and confusions. We have established trust by taking every opportunity to give these teachers the credit they deserve. We are the learners here.

"Ruby, I was interested in your response to the children's delegation about Easter," inquires John. "You turned the situation into a great opportunity to be inventive—'How can we create our own Egg Hunt?'—but you kind of avoided the issue."

"Maybe. Maybe not," says Ruby. "I wanted to figure out what the kids' issue was first before opening my big mouth and making everything all complicated."

"Sure," agrees Betty, "the hunting for treasure was what they wanted, and they discovered an acceptable alternative, with Ruby's help."

John still has reservations. "Let me try a 'What if?' on you. What if the kids had persisted in their demands for a *real* Easter-egg hunt?"

"I wasn't anxious to explain the 'boss's' rule," replies Ruby. "I'm not sure they would have even understood it, but the rule had to stand regardless of what I could make clear to them. We might have talked about how only some people celebrate Easter—and would it be fair. I'm not convinced they would have accepted my reasoning. Still, there are important *adult* reasons for why we don't support holiday curriculum here. You've heard me lecture the staff; that's hard enough, without starting on the children!"

18
April Visit:
Maps, Batman, and Baby Bats in the Bat Cave

At the Manzanita gate John discovers a map, clearly a collaborative effort by children and adults. The center's rooms and outdoor features are shown in outline, and teachers' names are written in each room. John remarks on it to Ruby when he looks into the office to say hello.

"Yes, the 5s came through," Ruby says. "I decided to support Bethany by visiting at group time to make an official request for a map. 'We've been having lots of visitors,' I told them. 'Some of them are parents who would like their children to come to this school, and they don't know where everything is here. Could you make a map that would show them?' That made sense to the kids. They'd been less enthusiastic about mapping the school just for the sake of mapping; after all, they *know* where everything is. But this was a real job to be done."[1]

Crossing the yard, John sees another map, now rain streaked, on the fence behind the garden. "We should have made this when we first planted the seeds," Dolores tells him, "but we didn't

think of it then. And so when things started coming up there was a lot of argument about whether they were weeds or not. Some things were so slow coming up that one morning we had to find a diversion for George, who was about to start digging to find them. So we got a big piece of paper and crayons, and we looked at the words and pictures on the seed packets (which we *had* put in the garden, on stakes), and I drew a map of our garden. I don't think

Representation As a Public Event

Why do people make maps and signs, write letters and books, give directions and lectures? To provide information needed by other people, and so the mapmakers and writers and speakers are motivated to communicate as clearly as they can. In contrast, children in schools are often asked to produce work for an audience of one, the teacher, for whom it serves as a test of children's competence rather than as useful information. Understandably, some children experience such tasks as busywork.

Alternatively, children may be invited to produce communications for a real audience whose members need the information the children have. A sign on a block structure asks others to be careful and not to knock it down; that's important. A map helps visitors know where to go; that's important. At the Diana Preschool in Reggio Emilia, Italy, the 5-year-olds have worked hard at the important task of creating Advisories for 3-Year-Old-Children—information about the school for the young newcomers. Here's a sample of their words from *Children's Environments* (they drew pictures, too):

As you get in, just past the hall, turn right and you'll find the classroom of the three-year-olds. There are some green tables there and you'll find, right straight, another door: if you find it unlocked, you can go into the courtyard. There is a blue carpet and three ladders are fixed to the wall: you can climb them and then you can throw yourself down those ladders! If you have just come to this school you must be a little more careful, but don't be scared because there are two very large yellow pads; just put them beneath where you are going to end up and you won't get hurt.

There are some windows that open on to the small gate. To say goodbye to our mom, we would take a chair and climb it to see her while she was getting through the gate.

If you can't help peeing, go out of the room, turn right, pass the wash-basins and you'll find the bathroom. Then, if you feel like going to the wash-basins and turning on the tap, you can have fun and take the water in your hands shaped like a cup, and get wet and sprinkle around. It's great fun but you don't need to do it very often."[2]

"The Children Get So Wrapped Up in Their Own Activities That I'm Not Sure How I Can Teach Them Anything"

"Rather than think their job is to present lessons on a topical theme, we hope," write Carter and Curtis, "teachers will see their role in terms of discovering the curriculum themes the children are already exploring."[3]

Using Carter's and Curtis's "provision-sustain-enrich-represent" formulation, teachers can be invited to identify themes they've recently seen in children's play and then explore related ways to carry out their teaching role. These authors describe the result of one group of teachers who tried this strategy:

Theme observed: hiding

Provision
  Bring in large boxes and sheets.

Sustain
  Notice what children are doing and affirm it.
  Add flashlights, pillows, clothespins, clotheslines, pulley.

Enrich
  Use descriptive language with words such as "underneath," "enclosure," "invisible," "perspective," "overview."
  Set up a tent and camping supplies.
  Extend to outside, build a fort, plan a tree house.
  Display pictures of different kinds of shelters.
  Explore concept of shelters for homeless people.

Represent
  Tell a story, create a song, record a video about the children's activities.
  Make blueprints or sketches of forts.
  Record the children's dictation about the activities; make a book.
  Take photographs and create a display.
  Make a video.
  Bring in related books from the library.[4]

the littler kids quite understood it, but it's good for them to know that grown-ups make pictures to help themselves remember things."

"Kids do that too," says John.

"And then it rained, as you can see. I'm glad I used crayons instead of markers."

John moves on. There's a blanket over a table, and he can hear giggling from underneath. "Do you suppose someone lives in there?" he asks. "Is anybody home?"

"GRrrrarhr!" Patty pokes her head out. "This is our mountain lion cave. We'll scratch you if you get too close."

"This is our baby mountain lion," adds Jody, poking the lion stick puppet out from under the blanket. "We're taking care of our babies."

"Do you have more babies?" John asks.

"Yes, lots, but you can't see 'em 'cause they're asleep. Go away." The heads disappear inside the cave.

This is wilder terrain than John had expected. And there's another cave in the vicinity; a big box near the climber is covered with a blanket, too.

"That's the bat cave," Bob tells John. "I've been getting really tired of Batman, but I can't get the kids to stop playing it. So I finally thought, 'Well, if you can't fight 'em, join 'em,'[5] and yesterday I checked the library for books about bats. I found some dandy pictures of bats hanging upside down in caves, and this morning I showed them to our Batmen. 'Bet you can't do that,' I said. They could so; they showed me, on the climber. I thought that was pretty cool. And then I said, 'Can your baby bats do that, too?'

"'We don't got no baby bats. We Batmen.' That was Frankie. But Justin was intrigued. 'They're in the bat cave,' he said.

"'Where's the bat cave?' I asked. We couldn't find it, so I asked if they'd like me to make them one. Even Frankie thought that was a good idea, so I got a blanket to put over the big box. They're in there now," finishes Bob.

But just then, here comes Justin. "I can't find the baby bats," he tells Bob, sounding worried.

"Did they fly away?" asks Bob.

"No, they're too little," Justin explains.

"Well, let's see if we can find them," says Bob. "I bet there are some baby bats in the scrap-paper box."

Justin looks doubtful, but Bob goes indoors and comes back with paper and scissors. "I think we need to hatch them," he says, folding a piece of paper and quickly cutting a recog-

nizable bat shape. He unfolds it and presents it to Justin. "Baby bat," Bob announces.

Justin is delighted. "More," he says. "Use this paper."

This paper is red, and soon a red bat has joined the original orange bat. Frankie arrives. "What's them?" he says.

"My baby bats," says Justin possessively.

"Baby bats is black," announces Frankie. "Not them colors. My baby bats is black. Like Batman."

John leaves Bob and Frankie on their way to look for black bat paper and moves on to Marnie's room, where she's sitting at a table with several children.

"Come see the Concentration game we made," she calls. "There's been lots of interest in animals and we've had this whole pile of wildlife magazines, many of them duplicates. So I pulled out the duplicates and asked the children if they could find two of the same picture. We cut them out and glued them on cardboard

Their Curriculum/ My Curriculum

Emergent curriculum reflects both children's interests *and* adults' interests and values. Some interests of children (especially, often, those interests promoted by commercial media and manufacturers to tap the child market) may be at odds with the values of the adults who care for those children. What options do children have? Carlsson-Paige and Levin offer four options: (1) ban, (2) permit/ignore, (3) permit with specific limits, (4) actively facilitate.[6]

As active facilitators, adults can draw on their own imaginations to intervene creatively in children's stereotyped play. Carlsson-Paige and Levin suggest,

For example, if a group of children always portray the "bad guy" as attacking them, the teacher might try to expand their concept of the enemy: "Where does the bad guy go when he's not fighting you?"

[A teacher can] bring in new content for the play, such as new props, roles, and physical settings, which grow out of the current content and will help children vary and elaborate the play. This is especially important for those children who seem to be following a television script or acting out the same theme over and over in the same way.[7]

squares, and now I'm teaching them to play Concentration. It's a good matching game."

Marnie returns to the game. "Right, Annie, you found the rabbit. See if you can find the other rabbit. Oh, too bad, you got the coyote this time. No, you have to stop looking, it's Paco's turn. Turn the cards over again, and let's see if he can find a pair.

"Excuse me a minute," says Marnie to John, turning her full attention to Annie, who is wailing because Paco got both rabbits and *she* wanted the rabbits. She finds matching a fine game, but taking turns is something else again. Solitaire, anyone?

Back outside again, John finds Bob scrunched into the bat cave, trying to hang baby bats by their toes "like in the book," says Frankie. He's begun with masking tape, but they keep falling down when bumped by Batmen's heads. John gets involved in problem solving: How about string loops on the ceiling and little hooks on the bats? Velcro? Safety pins? Sally checks in to see what's happening but declines to help; she's got another batty idea, she says, and is going to go work on it.

Speed, Strength, and Power

Children watching superhero dramas on television "like leading role models to be able to move quickly, be strong, and have power. Aggressive play in preschool has several components, which are important in children's development of competence and self-esteem, and which can be provided for through non-aggressive play activities," suggests Sally Skelding. She concludes, "The challenge to the preschool teacher is to find ways for children to experience speed, strength and power."[8]

Adults can invent a variety of activities offering new physical challenges to children. They can also think about strength and power in less literal terms, considering, for example, the power children experience through taking on nurturant adult roles (even as parent to baby bats!), through helping an adult complete a task, and through representing their actions in words and images.

19
May Staff Meeting: What Have We Been Teaching the Children?

As we enter the teachers' room, we see that there's a bat on the bulletin board. Sandra has a lion stick puppet in her hand; she roars it at Bob, laughing. Marnie is carrying her animal Concentration game in a zip-lock bag. Sally's hands are empty, but there's a gleam in her eye; she looks all ready for show-and-tell.

But Ruby, to their surprise and ours, doesn't begin the meeting with her usual "What's been happening?" question. Instead, she plunges in with *her* agenda. We wonder what's going on. Is she feeling stressed?

"We have a picnic to plan," says Ruby, "and there are lots of possibilities for going about it. The part I want to be directorial about . . . ."

"Ruby, is it possible that I heard you say 'dictatorial'?" asks Sally.

"No, you heard me say 'directorial,'" says Ruby, firmly. "There's a difference. One is authoritarian, the other is authoritative. You're all authoritative with children—on your good days, of course. You're competent adults, and I don't have to spend much time being any sort of overt authority. But this is one of those times

when I want you to do what I want you to do, and, if you'll quit interrupting, I can tell you what that is. No big surprise—we've been talking about it all year.

"The picnic is our opportunity to be serious about our obligation to communicate to parents—and to children, and *with* children—how our curriculum has emerged and what we've been learning together. We keep hearing some parental anxiety that 'All the children do here is play' and 'Why aren't we teaching them?' How clear and convincing can we be about all the things we *have* been teaching them? I think what we put up on the walls, and otherwise display, at this picnic is going to be important."[1]

"I've been thinking about that," says Bethany. "I hear more from anxious parents than the rest of you. '*Will* my child be OK in first grade when she's just been playing here? Maybe I should have sent her to a *real* kindergarten.' So it's clear to me that I need to document the curriculum, and I've started making a list of all the forms my documentation could take. This is what I've got so far. I thought maybe you could help me add to it."

Bethany reads her list:

curriculum theme webs
children's art and constructions
children's writing and scribed words
photos of children in action
child-made books

"Are you thinking about individual portfolios, or about what I think I heard Ruby say—displays at the picnic?" asks Sally.

"Both," says Bethany. "I think I should send some sort of portfolio home with each child, and I want to talk with the child about what we should put in it. But since Ruby's being directorial, as she puts it, I don't think I have any choice about making a splash on the walls."

"Looking at your list," says Marnie, "what about adding explanations of what children learn at each of the learning centers? I got those in my training program, and I've had them up in my room all year."

"I've noticed those, and I like them," says Sandra. "Did you invent them yourself?"

"No, one of my professors handed them out," explains Marnie. "I like not having to reinvent the wheel."

What Children Learn Here

Art

Art provides mediums of expression and enables the child to

- work with a wide variety of materials
- experience sensory pleasure by working with different media
- experiment with color, shape, and texture
- create an expression of self
- use visual expression as a means of communication
- develop small-muscle coordination
- develop eye-hand coordination
- work on cooperative or individual projects

Blocks

The block center helps the child to

- enjoy the manipulation of blocks
- enjoy the sensory and kinesthetic pleasure of the blocks
- improve small- and large-muscle coordination
- learn to share ideas and work together in a group
- develop concepts such as big, little, more than, less than, equal to, shape, size, etc.
- express creativity
- have the opportunity for nonverbal expression and emotional release
- understand that boys and girls can build with blocks
- develop physical concepts of balance, symmetry, and gravity
- work alone or in small groups on projects
- map out a real or imaginary world

Reading Center

The reading center is a relaxing center that encourages the child to

- handle books with comfort and independence
- "read" picture books
- browse through books for pleasure
- extend understanding of various media (photographs, illustrations, words) for expressing thoughts and feelings
- develop personal reading interests
- observe other children reading
- use books as reference materials
- use picture clues to predict fantasy or reality in a story
- explore the relationship of stories and print

Sand

Sand provides the child the opportunity to

- explore the properties of wet and dry sand
- find sensory pleasure in sand
- enjoy creating buildings of all types
- work cooperatively
- enjoy solitary play
- dig to one's heart's content
- create roadways, castles, tunnels, volcanoes, etc.
- work with evaporation and other scientific concepts
- enjoy the feeling of being "dirty"

Reprinted from "Interest Centers" (n.p.) by Kay Stritzel, n.d., Tucson, AZ: Borton Primary Magnet School. Copyright © by the author. Used by permission.

"Sometimes I like inventing my own to see if I really do understand what's happening for children," Sandra says tactfully. "I've put up Ruby's photos of my kids playing in the different centers, and I want to add my descriptions of what they're saying and doing. I wish I'd taken better notes while it was happening."

"Could you talk about the photos with the kids, and see what they remember about what they were doing in the picture, and write down their words *now*?" Sally asks.

"Great idea," says Sandra. "That way I can be a good teacher, leading a memory activity, instead of a bad teacher who should have been taking notes but wasn't. Thanks, Sal."

Sandra continues. "One thing I *have* done for most of the year is have children sign in when they get to school. My friend who teaches in Head Start has them do that every day, all year, and swears by it as the way children learn to write their names without direct teaching. I've only managed to do it on most Mondays, but I think that's been enough, and I've saved a sample list from every month. I'm going to use those as documentation for parents: This is how your child used to write her name, and this is how she writes it now (after she's been in our school!). I decided to make individual

books rather than a display, so parents wouldn't start comparing how well their children write. And we were going to do books anyway. We've gotten started on those; here are a couple that are done, if you're interested."

The books are passed around and admired. "Will they all be alike?" Gloria asks.

"No, not exactly," answers Sandra. "Every child will have a photo of him or herself and of the class and of Dolores and me, and I think we can get them all to draw a self-portrait and a picture of their families. Most of them already have. We have sign-in samples from everyone. We don't have photos of all the families, though.

Picking Up the Threads

Things happen rapidly in an environment filled with young children. The task of managing a group can mean that the meaning of words and actions becomes a blur; no adult can possibly keep up with it all. But any adult can reflect on what has gone on, think of things she or he has missed or wants to extend further, and return to them with the children. In this way, the threads of shared living are woven.

Signing In

The daily structure, after the first 6 to 8 weeks of the semester, begins with signing-in. Each day I post long strips of paper on the cupboard doors, having told the children, 'When you get to school, write your name here.' If a child says, 'I can't,' I don't give him a model (though he can find his name elsewhere in the room); I simply ask him to try. Any and all marks are acceptable, varying from an unrecognizable scribble for Jorge and a wobbly M for Marco to a carefully lettered ESPERANZA stretching the width of the page and on to the next line for ZA.

. . . By saving the first sign-in sheet . . . of each month, I accumulate a running record of each child's writing . . . . These are useful in planning,

September	November	March

for evaluating children and the program, and for parent conferences.

Reprinted from "It's All Academic!" (p. 94) by J. Meade-Roberts, in E. Jones, ed., Reading, Writing and Talking with Four, Five and Six Year Olds, *1988, Pasadena, CA: Pacific Oaks College. Copyright © 1988 by Pacific Oaks College. Used by permission.*

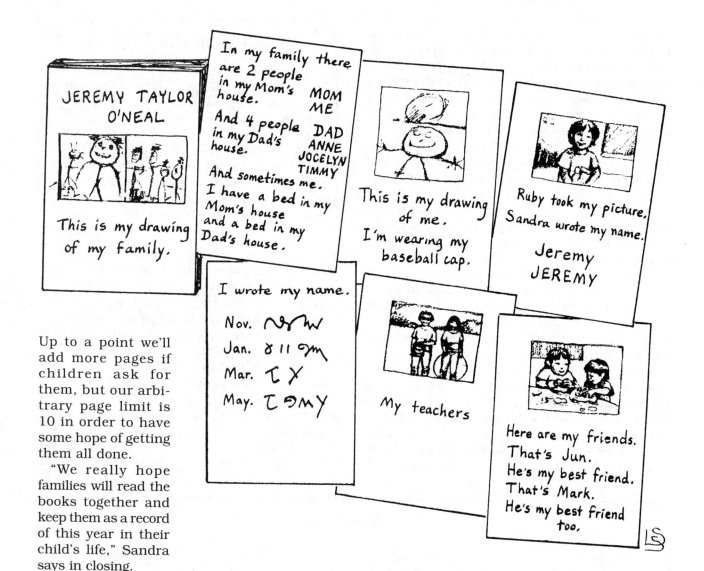

JEREMY TAYLOR O'NEAL

This is my drawing of my family.

In my family there are 2 people in my Mom's house. MOM ME
And 4 people in my Dad's house. DAD ANNE JOCELYN TIMMY
And sometimes me.
I have a bed in my Mom's house and a bed in my Dad's house.

This is my drawing of me.
I'm wearing my baseball cap.

Ruby took my picture. Sandra wrote my name.
Jeremy
JEREMY

I wrote my name.
Nov.
Jan.
Mar.
May.

My teachers

Here are my friends.
That's Jun.
He's my best friend.
That's Mark.
He's my best friend too.

Up to a point we'll add more pages if children ask for them, but our arbitrary page limit is 10 in order to have some hope of getting them all done.

"We really hope families will read the books together and keep them as a record of this year in their child's life," Sandra says in closing.

"You've certainly planned ahead. I'm impressed," says Sally. "But you'll be glad, Ruby," she continues, "I've been practicing planning and letting go, just like you said. Bats are evidence of my letting go of what I like and going with the children; I certainly never thought I'd be into bats. I have Bob to thank—or blame—for that. His Bat Cave really did slow down our Batmen. And I've been wanting to try storytelling to the kids about their play, and the other day I did. I couldn't bring myself to make it a Batman story; I'm so tired of Batman. I just began, 'Once upon a time there was a big, big bat,' and went on to tell about the baby bats in the cave. 'Again!' said several kids when I said, 'The end.' I decided I must be a pretty good storyteller, and I told it again. And then we all tried being upside-down bats.

"I want to make a bat mural as a follow-up, just for fun, but our kids don't do much representational drawing yet. Do you suppose it would be too uncreative if we provide some bat cutouts? Bob's already made some; we could just add more."

"That's a lot like using cutouts on a flannel board, isn't it?" asks Bethany. "You're doing storytelling, not creative art. If some of your kids want to try their own hand at bat making, can they?"

"Of course," says Sally. "We'll have extra paper and scissors handy. And I think I'll print my story on the mural for parents to see, even though our kids aren't yet much interested in the printed word. That lets parents know some of the things we do here. Maybe it will even give them some ideas for coping with Batman."

"I'll bet some of our kids will be interested in the words if you put your mural up outside," says Sandra. "And you know what? Some of our kids are into caves, too. Maybe we should collaborate on a display."

"How about expanding it to houses?" suggests Ruby. "Places where people and animals live. Most of you have done some Where do you live? and Who's in your family? activities. If we display home and family activities all along the porch wall, it would really look as if we plan curriculum at this school."

"We DO!" was the indignant chorus.

———

"You do plan curriculum, you know," says John to Ruby as we three linger outside in the warm evening. "You've been so relaxed about it all year, giving people lots of playful time together at meetings. In your place I would have been much more uptight. Were you uptight underneath?"

"Actually I haven't been, most of the time," says Ruby. "I trust the basic competence of this staff, and the old ones are good at including the new ones. Several of them have worked with me long enough that I can count on them to critique me when I need it. That keeps us pretty relaxed together.

"I don't like everything I see going on. But I choose carefully what to bring up because in my experience staff work a whole lot better if they get to operate pretty autonomously. It wasn't my idea to have age-grouped classes this year; at our old center the 3s and 4s were together, and I liked that. But the staff wanted to try it. Why, I wonder, when you move into a school building do people immediately want to play school? I decided not to buck them, figuring they have a right to identify their own sources of comfort. And in one way it's been OK; they've been busily mixing the children up all year.

"But having separate classes for 4s and 5s has had some of the impact I was afraid it would—pressure from parents concerned about school readiness. *Are* you teaching my child everything she needs to know? Why are you letting them play? And their concerns are realistic. I think we should be doing all we can to reassure parents, and ourselves, about the serious content of our curriculum. That's what you were hearing from me tonight."

"I've been impressed by how much of that you're doing already," Betty says reassuringly. "All the displays of kids' and teachers' work—they're exciting. Why the sudden dictatorial—no, directorial, you said—intervention tonight?"

"Oh, I don't know," Ruby shrugs. "There's always the risk, when people have gotten comfortable working together, that I'll fail to challenge them enough. There's the risk that we won't allow enough time for planning the picnic, and the whole thing will be chaos. There's the free-floating anxiety from the rest of my life. I've got that thesis to write. I spent two nights up with my sister when my niece ran away last week—she's back, it's OK—and I'm *tired.* And sometimes I just get tired of being a facilitator and want to be a boss and have people do what I say. If I knew how, maybe I would!"

"They wouldn't let you, you know," John adds, grinning. "You can't share power with people and then start wanting it back. But it was a well-timed challenge, I think, and they coped very well with you."

Adult-Made Patterns

Many classrooms are filled with commercial or teacher-made patterns for children to color, cut, or copy. In contrast, teachers who value children's creativity often refrain entirely from participating in children's work with art materials. Still other teachers find a middle ground, contributing their ideas and images side by side with children's, not as models or patterns but as one more source of good ideas to be shared.

As described in *Dimensions of Teaching-- Learning Environments,* a volunteer in one pattern-filled kindergarten classroom introduced a "making books" activity designed to be open ended but including precut pictures (elephant, dog, octopus, fish, and stoplights) and word cards (*Go, elephant. Stop, dog. Go, dog. Stop, octopus.*) Her description of the children's involvement reads,

> Most of the children responded to this new activity by concentrating on gluing the pictures . . . . [Some did match words and pictures.] As we ran out of pictures, children asked for more, and some of their requests were for different pictures, which I cut out for them— cat, ghost, footprints, hands, shark, dragon. Several tried cutting their own pictures; Aileen drew an octopus and tried to cut it, then asked for help in finishing. Some children just wanted pictures to keep; Humberto was gleefully hoarding red, green and yellow lights as I cut them at his request . . . .
>
> This was not an art activity; it was an opportunity for children to try a matching task, or just work with paper and glue. Scissors and extra paper were there for children who wanted to cut their own pictures; but the pre-cut pictures simplified the task and also were gifts from adult to child, especially those cut to order. This aspect was particularly important for Humberto, who takes things I bring and has difficulty returning them. These he could keep.[2]

20
May Visit:
Families in the Center, Families on the Walls

We've been invited to the picnic, and we're there a bit early in order to have time to look around before the families start arriving. Tables for potluck have been set up all along the porch, and on the wall behind them we see the Bat Cave mural, the various Families projects, and a new Hide and Find photo display that we haven't seen before. Patty and Jody, the resident mountain lions, pull us over to show us their story. They "read" it confidently to us; they've become fluent readers of these familiar words with many repetitions. "Sandra asked, and Ruby took our pictures when we popped out of the cave," they explain.

The 4s have made a mural, too. We recognize its language pattern from a classic picture book *Everybody Has a House*,[1] but children's spontaneous contributions add variations to the pattern. It's clear that adults and children have been inventing together all along the way.

Once upon a time
There was a big big bat
And there was another big big bat.
And they flew around and around until they were tired.

And then they flew home to their Bat Cave
Where all their little bat babies
Were hanging upside-down by their toes.
The End.

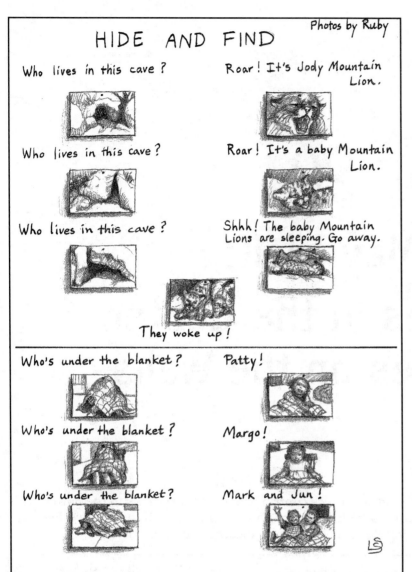

HIDE AND FIND

Photos by Ruby

Who lives in this cave?

Who lives in this cave?

Who lives in this cave?

Roar! It's Jody Mountain Lion.

Roar! It's a baby Mountain Lion.

Shhh! The baby Mountain Lions are sleeping. Go away.

They woke up!

Who's under the blanket?

Who's under the blanket?

Who's under the blanket?

Patty!

Margo!

Mark and Jun!

"Well, this isn't the time and place for that," says John. "Look what Bethany came up with."

Outside the 5s' room there's a large graph, How Many People Are in Your Family? It uses Bethany's strings of paper dolls, all the same size for graphing purposes, but the children have had the last word, we see; there's a Comments column to the right of the graph.

"We really struggled over this one," Bethany remarks as she comes by with a stack of plates and napkins. "I had decided it was time we did some real math, with a graph. The kids kept arguing about how the graph wasn't right, it left out all sorts of important information. I should know better than to keep encouraging kids to think independently all year if I want them to do what I tell them in May! Finally I came up with the Comments column as our compromise. 'If you'll count off the right number of dolls to go on these lines,' I told them, 'I'll write down what you want to say over here so people won't get mixed up about what your family is really like.' Most of them decided that was fair."

"My, I'm going to miss these kids! I hope their first-grade teachers don't squelch them too much."

John has a concern, though. "We're always oversimplifying things for children, aren't we?" he comments quietly to Betty. "Everybody *doesn't* have a house; there are homeless people all over this city. I think children need to know that, too."

Betty nods. "Keeping curriculum inclusive is a constant challenge. Some people would rather keep it simple, of course; but even those who are trying to be inclusive keep missing things. I think we all just have to keep reminding each other when we notice something that someone else didn't."

The birds have a nest and that's their house. The mommy and daddy feed them.
Margo

EVERYBODY HAS A HOUSE

The cow has a barn and that's its house.
Jeremy

My dog lives in my house but he sleeps on the back porch.
Rachel

The fish have an ocean and that's their house.
Rachel

The mountain lions have a cave and that's their house.
Grrrah!   Jody

HOW MANY PEOPLE ARE IN YOUR FAMILY?

Comments (or How not to lie with statistics, which never tell the whole story)

1 2 3 4 5 6 7 8 9 10

Althea
My family has __5__ people.
My daddy and my auntie and Booboo and Gramp. 1-2-3-4. And me. That's 5. My mama she's gone away.

Arnie
My family has __6__ people.
My mom and my dad and my sisters.

Clovisa
My family has __3__ people.
This one is me. This is my mum. This is my papa. Aren't they nice?

Danny
My family has __4__ people.
They aren't all the same like this. My daddy's bigger and my baby's littler. And my mommy - she's the Mama Bear!

Freddy
My family has __2__ people.
That's OK.

Greta
My family has __3__ people.
This is my mom Elsa. And my mom Sue. And me. They're bigger than me, you know. And we have a kitty.

Judy
My family has __3__ people.
But really it's 3 people and 2 dogs and 2 budgies. And my teddy bear. And when my Nana comes for dinner that's more.

Jorge
My family has __5__ people
But that's just in my house. In Jalisco we have a lot of family and we're going to see them pretty soon and I get to ride a horse.

Robbie
My family has ____ people. "I can't say that." Mom's house
I have two families so I need two places. My mom's house has my mom and me and Cindy. And George. And our cat.

"But we come too. Only you can't count us two times." Dad's house
My family has ____ people. "I can't say that."
And when Cindy and me go to my dad's house there are one, two, three of us. Other times there's just him. But sometimes Pam is there.

Kimiko
My family has __5__ BIG people. AND ONE LITTLE people AND WOOFIE AND THE CATS. MY CAT HAD KITTIES!
I can't use those paper dolls. They don't look like us. I'll draw us. See?

We find this invitation irresistible and tag along. Althea's dad pauses to look at the graph outside the door. "I see Althea right here," he says, pointing to her name.

"No, Daddy, that's not *in* the room. That's *outside* the room. I said, 'How many of my name *in* the room.' You need to listen."

Althea's daddy chuckles as she leads him, her grandpa and her small cousin inside. We don't interfere with their game, but from a distance we try playing it for ourselves: Where's Althea? "It's pretty easy to practice reading your name in a place where it's repeated eight times," John comments.

Does she have the number right?

1. On her cubby—that one's easy.

2. On the class list, where each child's full name has been carefully printed.

We see that Marnie has put up We Live in a House, which she showed us the beginnings of in March. No children's comments there; Marnie likes things neat and orderly. Gloria's quilt is indoors, we guess, but here's a photo display of a couple of adult volunteers and some children sewing on it. Yoshiko has grouped her child-and-parent stick people under their names.

Outside the staff room there's a web we haven't seen before; it looks as if Ruby has been busy, too. She's summed up all the different family projects that different groups have done and added some reassuring words about curriculum planning. Most of the time she seems really confident, but we guess maybe she gets anxious about what people think of the center. This picnic isn't just a party; it's an open house, too.

Several parents have arrived, and there goes Althea, running to hug her dad. "You need to come see," she announces. "I'm your guide, Bethany said so, and a guide gets to tell people where to go. You come see how many times you can find my name in our room. I'll give you a hint, it's eight. I counted them three times today just to make sure."

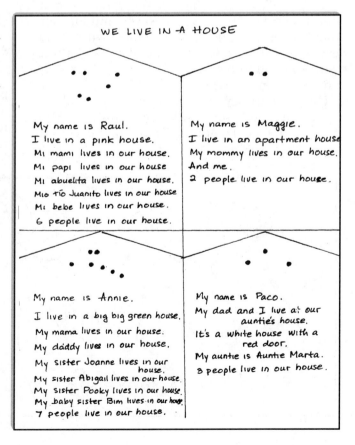

WE LIVE IN A HOUSE

My name is Raul.
I live in a pink house.
Mi mami lives in our house.
Mi papi lives in our house
Mi abuelita lives in our house.
Mio tío Juanito lives in our house
Mi bebe lives in our house.
6 people live in our house.

My name is Maggie.
I live in an apartment house
My mommy lives in our house.
And me.
2 people live in our house.

My name is Annie.
I live in a big big green house.
My mama lives in our house.
My daddy lives in our house.
My sister Joanne lives in our house.
My sister Abigail lives in our house.
My sister Pooky lives in our house.
My baby sister Bim lives in our house.
7 people live in our house.

My name is Paco.
My dad and I live at our auntie's house.
It's a white house with a red door.
My auntie is Auntie Marta.
3 people live in our house.

3. On the helpers chart, a pocket chart where names on cards can be inserted to rotate classroom tasks.

4. On the alphabet that circles the room. A is for Althea and Arnie, B is for Bethany . . . .

5. On a vivid painting of ladybugs, where she has printed her name herself and included every letter. "These are the ladybugs in our garden. They're spotty. They're real little." Bethany has scribed her words on the painting.

6. On a body tracing, where Althea has again written her own name. We recall that Bethany's intent was bones—What's inside?—but Althea is clearly more interested in what's outside. Her paper self is carefully dressed in a blue jacket with yellow buttons, purple skirt and socks, and white shoes, and there are tiny barrettes in her hair.

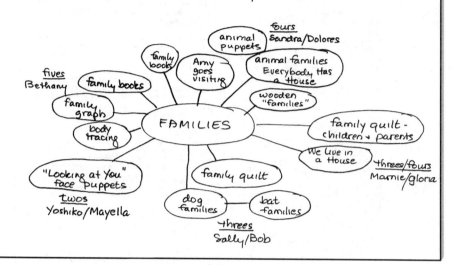

Social studies for young children begins at home. We've been studying FAMILIES in many different ways, as you'll see when you look around . . .

That's all we can find on the walls. Althea has taken the initiative, however, pulling her daddy over to the book display rack, which this evening is filled not with published books but with the children's own books. "This is mine," she proclaims. "'Who's in Your Family?' it say right there. It say 'Althea' right there, too."

"It sure do," says Althea's grandpa. "My, that's real nice. Lemme see that. You make that book yourself?"

This is Amy's family.

Number 7, then, is Althea's book, and we've found number 8 as well. There is a folder for every child—the portfolios Bethany was preparing with them—on the round table, and here's Althea's. We pick it up and leaf through it. Althea, Althea, Althea, on every page. She forgot to count these—but we're not about to tell.

"What's the matter, Patty?" Betty asks as we walk out on the porch, where Patty is sitting, crying.

"My mom's not here," she wails. "Jody's mom is here, and her brother and her baby and her auntie, and she won't stay with me. And I want to show Amy to my mom. I didn't ever get a turn to take her home, and my mom wants to see her."

"So do I," Betty says. "Could you show her to me while you're waiting for your mom?"

Clearly, Betty isn't the real thing, but she'll do in an emergency. Patty agrees to take her hand, and they go inside to find Amy the gorilla seated in state under a sign saying, This Is Our Friend Amy. There's a photo album of children signing, and Patty leafs through it to find her picture, which she shows Betty, saying, "This is me and I'm signing *I love you* so Amy will know."

"Can you show me how?" Betty asks, and Patty does. Betty picks up another album, which is labeled

EMERGENT CURRICULUM

Amy's Travel Diary. "Oh, look," she says, as she opens it. "Here's a picture of Jody with Amy. Are they at Jody's house?"

Too late, Betty realizes that was the wrong question. "Amy didn't go to my house, she only went to Jody's house," wails Patty—a tired and hungry Patty, it's evident. "I hate Jody. I want my mommy."

"Punkin, I'm sorry I'm late." It's Patty's mommy, enfolding her in a hug. "I left my brief-case in the office and had to go back for it and the office was locked and I had to find the custodian. It's been a long day—for you, too, I can tell."

Betty tactfully disappears, wanting to catch a look at Gloria's quilt before seeing what's for dinner. She finds John already there. The quilt is beautiful. We admire it together.

Mayella sees us. "I brought my quilt," she tells us. "You see it yet? It's in our room."

So it is. Mayella's story about her quilt is there, too.[2]

The potluck supper, we discover, is an amazing display of goodies. Its highlight is the salad bar, elegantly served out of a wagon in the garden by Yoshiko and several children. There is salad dressing and bacon bits as well as freshly picked lettuce, carrots, radishes, and beans. The tiny serving containers enable the harvest to be shared among as many diners as possible. There's lots to talk about.

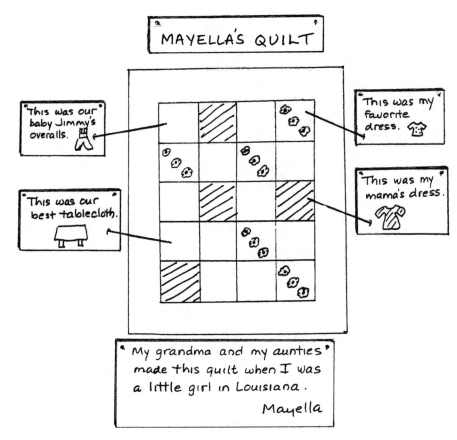

MAYELLA'S QUILT

"This was our baby Jimmy's overalls.

"This was our best tablecloth.

"This was my favorite dress.

"This was my mama's dress.

"My grandma and my aunties made this quilt when I was a little girl in Louisiana.
Mayella

"Did you really grow this lettuce?"
"We sure did!"
"This bean looks like a candy cane."
"Look at this one. It looks like a J. J for Judy—that's me."

After supper there's singing. Sally and Bob have brought their guitars, and the songs "This Little Light of Mine," "We Shall Overcome," and "I See the Moon" help to share some of the year's curriculum with families. Some parents sing along, some leave to put babies to bed, and some have just one more taste of that unforgettable pie.

21

June Staff Meeting:
Did We Have a Plan? Naming
the Emergent Curriculum

The school year began in September with a two-day staff meeting. It's ending with a Friday on which the center is closed (parents were notified of the schedule in September, reminded in February, and supported in networking with each other for shared care). Staff will spend the morning reflecting on the emergence of curriculum throughout the year, followed by a celebratory lunch and an afternoon of organizing their rooms.

This isn't the end of the school year, of course; child care is a 12-month commitment. But summer is a time of changes, staff vacations, and fluctuating attendance as families take time off. There are no official staff meetings in July and August. Yoshiko's husband is being transferred back to Japan at the end of July; she'll be leaving in June, as will Marnie, who's returning to Utah to plan her wedding. Bob will work through August and then, the tourist season over, take off with his backpack for a trip around the world—or as far as he gets, he says. We notice that he's letting his beard grow as part of his preparation for the trip. There will be some recombining of children's groups during the summer, and sand and water will be a focus of activity. The 2s' room can stay set up

as a nap room since it won't be used as a classroom until new 2s are admitted in September. So this is a time for winding down, for goodbyes, and for looking at where staff and children have been together.

———

"Thank you all, again and again, for the picnic," says Ruby when everyone has settled onto chairs and couches. (Sally is on the floor, her long legs stretched out and her feet bare.) You really outdid yourselves, and so many parents came! I think we're building a real sense of belonging here. Child care needs that. Mayella, thanks especially for bringing your quilt. That was wonderful." Mayella beams. She's dressed up for this day without children and is glowing in a new red-flowered dress.

"Remember the pieces of her favorite dress in her quilt?" Betty whispers to John. "It had red flowers, too."

"I liked watching the children explaining things to their families," volunteers Gloria. "There were so many places where they could say, 'Come see what we did.' 'Look, here's me.'"

"I think all of our displays made it easy for them to do that." says Sally. "There were times during the year when I thought you were going overboard on documenting everything, Ruby, but I have to admit you were right. I'm really looking forward to staying with my kids next year because they'll be older and I can do more."

"Thanks, that's reassuring," says Ruby. "This is a new focus for me, too, and I've worried about being too pushy. But you folks have really come through and sometimes even looked as if you enjoyed it."

"I did," says Sandra. "I need new mental challenges when I'm working with kids, or it just gets too daily, and I get lazy and then bored. Inventing ways to look at what we're doing and naming that part of what we do together—I'm going to be learning about that for years."

What emerged?

"Thank you for the lead-in because that's what I want us to do this morning," says Ruby. "I want to look at what we've done—the curriculum we've helped emerge—and then try several ways of sorting it out. What have we done with children this year, and why did it happen that way? Could we begin by just brainstorming a list—not a web, just a list—of all the names of memorable activities or themes or whatever that come to mind? Sally, could you write it, large, up here? You're good at talking and writing at the same time."

"Go!" And Sally does.

"There's no more room on the page," announces Sally after a while. "Can I stop?"

What was important?

"That's fine," says Ruby. "This could go on and on; an awful lot comes up during a year with children. Let's move on and do something else with the list. I'd like each of you to identify five items on the list that seem to you to have been especially important for any reason, for you and your kids or for the center as a whole.

"Choose yourself a colored marker and write your initials up there with it in case we want to know who's who when we're talking about it. Then circle your five choices. I think two people can do it at the same time, and it's OK to have more than one person circle an item. Sally, go for it! And Dolores?"

———

So much has happened since Ruby asked this same staff to brainstorm and circle *their* passions just 10 months ago. It's interesting for us—watching the circling going on. Some people bounce through it impulsively; others take their time over each choice. When they're through, it appears that everyone has chosen some item that no one else has circled, but there's a lot of convergence as well. Harvest, garden, Martin Luther King, quilts, sand, families, Legos, and digging—each have many circles around them.

———

"What's different about the ones with lots of circles?" wonders Bethany aloud once all the choices are made. "What have they got in common?"

"Most of those are things that became community events, aren't they?" asks

garden	Legos	ocean
cooking	houses	bones
families	graveyards	animals
masks	calaveras	dinosaurs
treasure	digging	bats
Amy/sign	baby birds	caves
weaving	Martin Luther King	Batman
quilts	hiding	stick animals
sewing	stick people	pumpkins
Easter eggs	maps	squash
shadows	concentration	harvest
light in darkness	mouse skull	our harvest
Magic Mouse	I See the Moon	bugs
gunniwolf	Carrot Seed	little cars
housekeeping	sand	road building
Barbies	water	monsters
Beauty + the Beast	weaving	

Gloria. "We invited parents to a celebration or did major displays."

"But not all of them," says Sally. "How about sand and digging? Those are just activities that happened practically every day."

"How about Martin Luther King?" asks Ruby, "We didn't really involve parents, though we probably should have. And that was mostly a one-day event."

"But it was so personal," says Sandra. "You and Mayella made it clear that all of us needed to pay attention because this was important in your lives—and in all our lives. This wasn't just 'Go have fun in the sand if that's what you want to do.' Most of our activities are choices, but this wasn't a choice. Maybe that made it memorable."

Why did we do what we did?

There's a pause while people think about that idea. Then Ruby says, "Suppose a parent or someone else came in right now and saw our list. Do you think we could convince them that we have a sensible curriculum at this center? Did we have a plan?

"What do you mean, a sensible curriculum?" asks Marnie. "That's a really odd question."

"It's one you've asked from time to time, using other words," Ruby responds. "And it came to me when I looked at our list. How can anyone justify a preschool curriculum that has masks, maps, sewing, hiding, and graveyards all jumbled up like that? It looks as if we have no plan for what we're teaching the children."

"Well, you're the one who encouraged us to make a jumbled list," says Sandra. "What do you want us to do with it now—web it?" A groan is heard from the couch.

"That had crossed my mind," admits Ruby. "But I won't ask you to go off and web in small groups or anything like that. Let's just try talking through some of it, and if my notes end up looking like webs, that's my problem."

"OK. Did we have a plan?"

"Not *a* plan," says Sally. "We had lots of plans."

Why shadows? Where did they come from?

"How come *shadows* is on the list?" asks Ruby. "Just as an example, why should children be learning about shadows?"[1]

"I started that one, didn't I?" says Sandra. "I don't know if anyone else got into it ('We did,'

Bethany reminds her), but let me try remembering how it happened. It was winter, and it got dark early; we started doing Candle Time, and in candlelight there are lots of shadows. Wow, fluorescent light has really changed people's experience of the world, hasn't it?

"So there we were with light and shadows, and without even thinking about it I started making animal silhouettes with my hands because that's what you do at bedtime. It's what we did in our family when I was little. Our uncle showed us how, and my sisters and I used to make animal shadows on our walls when we were supposed to be going to sleep. The streetlight shone in our window."

"And why are you doing that with children now?" prompts Ruby.

"Oh! Why? Because it's what my uncle did with us," continues Sandra. "Because it's what loving grown-ups do with children. It's a happy memory from my childhood and I want to pass it on to this generation of children. Is that a good enough reason?"

"Yes," says Gloria firmly. "We are handing along our heritage to children. We're including them in our community. How can we do that except by sharing our lives with them?"

"But parents want to know what we're *teaching* their children," says Marnie. "If we're talking about shadows, shouldn't we identify the scientific ideas children can be learning from a study of shadows?"

"Remember, I did ask about whether shadows are longer in summer or winter," says Sandra. "There's a good scientific question for you."

"What did you find out?" asks Sally.

"I didn't," admits Sandra. "I think it was at that point that Bob got the idea of teaching Sign; I brought Amy to school, and we left shadows behind."

"I did," says Sally. "Find out, I mean. Not with the kids, for myself, because when we talked about it at that staff meeting I couldn't remember the answer. But I cheated; I looked it up in a book instead of finding it out for myself."

"And which is it?" asks Marnie.

"I'll tell you later," says Sally. "Remind me."

Bob enters the discussion. "But Sandra, you make it sound like Sign and Amy just squeezed out the shadow research. I don't think the length of shadows was an important question for the kids."

"I didn't follow through on that question with the kids, either, even though I think I said I was going to," says Bethany. "Maybe we could

Shadows and Seasons

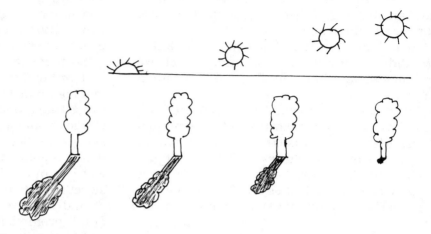

"Just as shadows feed the imagination so they can also stimulate intellectual reason," Guido Petter tells us in the catalog of the Reggio Emilia exhibit. "A shadow changes according to the slope or type of the surface on which it is projected, or according to the position of the light source. A shadow can grow longer or shorter, become wavy or even zigzag. During the summer, at midday we can hardly see our own shadow because it is so contracted, but in the evening it lengthens dramatically."[2]

Shadows are longer in winter than in summer, just as they are longer early or late in the day than at noon. The reason is essentially the same: The sharper the angle at which the sun's rays hit the earth, the longer the shadow made by any object that blocks those rays. Both in winter and in late afternoon or early morning, the sun is "lower in the sky."

In winter the sun's rays hit the earth at a sharper angle, creating less heat and longer shadows. This effect varies, of course, with latitude. There is no winter at the equator; whereas near the poles there is very little daylight in winter, and the shadows are very long indeed.

---

have found ways to sustain their interest, but you could be right, Bob. There's so much to keep track of in an emergent curriculum.

"I did, though, get them making shadow drawings on the asphalt. Remember when we were weaving on the fence and trying to draw its shadow? A few kids really got into that for a week or so."

That was . . . when?" asks Ruby. "In winter, I remember. "And then what happened? Has there been any interest in shadows since?"

"Just the other day, since the sunflowers have gotten so tall," answers Dolores. "Several kids started measuring themselves against the sunflower plants, and then they told me to come stand by the sunflower and were amazed to discover that it was even taller than me. I happened to remember, Bethany, that these were the same kids—your Pauline and Althea—who were drawing the fence shadows way back when, and so I said without thinking, 'Is the sunflower taller than my shadow?' That started a big argument over whether you could measure my shadow against the sunflower or only measure it against the sunflower's shadow. That was too much for me. They're your kids,

Bethany. You can do something with it if you want to. Not me."

Ruby has been making notes all through this discussion, and now she holds them up for all to see. "I've been webbing, as you knew I would," she explains, "but the web isn't big enough for you to see so I'll just talk it. It sounds as if no one started out intending to study shadows. They just happened along because candles make shadows and Sandra noticed. She made animal shadows because that's what her uncle did when she was little. You did tell the kids about that, right, Sandra?"

"Oh yes," says Sandra, "and we had several days of 'Bedtime for Sandra and her sisters' stories. And, of course, children started talking about what happens at *their* bedtimes. We wrote down some of their words—I'd forgotten that—so that we could all remember them. And we went looking for books about bedtime, too, and those became Candle Time reading."[3]

"Was that as far as shadows went, in your class?" asks Ruby.

"No, Sandra forgot to mention our attempt at shadow plays," says Dolores. "When my daughter went to camp they had a parents' night and put on shadow plays—you know, like the one about doing surgery with a saw and yards and yards and yards of rope? She loved that—real 10-year-old humor—and I remembered it. So Sandra and I put up a sheet and tried doing shadow plays a couple of times, but it got too crazy with 4-year-olds. We had the whole group, and we hadn't talked about how to organize it. They ran around and knocked the sheet down and tangled themselves up in it. We gave up. I think you could do it with just a few kids, though, and maybe I'll try something like that next winter."

Ruby adds a few more bits to her web and then puts it down. "This is helping me think," she says. "If you look back at our big list, you'll see that no one circled *shadows* when I said to choose the five you thought were most important. There are lots of uncircled items, and I picked this one at random to see what happened with it. The two oldest classes did some shadow activities, 4s in the whole group and 5s with just a few kids. These didn't last long, but they made a bridge to some other activities that have lasted longer—learning Sign, especially, which Sandra and Bob have continued all spring. Shadows weren't a preplanned idea; they emerged one day out of another, larger idea.

"So, what would you say about shadows as curriculum?" Ruby concludes. "Were they important? Or shouldn't we bother to mention them?"

"We have to mention them," Sandra says quickly, "because we did do something with

BEDTIME STORIES

Jody: My mom turns on music. My bear sleeps on my pillow.

Mark: Me and my brother, we tickle.

Jun: My papa reads to me.

Jeremy: I better be quiet and go to sleep right now.

Luisa: I go to sleep in front of TV. And then my papi puts me in the bed.

them and so they really were curriculum—an idea we were exploring together. Shadows just didn't turn out to be a *big* idea this year. In another year they might. Or they might not happen at all, at least not that we notice."

"But shadows are always there as part of the world we live in," says Sally, thinking hard. "So whether or not any of us are consciously paying attention to shadows at a particular time, they're *potential curriculum*. They become actual curriculum when any of us—kids or grown-ups—start paying attention. Wow! I like that." She pauses and then goes on.

"There are lots of bits of curriculum, aren't there? One child can get absorbed in puzzles, and that becomes significant curriculum for him for days. Or putting the babies to bed is what a couple of girls do in the house corner every time they play there, with variations. But they don't play there every day. Sometimes they drive trucks in the sand, and sometimes they're on the climber. And when I read *Blueberries for Sal*[4] to the whole group because I love it (after all, it's about me!), they're there, and that's part of their curriculum, too."

"So can we say that any part of curriculum is more important than other parts of it?" wonders Bethany, aloud. "Does it matter how

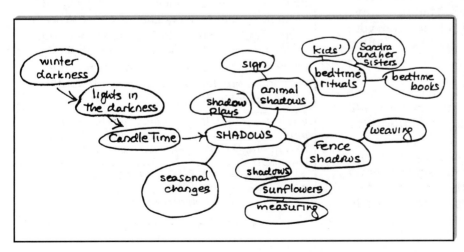

many kids are doing it, or for how long, or whether it was my idea or theirs? Is Batman or Little Mermaid curriculum if children are busy playing it, but I'm trying to divert their attention to something I think is more important and appropriate? There's a good deal of my curriculum versus their curriculum; I've been experiencing that all year as I try to figure out what a kindergarten teacher is supposed to do. Maybe I should have stayed with the 4s."

"We're trying to get the big picture, and it's complicated, isn't it?" says Ruby. "Can we go back to concrete examples for a little longer? Shadows seems to be an example of a little curriculum piece or maybe a middle-sized piece. It wasn't a beginning idea; it spun off from something else. It involved all the 4s in a couple of activities and a small group of 5s in a different activity. It stayed in Dolores's head so that months later she tossed it out casually to a few of the 5s, and we're now waiting to see whether their teacher will pick it up. And it was a bridge to teaching sign language to all the 4s.

"Shadows was one way an idea can develop, sort-of-by-chance," says Ruby. "Now, what if we compare it to another on your list—say, one that a lot of people circled, like *Legos*? Where did that one come from? Why should children be learning about Legos?"

Why Legos—by design?

"That's obvious, isn't it?" asks Marnie. "They're designed to be an educational activity. Children sort them by size and color, and practice fine-motor skills by putting them together, and use them to represent houses and train stations and stores. They're a *manipulative*, and that's one of the areas in a good classroom."

"You're so good at logical, Marnie," says Bethany. "I need to learn some of that from you; I always get stuck in the story of how a thing happened and don't think in terms of what's *supposed* to be happening. So far, though, you've left out the story, and I remember some of that because we were in the same small group at that first staff meeting when Ruby had us all webbing, and you webbed Legos."

"And Ruby said it was a planning meeting," Marnie adds, jumping back in, "only it didn't feel like one to me. So I took the 'plan' I made—the Lego web—and used Legos to teach classification and wrote children's words about Legos,

and then I ended up with everybody's Legos. That wasn't part of my plan, but it was nice."

"Why did you all circle Legos on the list, those of you who did?" asks Ruby. "Why was it important?"

"I did," says Sandra. "I really remembered all those tubs and tubs of Legos, out on the porch, and all the things kids did with them. And Marnie did a really nice job of calling attention to them with her web, and signs, and children's scribed words. I remember there was a lot of interest among parents, and conversation about Legos between parents and kids."

"Is that why you keep talking about documentation, Ruby, and pushing us to do it?" asks Gloria. "Because it gets parents involved?"[5]

Communicating with Parents

Family participation requires many things, but most of all it demands of teachers a multitude of adjustments. Teachers must possess a habit of questioning their certainties, a growth of sensitivity, awareness, and availability, the assuming of a critical style of research and continually updated knowledge of children, an enriched evaluation of parental roles, and skills to talk, listen, and learn from parents.

Responding to all of these demands requires from teachers a constant questioning of their teaching. Teachers must leave behind an isolated, silent mode of working that leaves no traces. Instead, they must discover ways to communicate and document the children's evolving experiences at school. They must prepare a steady flow of quality information targeted to parents but appreciated also by children and teachers. This flow of documentation, we believe, introduces parents to a quality of knowing that tangibly changes their expectations. They reexamine their assumptions about their parenting roles and their views about the experience their children are living and take a new and more inquisitive approach toward the whole school experience.

Reprinted from "History, Ideas, and Basic Philosophy" (pp. 63–64) by L. Malaguzzi in C. Edwards, L. Gandini, & G. Forman, eds., The Hundred Languages of Children: The Reggio Emilia Approach to Early Childhood Education, *1993, Norwood, NJ: Ablex. Copyright © 1993 by Ablex Publishing Corporation. Used by permission.*

"Yes, that's one reason," says Ruby. "And because it helps us to pay attention to what children are doing. If you're writing down children's words or taking their pictures, you have to observe them and find out what's really happening in their play."

"And then *they*—the kids—notice that we're noticing them," says Sandra, "and so we must think what they're doing is important. So they look at their pictures and their names and talk about them and start trying to read them. I've found that so exciting this year. If we keep a record, which we share with children, it helps them develop both literacy and self-esteem. Awesome!"

"You know what else?" says Bethany. "We start paying more attention to each other. If Marnie had just been doing Legos in the room and not saying anything about it, she would have done her thing, I would have done mine, and so would the rest of you. And we wouldn't have thought of sharing them and there wouldn't have been Lego land and Legos wouldn't have ended up on our *important* list."

"You folks are so good at sorting out all these ideas," says Ruby cheerfully. "I just get you started, and it happens. It *emerges*. Go on with the story, Marnie. What happened with Legos after October, or was it November? Did they go on?"

Marnie stops to think and then begins, "I guess pumpkins and then the harvest festival came along, and everybody got involved in those. And it was getting chilly on that shady porch in the morning, so I moved our Legos inside and gave back everyone else's. They stopped being special. Some children played with them all year, but a lot more children got into large-scale building with blocks and into exploration of the other kinds of manipulatives."

Why sand?

"Has *sand*, which is also on our *important* list, had the same sort of history as curriculum?" asks Ruby. "I'm sorting out an idea here; bear with me. Like, was it big for a while, and then it just became part of the scenery?"

Everybody stops to think.

"No, that doesn't describe it," Bob says. "There's *always* someone in the sand, isn't there? But sometimes there are major projects—treasure, bones, dinosaurs, digging to the center of the earth (Did I tell you about that one?), riv-

Digging to the Center of the Earth

Bob's story

We got some new shovels a couple of weeks ago, which stimulated renewed interest in digging by some of the older kids. I was out there by the sand one day when tempers were rising; the conflict was territorial. To defuse it I tried a challenge: "How far down in the earth do you think you can dig?" The idea really grabbed them. "You'll get there faster if you work as a team," I said. The group dynamics improved instantly, and they pursued their common goal with much discussion.

One girl thought they could go as far as the devil.

Another thought they'd get to China.

A boy said they'd go until the ocean.

Another mentioned that he didn't think they'd get very far because the walls would cave in.

All the while they dug, and at the end of the day someone said they should measure the hole and keep a record. Bethany says they've been measuring everything in sight ever since.

ers and dam-building. There's so much you can do with sand, especially with sand and water. And there's room for lots of children doing different things."

"Sand's more . . . what? . . . more *basic* than Legos, it seems to me," says Sandra. "It's a raw material—the rawest of raw materials—like dirt. Nobody planned it to be neatly educational; it's just *there*. You can do anything with it; it's wide open. And the kids do."

"They add all sorts of things to it," Sally says. "Shovels and cooking tools and water and sticks and leaves and little cars and on and on. It isn't the sand so much as what you can do with it, all the things you can play with it."

"You can't build with it the way you can with Legos," Bethany comments. "But you can't build with Legos the way you can with blocks; they're not big enough or versatile enough. I notice that as kids get seriously into building in support of dramatic play, they prefer the unit blocks and, increasingly, the hollow blocks and boxes and boards, with which they create their own play centers. Bigger kids don't need a house area; they'd rather build their own."

"And besides, why limit the area to houses?" adds Bob. "They need post offices and restaurants for their play, too."

Playable big ideas

Yoshiko, who has been listening intently for a long time, suddenly looks up. "Please, may I tell something? You are now talking about play materials. Sand is a material. Legos are a material. Blocks are a material. Materials are not the same thing as curriculum. Curriculum is ideas."

She looks around anxiously; does anyone understand? Marnie thinks she does and responds eagerly, "Right! That's what I keep trying to say, too. Curriculum is the important concepts children learn by working with materials."

Yoshiko shakes her head. "You keep saying classifying and counting," she answers, "that is not what I mean. Those are important skills, yes. Children will learn them, and we help.

Play Scripts

A script is a play theme based in the child's real or fantasy experiences. It is the dramatic portrayal of a sequence of events, with predictable variations. Children playing together keep it somewhat unpredictable by adding new ideas and dialogue as they negotiate the emerging script with each other. The "cooking" script may include play behaviors such as taking food from the cupboard or refrigerator, putting it in a pan, turning on the stove, stirring, turning off the stove, putting the food on a plate, putting the plate on the table as part of a table setting, and sitting down to eat. The "baby" script may include the baby's crying, picking up the baby, changing its diapers, warming a bottle, giving the bottle, burping, wrapping the baby in a blanket, taking it out in the stroller, coming home, and putting it to bed . . . .

Young children, new in the world as they are, play in order to find their way around in what is for them the foreign country of adults, to master its daily scripts.

Reprinted from The Play's the Thing *(pp. 9–10) by E. Jones and G. Reynolds, 1992, New York: Teachers College Press. Copyright © 1992 by Teachers College, Columbia University. Used by permission.*

"Pardon me, I contradict you. That is rude. I think *ideas*—the word I said—is the wrong word. What I want to say is, what is really important is the *society* in which children live. They must learn how we live together in families, how we care for each other, and how we celebrate together."

"*Oh*," says Bethany, who has been trying to understand. "Of course. Those are all the experiences children play, aren't they? Living together and taking care of each other are made up of all sorts of activities—cooking and shopping and driving cars and fixing cars and having birthdays. They play those things over and over again."

"Does it help to think about the *scripts* children play?" asks Ruby. "I got that idea in a class I was taking last fall, and it connects, for me, with what Yoshiko is saying—that children need to learn about the society in which they live. Some of the topics on our *important* list fit into what I like to call *playable big ideas*. Families, for example."

"Is *families* what you mean by a play script?" asks Bethany, looking puzzled again.

"It's dozens of play scripts, hundreds," Sandra says. "You don't play 'families,' just like that. You play all the different things people do in families."

"Yes. And so if teachers decide, as we all did this year," explains Ruby, "that they want children to learn about families, then that's a big enough idea to go on for a month, or a year, because there are so many stories in it—so many play scripts. Whenever we find a playable big idea, curriculum will emerge from it for a long time. That helps us to think logically and creatively about curriculum and to investigate an idea in depth, rather than rushing on to something new.

"Was families our only big idea? What about the rest of the *importants* on our list?" Ruby adds.

"Garden, harvest—those go together. There's another big idea," Dolores says.

"There's no way *not* to extend that over time," says Bob. "Plants take a long time to grow."

"Garden and harvest were different, weren't they?" says Gloria. "I don't think it's accidental that we listed both. Harvest was our celebration. I liked it, Yoshiko, when you said that children need to learn how we celebrate together."

"Gardening is more like science," says Bethany. "People invent celebrations, but people don't invent how plants grow. They have to *learn* how plants grow if they want to be able to cultivate them for food or flowers."

"That's like lights in the darkness," says Sandra. "Light and dark are there in the world. In winter there's more dark and less light, and people—who are diurnal animals!—make festivals of light and look forward to sun's return."

"People invent candles and electric lights, too," says Bob. "People are the animals who do something about the way things are; they invent technology to make themselves more comfortable."

"This is getting to be a very adult conversation, isn't it?" Ruby comments. "Does it feel like we're still talking about curriculum for young children?"

"Well, I don't need to tell young children all these things, but thinking about them really helps me get my head together. It's like the question about when are shadows longer. I went and looked it up, not so I could tell the kids but just because I wanted to know. If I'm an adult who keeps wanting to know things, I think kids pick that up from me. You know, I'm a model for them. We're teachers, and so it makes sense that we want to know more about how to plan curriculum, and how ideas hang together at an adult level." Sally pauses for breath, deciding she's said it all.

The clock says lunchtime. Bob's stomach growls. "Sorry," he says. "I skipped breakfast so I could sleep in."

Ruby has beamed her appreciation at Sally, but wants the last word. "If we offer children interesting materials in an organized environment, with time to make choices and see them through, I believe we've got our solid curriculum base in early childhood. Children will explore the materials and each other and use them to play out all the experiences and issues that happen in the rest of their lives. If we observe their play and help them extend their ideas, there will be a whole lot of important learning going on.

"The other challenge, which we've been investigating together, is about providing continuity and depth in some of the things we do—'engaging children's minds' and our own.[6] That seems to me to become increasingly important as kids get older, in our program for the 4s and 5s, but it may always be important for adults working with children. That's where adding the 'playable big ideas' to all materials and to all the little ideas comes in.

"Lunch, anybody?"

22
Epilogue:
Talking It Over

A couple of months after the June staff meeting, Ruby arrives at our college office for a meeting to discuss her thesis—a documentation and analysis of the year's emergent-curriculum process. Her rough-draft narrative is in good shape; now she wants to talk about her conclusions. We'd like to talk about them, too, to reflect together on what we've all been learning. We have really become co-learners, and this conversation proceeds much like our conversations at the child care center, with all of us trying out ideas on each other.

To reflect on experience, organizing concepts are helpful. Ruby has introduced several such concepts to her staff during the year (for example, loose parts, softness, and scripts children play), and she has read and thought about others. In our discussions with her and in our observations at her center we, like her staff, have been engaged in the classic dialectic process—thesis, antithesis, synthesis—which we like to translate as *my idea, your idea, our collaborative idea;* or alternatively as what was planned, what really happened, and what I learned from the resulting disequilibrium. New learning happens because we need to accommodate to the unexpected. In our experience,

this practice-to-theory-to-practice-to-theory sequence is how understanding of the complexity of teaching and learning grows. Always, it happens best in collaboration, which Ruby is making possible for her staff.

Our shared agenda for today is partly planned, partly emergent. We know we want to look at the sources of curriculum ideas, the process of generating ideas and of turning them into teaching plans, and the larger so-what questions—What's important about these ideas? What values do they reflect? What are the program's goals?

Sources of emergent curriculum

Some years back, Betty made a list, Sources of Emergent Curriculum, which is one of the organizing concepts she has introduced to Ruby. "Has the Sources list been helpful to you, Ruby?" she asks now. "Will you be using that as one way to organize your analysis?"

"Yes, I'd like to," says Ruby. "Could we chart it? I brought the staff's brainstormed list of emergent themes. We can go down that, I think,

Emergent-curriculum planning happens best in collaboration. In programs with a large staff and facilitative leadership, the stage is set for active thinking together. But many adults who work with young children do so in the relative isolation of family child care, one-classroom sites, or centers where no one else seems to be interested. If they want colleagues to think with, where can colleagues be found?

The NAEYC book, *Growing Teachers: Partnerships in Staff Development,*[1] addresses staff developers primarily, but it could be read as well by teaching staff looking for resources for their own growth. The projects described in this collection of stories of collaborative learning variously use the resources of the Child Development Associate (CDA) credentialing process; adult-school consultants; teacher-center staff; college instructors; mentor teachers visiting teachers in other programs; and teachers from different programs meeting together to discuss a common curriculum interest. Professional meetings also offer opportunities for teachers from different programs to meet and talk and, perhaps, follow up by getting together informally for coffee and conversation.

Inspired by a workshop or an article, some teachers recruit teachers from other programs to join them in a study group working on a new challenge: How can I make my program culturally relevant? How can I encourage children's spontaneous development of literacy? Especially in parent cooperative preschools and family child care, some parents may be potential collaborators in curriculum planning.

It's more work to seek out colleagues than to go it alone. But cooperative play, at any age, is more likely to stimulate growth than solitary play because it offers the challenge of different ideas. Emergent-curriculum planning is a form of teacher play.

---

and organize topics by sources. *Children's interests,* first; there were lots of those."

"Batman, Barbies, Beauty, dinosaurs," says Betty, reading from the list. "And treasure was their idea, too, wasn't it?"

"Masks," adds John. "Graveyards and funerals."

"Well, but wait a minute," says Ruby. "Children didn't start the graveyards. Staff did, with *Día de los Muertos.* That was an *adult interest.*"

"And a *cultural value,*" says John. "And then some children carried it on to connect with Martin Luther King's birthday, which is another adult interest and cultural value."

"Bethany was trying to promote bones even before *Día de los Muertos* came along, as I recall," Ruby says. "That's a good example of an adult interest that didn't particularly interest children, until much later in the year when the mouse skull was discovered. There's *serendipity* for you."

"The kids ignored some adult interests, and made changes in others, and did just what was expected with others, didn't they?" says Betty.

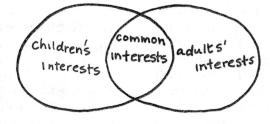

"And as I think about it, adults did the same with children's interests. They tried to ignore Barbies and media themes. When Bob found he couldn't ignore Batman any longer, he transformed the play into something more complicated and more in tune with his values. Bethany used kids' interest in treasure to push her interest in maps. Marnie's interest in Legos got everyone interested in Legos."

"We've mentioned *values* a couple of times," says John. "In their curriculum choices, staff were making significant value statements: We respect diversity. We honor people who have been courageous in social action. We discourage violence. We value children's initiative and creative ideas. You could make a whole list of those."

"My emphasis on documentation reflected my concern for something parents value: preparation for school success," Ruby says. "Parents want their kids to learn academic basics; that's part of being a good, responsible parent. I share that value, but my developmental idea of how young children learn those things

Sources of Emergent Curriculum[2]

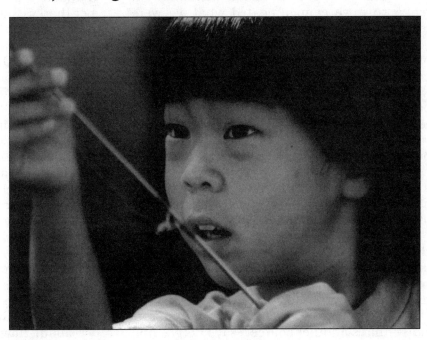

Children's interests. Children whose own interests are acknowledged and supported don't need to be motivated to learn; their own excitement will keep them learning. Different children have different interests; how many of them can be built into the emerging curriculum?

Teachers' interests. Teachers are people with interests of their own which are worth sharing with children. By doing some things *they* like, they can model knowledge and enthusiasm—even adults keep learning—and stay interested in teaching.

Developmental tasks. At each developmental stage, there are tasks to be mastered: crawling, walking, talking, pouring, cutting, skipping—the list goes on and on. Appropriate curriculum provides many opportunities for children to choose activities providing spontaneous skill practice. Similarly, appropriate curriculum is responsive to the social-emotional issues which characteristically surface powerfully at different stages: autonomy, power, strength, and friendship among them.

Things in the physical environment. Children's experience of place is unique to the place they are in. The man-made things in their physical environment are typically standardized and predictable; thus unit blocks facilitate orderly building. The natural things are unstandardized and unpredictable—each plant and animal is different—and reflect the local climate and terrain. Children need experience with both.

People in the social environment. Children are interested in all sorts of people, who they are and what they do. Parents and cooks and big brothers and librarians and custodians and bus drivers and neighbors are right there to learn about and relate to.

Curriculum resource materials. Teachers need not reinvent the wheel. Libraries, exhibits at conferences, school resource centers are full of curriculum ideas ready to use. Use them *and adapt them* to your own setting, your teaching style, and your children's interests.

Serendipity: unexpected events. When the unexpected happens in the classroom, the community, the natural world, teachers have choices. They can try to ignore it, or join in briefly, or invent ways of incorporating it into their plans, short- or long-term. It's important to become skilled in on-the-spot decision making.

Living together: conflict resolution, caregiving, and routines. Cooperation, expression of feelings, conflict resolution, and all the daily tasks of living together are potential curriculum for young children. Physical care, self-help skills, eating and resting and washing and dressing are the everyday life experiences that nurture the growth of young children. Caregiving and the resolution of interpersonal issues are not interruptions to the curriculum, they are basic curriculum.

Values held in the school and community, family, and culture. It is important to be accountable to others' expectations and to *evaluate* programs in that framework. It is not necessary to *teach* directly from expectations; learning activities should be developmentally appropriate and adapted to the situation. It is important to define the curriculum planning process clearly so that you know when you are actively engaged in it.

isn't necessarily familiar to parents. So I worked hard—and even got directorial with staff—to make sure we communicated what we were teaching and what children were learning."

"*People in the social environment*—that's another source, and your Families curriculum certainly focused on some of them," says Betty. "So did visiting the *mercado*, introducing some of the children to a language and culture new to them while providing familiarity for others."

"How about Sandra's gorilla? Is she someone in the social environment?" asks John.

"Amy? She certainly is," grins Ruby. "That's an interesting way of thinking about persona stories, isn't it—that they introduce new kinds of people into the children's environment?"

"*Living together* as basic curriculum—you do that all the time," John says. "I've been impressed by the staff's competence in conflict resolution; they really take time to help kids problem solve together."

"Marnie makes good use of *curriculum materials*—that's another source," says Betty. "And didn't Yoshiko mention that she was reading American books for curriculum ideas?"

"Yes, that's where she got the idea for her stick people," says John. "That's actually an idea I had written about, and Ruby has the book and loaned it to Yoshiko.[3] But she took it further than we did, with photos of parents as well as of children. That's so perfect for 2s."

"Which takes us to *developmental tasks* as a source," says Betty. "Those are so basic, I didn't include them on the first version of the Sources list, but they do belong there. The 2s and 3s are practicing basic physical skills, so all the digging and filling and pouring that took place because sand and water and tools were available were important curriculum."

"And those are things in the *physical environment*, which for me is always the primary source of curriculum," says Ruby. "So are Legos. They speak directly to kids, who get busy investigating them. Thoughtful, clear setup of the environment really helps kids get started. I loved what happened when all the Legos came outside. It created a 'Wow, look what's here!' feeling to have so much—sort of celebratory."

"You know, Ruby, I had questions in September about how much staff meeting time you took to investigate and talk about the outdoors," says John. "But that was the common space, right? Did you know that's what you were doing—stimulating collaborative use of space?"

"Not exactly," says Ruby. "But I had a gut feeling that I really wanted the outdoors used well. I didn't know then that people were going to decide to change the schedule and to share the outdoors. I saw that as ideal, but I let staff choose how to organize classes and schedule, and at the beginning people didn't think sharing would work. Then Sally wanted more outdoor time, and things got changed all around, and we ended up with lots more mixing of ages. That really feels serendipitous to me! I unexpectedly got what I wanted after all, having decided not to make people do what I wanted."

"Did you ever mention this to them?" asks Betty.

"No. There's lots I don't mention," says Ruby with a smile. "I see better teaching happening when I'm not trying to make it be exactly what I'd do if it was me doing the teaching. I think kids learn more when they get to do lots of things their way. Adults do, too."

Using the Sources of Emergent Curriculum list—knowing where curriculum begins—has proved to be a useful starting point in our discussion. Ruby is anxious to move on to the doing piece and suggests, "Now I'd like to talk about webbing as a strategy for working with staff in planning curriculum."

Collaboration and Fruitful Conflict

Knowledge is the result of individual constructions of reality. . . . Learning occurs through the continual creation of rules and hypotheses to explain what is observed. The need to create new rules and formulate new hypotheses occurs when the [learner's] present conceptions of reality are thrown out of balance by disparities between those conceptions and new observations.

. . . Within a context of growth and cooperation, conflict is the source of developmental progress. It is not the teacher's intent to structure a classroom in which conflict is avoided. Rather, it is the teacher's job to help [learners] negotiate the frictions that inevitably arise in settings that provoke them to challenge ideas, most often their own.

Reprinted from "Teachers and Students: Constructivists Forging New Connections" by J. Brooks, 1990, Educational Leadership, 47 *(5), pp. 68, 70. Copyright © 1990 by the Association for Supervision and Curriculum Development. Used by permission.*

Webbing

"In my experience," begins John, "webbing so often feeds into a thematic approach and simply becomes interior-decorating curriculum. A pile of ideas is generated with a superficial connection to each other, and they're used to fill in slots in the weekly schedule. You end up with pumpkin this and pumpkin that. But I didn't see that happen with your staff."

"When I began with these folks in the fall," responds Ruby, "I actually started with a couple of the curriculum sources: What are things children like to do? And what are things you as adults like to do? But all that gets you is a list, not a plan. And I don't think you need webbing for planning for materials, even though the first time I ever heard about it, a workshop leader was demonstrating how you could web from *blocks* as the starting point.

"You *can* web from blocks or Legos or play dough or easel paint, but what you're usually doing is just listing ways you can vary or add to the materials or identifying what kids can learn by playing with them.

"To get a plan, we chose *an idea* and brainstormed ways that children could play it—hands-on activities we could provide. Putting all the activities on a web gives you a road map full of possible journeys. It's like buying one of those three-month bus or train passes you can use to go anywhere with. That's real different from having a nonrefundable, nonstop ticket from Los Angeles to Seattle."

"I love it," says Betty. "I hadn't thought of that analogy before. A conventional lesson plan has one activity designed to get all the children to one objective, and if anyone misses the plane, that's tough. It's proof they're not responsible, or not ready. But if you've got a bus pass, you can get off to smell the flowers, or have dinner at the diner, or go fishing. And pretty soon the next bus will come along, and you can get on, after checking to see if it's going somewhere you want to go. And so you practice making choices, at your own pace."

"But Ruby, have you really seen staff using the webs that way, as road maps?" questions John.

"Probably they hold ideas in their heads more than they actually go back to the webs," says Ruby. "For most of this staff, I think webbing has been more important as a process than as a product. But I've loved the webbing, even though folks started teasing me whenever I mentioned it. And I do think most of them appreciated its usefulness as a planning tool. It's fun, for one thing, unlike writing old-style lesson plans. You can play with it. It doesn't have to be logically organized."

"Webbing isn't always approached that open-endedly," Betty remarks. "Have you had time to go through that collection of articles I gave you?"

"Yes, because I was particularly curious about them," says Ruby. "I have to admit that you've given me lots of other things I haven't looked at yet, though. There's never enough time."

"And what did you think?" Betty asks.

"Well, I didn't much like the ones that *organized* the webs into subject areas—you know, science and social studies and language arts," Ruby replies. "I mean, I'm sure that's useful in being accountable within a prescribed curriculum, but in planning with this staff I think it would get in the way. They'd stop being playful and start trying to find right answers, and they'd look at me to see if they were doing it right. I think they'd get resistant real fast, and it's an anxious sort of resistance I don't want. It's different from their teasing me about too many webs. That just means they're tired of playing this game (or they just feel like teasing me!), not that it's too hard."

Adults as playful learners

"You know the whole idea of open and closed tasks?"[4] Ruby asks. "I think that applies to adults, too. I think a staff needs to *play* together, and they can't do that if they're trying to figure out right answers. Staff meetings are different from a college class, to which students come expecting to be taught. My staff came to the center to work with children. They don't much like evening meetings, but they like thinking about working with children. Most of our discussion stays concrete, and I think it should. Our responsibility is to these children and their families."

"But people were having real, intellectual ahas all year," says John. "You were teaching some theory along the way, and some of the staff got it or came up with their own. Think about Bob's realization that kids play whatever they're trying to understand and Sandra's excitement when she noticed the way some ideas kept reemerging all year."

"Those were spontaneous discoveries by individuals," Betty says. "I think Ruby's right. Staff meetings need a playful quality, out of which good ideas hatch. Ruby set them up that way from the very beginning: What are all the things we can think of together? rather than What's the best way to do this? And everyone contributed—some more than others, of course. But if there were right answers to be found, a few people would take over, and everyone else would feel less competent. That happens all the time in college classes."

"All along, you've been thinking as much about how to work with adults as how to plan for children, haven't you?" John asks Ruby. "So the conclusions in your thesis will be looking at both those things? What we've just been talking about is staff process: How do you create a climate in which staff become mutually creative thinkers?"

"That's really my priority," Ruby agrees. "If that doesn't happen, nothing else will. I can't legislate emergent curriculum; it's got to emerge out of reflection and dialogue. And at the end of a long day, staff need to be energized enough to engage each other. I call that play.

"If you noticed, I emphasized the rules of brainstorming in September and enforced them all year. Brainstorming is play. It's open ended; it doesn't let you box things into right ideas and wrong ideas, possible and impossible. That's how little kids play, too, though they're mostly doing rather than talking. I think adults as staff need to master the same sort of cooperative play, and I think these folks have done it really well."

"I agree," says Betty, and John nods enthusiastically.

Objectives, and the values they reflect

John's got another question. "All this playing together and emphasis on process is great, and we've seen its outcome in the quality of your program this year," he says. "But when you give up reliance on linear planning, what happens to objectives? What are your objectives for children, for the program as a whole? There's no question that you have them; we've been watching them in action. But you haven't talked about them much.

"Remember, at the June staff meeting, you kept asking, 'Did we have a plan?' And some great processing went on around that, and it was Yoshiko who said—it's in my notes right here—'Curriculum isn't materials; curriculum is ideas.'"

"Oh, I remember that," says Betty. "And Marnie said, yes, of course, curriculum is about developing cognitive concepts . . . ."

"And Yoshiko actually contradicted her; that *was* memorable," Ruby recalls. "And she said . . . what do your notes say she said, John?"

John reads from them. "'Really important—society. Children must learn living in families, caring for each other, how we celebrate.'"

"She was talking about *values,* wasn't she?" says Ruby. "That's why she was being so assertive; she wanted us to pay attention to what's really important in our work with children. Shall *we* talk about values?"

"Good, you have just gotten back to my question," says John. "What are your objectives in the program, Ruby?"

"Are values and objectives the same?" Ruby asks, puzzled. "That's not what I learned in my curriculum and instruction class, where they spent a lot of time defining things like that."

"Technically, I suppose not," says John. "But objectives reflect values. The real question is, What do we want for our children? Yoshiko is clear: We want them to learn to live together and care for each other. Marnie is clear: School is about developing cognitive concepts."

"Maybe I'm not that clear." Ruby is thinking out loud. "I'm closer to Yoshiko's view about living together as basic, but I certainly want children to develop intellectually, too, for their own sake as well as for success in school. And I think of this staff as very values oriented. Now that we're talking about it, I realize that strong value commitments are something I look for when I'm hiring staff. Should we be talking more about this, and not just taking it for granted?"

"There were some staff meetings this year at which values came up, especially around holidays and cultural sensitivity," Betty remembers. "I don't think you ignore values, Ruby, in your discussions. They come up in the context of program planning, and that makes sense, as you've said. Teachers at work are necessarily practical folk."

"Let me try to give a name to what I've seen as your program's basic value orientation, Ruby," says John. "I think you're committed to building an adult–child community in which diverse people care for each other and think effectively together about the issues in their lives. Does that say it?"

Ruby smiles, wonderingly. "Yes, that says it. And you've seen it? That's what I want to do, but I'm always aware of all the ways it isn't happening. It's so affirming to have someone else say that it is. And now I have some words to name it and think about it."[5]

Going into depth

"If adults and children work *together*, that's very different from children's doing worksheets while a teacher makes them stick to the task," says Betty. "Creativity that results in a product—a fruitful garden, a handmade quilt, an inspiring curriculum—requires a lot of work. A completed worksheet isn't a significant product in the life of the community. A teacher's pretty bulletin board made with no help from children has some of the same meaninglessness. What tasks, what ideas, have significance to both children and adults—and not only to teachers but to parents and other community members as well?"

"That's what you were doing with the Families curriculum," John says to Ruby. "You encouraged everyone to investigate it in depth rather than rushing on to something new the way I see in some other programs, where there's a weekly theme that may have no relation at all to the theme of the week before."

Betty joins in. "When that happens, I think it encourages a 'shopping' mentality—Cinderella at the mall—in both adults and children instead of encouraging them to investigate important ideas in depth and look at them from many angles. Slow down and pay attention—that's a value I have for everyone in early childhood programs."

"Some kinds of curriculum won't happen unless staff plan way in advance, I realized," says Ruby. "That's an important point for me to remember even as I keep on emphasizing spontaneity."

"Gardening has to be planned ahead," agrees Betty. "And it's a wonderful slow-down-and-pay-attention theme. Plant a seed, and wait, and maybe a plant will come up. Watch it grow, very slowly. Take care of it; weed it and water it. Wait some more. Don't pick that one, it isn't big enough yet. Gardeners need a lot of patience."

"In September I did begin with child and adult interests," Ruby recalls. "But I also began with the outdoor environment, as you've pointed out. How does that fit into this scheme?"

Beginning with the environment

"Beginning with the environment, you're setting the stage," says Betty. "As Gretchen and I wrote in our play book,[6] 'the teacher's first job is to be stage manager.' This seems to be the easiest teaching role for adults to learn, too. Most adults like playing with space and time, and moving things around to fit in them."

Teacher Role Development

Like children at play, adults who work with children grow in their mastery of role behaviors . . . . *Stage manager* is the most basic of the roles, to be mastered by all staff. In a well-ordered, well-provisioned environment with plenty of time for play, most children will be able to create and sustain their own play as they have always done in homes and neighborhoods. Play in itself meets many of young children's growth needs. It is a self-teaching, self-healing process.

Fortunately, stage management seems to be the easiest role to learn. Nearly all adults are experienced in organizing and managing living spaces and time schedules for themselves; this experience transfers directly to the preschool. And it is easier and more appropriate to learn to manipulate environments rather than to manipulate children.

Reprinted from The Play's the Thing *(pp. 112–13) by E. Jones and G. Reynolds, 1992, New York: Teachers College Press. Copyright © 1992 by Teachers College, Columbia University. Used by permission.*

"I noticed you didn't say much about the indoor space in staff meetings, Ruby," says John. "You only talked about the outdoors. Why?"

"Oh, I've got a whole list of reasons," says Ruby. "Want them?" We nod.

"OK. First, it was September when we moved into the space, and it was hot. Outdoors, with lots of water, was the sensible place to be.

"Second, as you mentioned earlier, our outdoors is shared space. Yoshiko sensibly asked for separate space for the young 2s, but everyone else had to collaborate. I decided to let them have their rooms as their own territory (which I could talk about with them individually) and to focus our collective attention on the outdoors.

"Third, it really bothers me that most schools don't use the outdoors as a learning environment except for large-muscle activities. I think the outdoors is also the best setting for most sensory activities including art, and for science, and serendipity, and finding spaces of one's own. I wanted to push it for all those reasons.

"I knew that Sally, who loves to be outside, would be with me. Bob was, too, as it turned out. And Yoshiko really showed us some new ways of thinking about the environment. It was a chance for her to share her sophisticated knowledge, which sometimes didn't get through when she was struggling with English."

"Oh, I remember Yoshiko at the September meeting," says Betty. "What was it she said? She was so clear about it, when she'd been quiet most of the day before. Something like ' The child must learn to know each rock'—must be able to walk on uneven terrain, to gain poise and balance in unstandardized physical space. It really grabbed me. It brought back memories of taking my own kids on hikes up a dry stream bed, with the big kids leaping from rock to rock and the 2-year-old stumbling along, dragging at my hand. I wanted my kids to be confident walkers in stream beds, not just on sidewalks and floors. Somehow, rooms seem to belong to adults, who don't want children to make messes in them. But outdoors is the children's."

Children and the Outdoors

Much of the "man-made" environment, especially in an industrial society, is mechanistic and linear. As we become accustomed to this functional order, we may rely on its predictability and prefer it aesthetically as well; the clarity of tulips in arrays becomes preferable to the random wildness of marsh or field. Tame replaces wild, and we breathe a sigh of relief; we have created safety for ourselves.

The wish to keep young children safe is strong in nurturant adults. It is reflected in many of the environments we provide for children—clean, neatly ordered, and devoid of risk. We keep an eye on every nook and cranny, removing spiders and splinters and dust bunnies, and admonishing children to clean up their messes.

Sensible children escape outside, if they can, where adults are less vigilant. If you ask any group of adults, "Where did you like to play as a child? What are your memories?" most of them will talk about explorations of the natural world, the underlayer of which adults are often unconscious. Roger Hart, emphasizing "the satisfaction children find in the process of transforming the physical world," and deploring "adult ignorance of what places and equipment are important to children," tells this story:

> Johnny is really upset. He arrived at his home from school 15 minutes before me, and now with eyes tearing he is sitting on the three-foot stump of what had been a very old elm tree when he left for school. With little control in his voice he shouts, "That was our tree, we used to play under it all the time—it's not fair, we didn't even know they were going to do it." His tent had even been tied to it when they came to chop it down.
>
> There has been no play on the driveway since last fall, when stones were laid down in order to improve parking during the few days of the spring "mud season." Last summer almost half the activity of the children was in this dirt driveway. Not only had it been central for all of the children's homes, but the dirt was said by the children to be excellent for building with. I am certain that children's use of this area never entered the landlord's mind.[7]

Pour More Water, Fernando

Some children are playing at the edge of the sand area, safely in view of the teacher supervising a table activity on the porch, but comfortably out of earshot across the large yard. The day is warm and sunny.

Nicole picks a tuft of the grass that is growing along the paving stones. She carefully puts it in the sand and stirs it, asking the observer, "You want some dinner?" She brings more grass; then, leaving it cooking, she begins weeding out all the little tufts of grass and tossing them into the sand area. "Yuk."

Fernando picks up one of the tufts: "Hey, look at the . . . ." He dusts it off, throws it, makes sound effects, and weeds the last remaining tuft. Nicole adds leaf-bits to her dinner, then continues weeding. "Are you going to be in our class while we sleep?" she asks the observer. She adds sticks to her dinner.

Fernando brings a bucket of water from the drinking fountain. "For you," he says to the observer. "Gimme it," says Nicole. They are both holding it and he looks uncertain. "Nicole might like some water for the dinner she's cooking,"

says the observer, deciding a little conflict resolution is in order. He decides to share and both are pleased as the water is poured in the sand. "You can't have no dinner."

Nicole: "Pour more water, Fernando." He does, and they giggle, adding sand.

Fernando: "More?"

Nicole, adding more sand: "Go get some more water." He does.

Nicole: "Lookit, big turkey! Big dinner. Salad in there. Here we go...." She brings more grass. "He's gonna pour some more, OK? Want some more dinner? Here he goes. Fernando! Fernando!"

Fernando is walking slowly across the yard with a full pail. Michael stops by on a bike: "You making mud?"

Nicole: "No, I'm making dinner."

Reprinted from "Observation Notes: Play and Language Development" (v. 1) (n.p.) by E. Jones and G. Reynolds, Pacific Oaks Occasional Paper, 1989, Pasadena, CA: Pacific Oaks College. Copyright © 1989 by the authors. Used by permission.

Safety and risk taking

"The risk of putting children in child care is similar in some ways to the risk of raising children in unsafe neighborhoods, isn't it?" muses Betty, making a connection.

"What do you mean?" asks John.

"In child care, kids are watched all the time to keep them safe," Betty goes on. "If you're trying to be a responsible parent in an unsafe neighborhood, you watch your kids all the time to keep them safe. But growing up in safe neighborhoods, or in the country, children haven't been watched all the time; adults were busy doing other things. So children had freedom to roam (within sensible limits depending on how old they were) and were expected to be responsible. Roaming children have always sought physical challenges for themselves in the outdoors. They've gotten dirty and wet and cold, and made choices and taken risks. That's how kids develop physical and moral competence.

"Liz Prescott and I were talking not long ago and she suggested that many children these days are suffering a sort of sensory deprivation. They don't have enough opportunity for hands-on experience with real things—the messing-about that leads to in-depth knowledge of materials, tools, bodies in space, and competence in predicting cause-and-effect. Perhaps, then, it is no surprise that our adolescents crave sensory experience of all kinds but often display poor judgment in handling it. 'They're trying to wake up their bodies,' another friend remarked. It's an idea that keeps coming back to me," Betty says.

"Hmm," says Ruby. "I hadn't thought about that, but it makes sense to me. My own outdoor childhood was really important to me, and I want that for other children. Even in child care. Especially in child care."

Adults as theory makers

"Looking at the environment helps us stay in a hands-on mode, doesn't it?" says John. "It's when academic types (like us) lose track

Letting Children Manage Their Own Risks

When bits of trash blow through the fence from the junior high school yard next door, preschoolers often improvise play with them. This morning they're delighted to find a large piece from a cardboard box, near the slide. Three boys and a girl improvise a game in which one child puts the cardboard on the bottom of the slide and the rest slide down together to push it off. Spatial directions are freely given:

Ready, go! Ready, go!

Put it on the side. Up high! Higher! Higher!

Amigo, put the box up! Higher! Put the box up here!

OK.

Put it up high. Open it up. Up high. Not that way!

OK, this way?

Yeah.

Wait. OK, go.

No, put it up high!

This way?

Yeah, that's good. Let it go.

Shamika lets go and the boys slide down. Then she runs to the top and says to Darrell, "It's me and Pauly's turn." Pauly hugs her, and they slide down in a hug. Shamika gets bumped at the bottom but shakes it off.

That was fun. Now let me go in the front.

Lie down. Push back. Wait, don't go yet.

I'm not your friend!

Fast pileup sliding is the game, competently handled; these children have already mastered basic sliding. Sometimes they go back up the ladder, sometimes directly up the slide. Physical contact, both hugging and bumping, is part of the fun; when the boy arranging the cardboard is bumped by the sliders, he is surprised but pleased.

The yard is large, and the supervising adults are far enough away to give children some opportunity to choose and manage their own risks. Eventually, however, one of them arrives. She's looking for Darrell, who had ignored the call that it was his turn for an art activity, but she decides the sliders need her advice. "OK, one at a time. Yes, come on down." She stops a child from climbing up the slide because another is waiting to come down. They had this all organized for themselves before she came; she has just destroyed complex cooperative play. They wander off.

Adult concern for order and safety often invades children's play, sometimes necessarily but at other times thoughtlessly. Pause to pay attention if there's no immediate danger. What's going on here, and are the children handling it?

---

of the concrete and get infatuated by their words that they become irrelevant for teachers—the very ones who are dealing with the real world of children every day. I'm only a couple of years away from the classroom, and I'm already losing sight of what it's really like. Being with you all year, Ruby, has been a good opportunity for me to see which organizing concepts catch on with teachers—which concepts represent their experience for them.

"As I've been trying to see the whole picture in my head," John continues, "it seems to me that there are three main levels at which we can talk about curriculum. One level is *materials and tools*—the things we put in the environment for children and the things already there for them to discover, outdoors. Another level is what we're calling *playable big ideas*. I think of these as ideas that both children and adults can understand and talk about together and that have lots of potential play scripts in them, through which children can keep constructing knowledge. Families. Gardens. Harvest festivals. Lights and festivals of light. Animals.

"My last level is the *construction of theory* as a form of adult play. You've been teaching theory to the staff, Ruby, and some of them have been having real ahas in response."

"I like it when that happens, but I have to be careful," Ruby says. "Some folks will back off real fast if they think I'm trying to play teacher during our meetings. I can't just *tell* them things I'd like them to understand. But I can try to set the stage for them to figure out some of those things."

John nods and adds, "Much of the time adults are concrete thinkers. But Piaget said that they're also capable of formal thinking,

thinking about ideas, in those areas where they have enough hands-on experiences. Then they can see the larger patterns that give meaning to many different experiences. Theory making—*that's* my third of three levels."

"Are you talking about teaching teachers theory or having them construct it for themselves?" asks Ruby.

"Well, the process reaches beyond just one individual," says John. "If I teach someone else's theory about an experience you've had, and if you like the theory because it adds to your understanding, you'll begin the process of making it your own. You'll look for new examples of the theory in action and keep naming them for yourself. 'Till someone else offers a new perspective."

"I don't know how comfortable I am with the word *theory* here," says Ruby. "What I want staff to do is to reflect on their experience. I want them to discover patterns in it and to get excited by their discoveries.

"An example of a memorable pattern, this year, was *hiding and finding*. That one kept popping up all year. I remember Bethany's naming it once, during a conversation about treasure or masks or something. But that's not theory, is it? It's more of a metaphor."

"Gloria said it another way at one meeting," Betty says. "I made a note of it because it really hit me. She said, very quietly to herself, 'What's behind the mask?'"

"And here comes developmental theory," exclaims John grinningly, "with issues like separation and object permanence, and why peekaboo is so basic for babies, and intimacy in adulthood."

Where Stories Start

It will make much sense to teachers to be reminded that the easiest place to start in planning is the midlevel. This is the arena where stories start, the human perspective in which thought and feeling are inseparable. The midlevel, the "playable big ideas," provides the connective tissues between the stuff we use and the abstract concepts that provide the rationale.

From personal communication by Carol Anne Wien, Faculty of Education, York University, Ontario, Canada. Used by permission.

"And that takes you right to the existential dilemma: Do we ever see behind another's mask?" says Betty. "That's the stuff of drama all down history. We're back to metaphor and all the arts. Arts and sciences both deal with universal human issues and both create patterns to help us understand those issues."

"Yoshiko's *looking at you* is connected to hiding and finding, too," says Ruby. "It has to do with learning to see oneself. Yoshiko put photographs on sticks. Gloria did skin-color handprints. Bethany wanted children to Look Inside You, with bones; but when the kids finally got into body tracings, in the spring, more of them were interested in painting clothes on their bodies than in putting in bones. Body adornment is certainly a universal human theme; maybe that's another way to go with it."

"We do like this kind of play," observes Betty happily. "You've really got us going, John. Ruby, can you think of other examples of adult-level ideas that have been important in this year's curriculum?"

Ruby thinks. "The idea of *social justice* has certainly come into our curriculum," she says. "I talk to kids about Martin Luther King because he's a symbol of social justice for me. I teach them conflict resolution because it's a way to get social justice. At age 4 they aren't going to understand justice as an abstraction, but *fair* is a word that makes sense to them when it means getting their share, and they're trying to learn about other people's shares, too. Antibias curriculum is about social justice."[8]

"So are we saying that teachers should be not only playing with theories and metaphors, but also planning curriculum from them?" Betty asks. "I'm not at all sure that's what they do."

"Actually, I don't think I *plan* from social justice, even though it's very important to me," says Ruby. "I plan from things that are real, like Martin's birthday or having to ride at the back of the bus. But I know how those things are connected and that keeps me on track. It's how I draw on my values as a source of curriculum."

"Are the three levels useful, then?" asks John.

"Yes, I think so," says Ruby. "The first two—materials and tools in the environment and playable big ideas for children—are what we plan from. The third—theories and metaphors—isn't for planning from. It's for having ahas with, as you rediscover that what you're teaching really is important in the larger scheme of things."

Theory making as an inclusion issue

"I do see some staff members eagerly looking for ahas," Ruby continues. "They *like* theories and metaphors; they're the big-picture thinkers, confident players with abstract ideas.

"But in a staff with as much diversity in education and age and culture and personal style as this one, you can get a real range of reactions whenever anyone starts talking 'that college talk,' as Mayella put it one day. For several folks, including me, that's just the way we talk. But it excludes some other people. Bethany was always going on about abstract ideas when she first came on staff, without noticing people's reactions. She monitors herself better now that she's come to know them, and I do a lot of monitoring, too. It's important to me that everyone feels their knowledge is valued and knows

---

Supporting the Role of Teacher As Learner

A view of teacher as a collaborative and action-oriented researcher not only contributes to the determination of developmentally appropriate practices with young children, but provides a vehicle for teacher development as well . . . . An expanded understanding of developmental appropriateness must take into account not only the lives of children, and the course of their development, but also the lives of adults (both teachers and parents), and the cultural and societal contexts in which those adults and children live. That is, development is not a phenomenon limited to young children. Rather, it is a process also experienced by adults and by society in general. Children *and teachers* require learning environments that allow them to hypothesize, investigate, experiment, and construct new understandings of themselves and others with whom they work . . . .

Reprinted from "Culture, Child Development, and Developmentally Appropriate Practices: Teachers as Collaborative Researchers" (pp. 77, 78) by R.S. New, Chap. 3 in B.L. Mallory & R.S. New, eds., Diversity and Developmentally Appropriate Practices: Challenges for Early Childhood Education, *1994, New York: Teachers College Press. Copyright © 1994 by Teachers College, Columbia University. Used by permission.*

---

they're expected to share it. That won't happen if a few people use a lot of big words.

"When Dolores starts feeling out of her depth, she gets quiet. Yoshiko has been quiet a lot because English is a challenge for her. Mayella is more likely to mutter, often loudly, and I tend to call her on it. Her reaction to 'college talk' is generational and social class based, but it's also a self-protective defense that I don't want to encourage here. Mayella has no problem at all being articulate about a big idea like social justice. She's a model for me in that, and I want to push her in other directions. I do wish I could talk her into working on her CDA, but she just starts 'Oh, come on honey'-ing me when I push too hard." Betty and John both smile, knowing that Ruby not only respects and loves Mayella, she also appreciates her immense experience and connections with the local community.

"I've loved discovering the recent writings on the teacher as researcher. That's how I'd like our staff to behave," says Ruby. "But I sure wouldn't use the word *researcher* around here. We're just teachers. But I hope we're growing teachers."

"A great many folks in early childhood education feel intellectually inadequate, don't they?" Betty observes. "That's probably the message they got in school. So they grew up as solidly intuitive, concrete thinkers and discovered early childhood education, where their concreteness keeps them actively in touch with kids and where they encounter some other folks whose intellectual curiosity about children is what got them into teaching. Ruby, I think you manage to include everybody, without implying that one style is better than another."

Ruby smiles. "Now, where were we?"

Private vs. public curriculum

"I have one more floating question," says Betty. "In all of our discussion of curriculum, we've been talking about planning for the group—the *public* curriculum. And in that process the teachers of the older kids and those who are most into planning—like Bethany and Sandra and Marnie—usually have the most to say.

"But what about people like Sally and Mayella, who are really aware of many of the private moments in their kids' lives and are not particularly into project-type planning? As Sally has insisted to Bob, large-scale project ideas aren't where young 3s—and 2s—are at. They're just *doing*, exploring the things and

Teachers Challenge Each Other

This day-to-day work . . . involves constant challenge and decision making because of the use of emergent curriculum . . . . Teachers believe that by discussing openly they offer models of cooperation and participation to the children and parents and promote an atmosphere of frank and open communication . . . .

It is important to note that analysis and feed-back in Reggio Emilia involves both support and criticism. In contrast to a system where concern for hurt feelings or ownership of ideas prevents extended examination and argumentation, in Reggio Emilia intellectual conflict is considered pleasurable for both adults and children . . . . The point of a discussion is not just to air diverse points of view, but instead to go on until it is clear that everyone has learned something and moved somewhere in his or her thinking. A discussion should go on until a solution or next step becomes apparent; then, tension dissipates and a new, shared understanding provides the basis for future joint activity or effort.

Reprinted from "Partner, Nurturer, and Guide: The Roles of the Reggio Teacher in Action" (pp. 157, 159–60) by C. Edwards, in C. Edwards, L. Gandini, & G. Forman, eds., The Hundred Languages of Children: The Reggio Emilia Approach to Early Childhood Education, *1993, Norwood, NJ: Ablex. Copyright © 1993 by Ablex Publishing Corporation. Used by permission.*

people in the environment. So a chart of their curriculum might not look as if they have any."

"But the kids are busy doing things, and if you define curriculum as what happens, then that's their curriculum," says John. "It's largely individual, not group, because the younger children are less collaborative in their play. Does that make it *private* curriculum?"

"At least it's more individual," muses Ruby. "The words *private curriculum* have suddenly reminded me of when I was in school, and we kids had all sorts of lively interests that were forbidden in the classroom, from baseball cards to boyfriends. Those were *not* part of the teacher's curriculum, and hers was the only curriculum that was supposed to happen. So we learned to be sneaky with our interests. I had to be especially sneaky because I loved fairy tales and among my friends that made me weird. I read them at school whenever I could get away with it, but I didn't talk about them with anyone else. They were my private curriculum. My teacher didn't approve, and my friends didn't approve; but I read them on school time, and I learned by doing it."

"At the center you don't forbid curriculum ideas the kids bring, though," says John.

"Well, not many. If a child brought a gun to school, we wouldn't let him play with it there. And there are a good many play activities that teachers don't forbid, but they certainly ignore. Some of these flourish anyway, because they fascinate several kids. If they fascinate only one kid, and it's a really little kid or an older kid

Developmental Theme Names

A developmentally appropriate curriculum is neither teacher nor child directed but a result of interaction between teachers and children, with both contributing ideas and reacting to them to build on appealing and worthwhile themes . . . .

If a teacher-initiated topic is not "appropriate" for the group, this will become evident from the children's waning interest. In contrast, other ideas will catch on and be extended into a multitude of learning experiences through questions and activities initiated by children and teachers . . . .

"Units" in a developmentally appropriate classroom are not preplanned activity seg-ments with a standard time length. Themes that emerge from brainstorming, a happening, or introduction of materials are interconnected and flow from one to the other as children ask questions and develop new interests.

Reprinted from "The Grassroots Curriculum: A Dialogue Between Children and Teachers" by D.J. Cassidy & C. Lancaster, 1993, Young Children, 48 (6): pp. 47, 48, 50. Copyright © 1993 by NAEYC.

who likes playing by herself, then she can sus-tain her little private curriculum, the way I did. But if she tries and tries to get other kids inter-ested because what she really wants is someone to play with, then an adult is likely to notice and suggest a new curriculum idea that is more likely to help her make friends. There's a continual flow of new ideas coming from everyone in the place. Some of them make it; some of them don't."

Being accountable

"You're fortunate," comments Betty, "that in this center you don't have to follow someone else's formal curriculum categories. You can begin with the lives of children."

"That's what I like to do best," Ruby says. "But I'm equally responsible to the parents and to their aspirations for their children. Lots of our kids are really up against it when they get to school; some teachers have built-in low expectations for kids from this side of town.[9] I keep struggling with Lisa Delpit's challenge: How do we support kids' pride in who they are, while teaching them school survival skills?[10] I'm not willing just to build in arbitrary lessons on shapes and colors; that's not my understanding of what young children need to know or how young children learn. But that means I have to be really clear in letting parents know that we do take re-

Play—Debrief—Replay

Providing opportunities for creative, investigative play, followed by helping children to reflect on their play experiences and then encouraging them to build on earlier experiences through replay, does what it claims: Children who learn under these classroom conditions are empowered. They learn habits of thinking, and they become more self-initiating, responsible, creative, and inventive. They grow in their capacity to understand the concepts or important ideas within the curriculum. Within their play, different learning styles, different learning tempos and different talents are all naturally accommodated. Concepts are learned and understood via the primary route of practical experience, the only way in which learners at any age actually learn to understand.

Teaching from Learners' Objectives

The learning event belongs to the student, and the teacher experiences it through inclusion. The teacher thus bears a tremendous responsibility. Striving always to see the learning event from the standpoint of the student, the teacher teaches by actively pursuing the student's objective, an objective that teacher and student have together constructed. In a caring relation, the student responds by engaging fully in the event. He or she grows, and the teacher seeing this knows that teaching has had a desirable effect.

sponsibility for their children's learning. As you've seen, I can get pretty anxious about that."

"You're able to define your own accountability out of your commitment to the kids," John responds. "But in lots of places, staff are accountable for teaching within prescribed categories. That's true in preschools as well as in elementary schools. So, learning how to categorize curriculum by subject matter and by learning objectives is at the very least a useful survival strategy for teachers. And I suspect that it's useful practice in systematizing one's own thinking, as well."

We all look at each other. Have we gotten anywhere? Is Ruby being helped in organizing her thesis? "What do you think, Ruby?" asks John. "Can you use any of this?"

"Yes, actually I can," says Ruby. "I appreciate the chance to talk it through. I'm ready to be *done* with the thesis, but we certainly haven't figured everything out, have we?"

"Well," says Betty, as she picks up her notebook and looks at her watch, "maybe we should just look at this conversation as one more example of the curriculum questions that never get resolved and will always be there for each group of teachers to struggle with: What's the right balance between spontaneity and planning? How much subject matter knowledge does a teacher of young children need, and are you a better teacher if you're full of answers or full of questions? How much should adults scaffold children's learning, and when should children just be left alone to explore at their own rate? It's the continuing dialectic process again; it never stops. And so learning isn't a destination, it's a journey. To learn is to be alive, discovering new possibilities we hadn't thought of before."

John agrees. "Really, it's Yoshiko who said it for us: 'The child must learn to know each rock.' Each rock is individual; experiencing and learning the variety of rocks, the child discovers how to adjust her body to walk upon each one. I find that a really powerful metaphor for teachers learning to adjust curriculum to each child, and for teacher educators learning to support each teacher's individual growth."

Ruby's face glows with pleasure. "It's a balancing act," she says. "Walking on rocks is a process of continuous balancing. Working with children and adults is a process of continuous balancing, adjusting, losing equilibrium, and finding it again, in response to unique moments in time and space."[11]

Notes

Chapter 1, pages 1–5.

1. B. Cambourne, & J. Turbill, "Teacher as co-researcher: How an approach to research became the methodology for staff development," in *Frameworks: A literacy and learning staff development program, K–8*, eds. J. Turbill, A. Butler, B. Cambourne, & G. Langton (Stanley, NY: Wayne-Finger Lakes Board of Cooperative Educational Services, 1991).

2. E. Jones, ed., *Growing teachers: Partnerships in staff development* (Washington, DC: NAEYC, 1993).

3. E. Jones, & E. Prescott, *Dimensions of teaching-learning environments: A handbook for teachers in elementary schools and day care centers* (Pasadena, CA: Pacific Oaks College, 1984).

4. Thanks for this phrase to Cirecie Olatunji, New Orleans site coordinator of the Culturally Relevant Anti-Bias Education Leadership Project.

Chapter 2, pages 7–16.

1. B. Bowman, & F. Stott, "Understanding development in a cultural context: The challenge for teachers," in *Diversity and developmentally appropriate practices*, eds. B.L. Mallory, & R.S. New (New York: Teachers College Press, 1994), 128. Copyright by Teachers College, Columbia University. Reprinted by permission.

2. J. Gonzales-Mena, *Multicultural issues in child care* (Mountain View, CA: Mayfield, 1993).

3. H.C. Holling, *Pagoo* (Boston: Houghton Mifflin, 1957).

4. M. Hohmann, B. Banet, & D. Weikart, *Young children in action: A manual for preschool educators* (Ypsilanti, MI: High/Scope, 1979).

5. J. Nimmo, "Unique curricula for day care: Considerations for future directions," *Australian Journal of Early Childhood* 11, no. 1 (1986): 10–14.

6. S. Goldenberg, "Publishing children's writing," in *Reading, writing and talking with four, five and six year olds*, ed. E. Jones (Pasadena, CA: Pacific Oaks College, 1988), 221–31.

7. B. Waber, *Lyle Lyle crocodile* (Boston: Houghton Mifflin, 1965).

8. T. Ungerer, *Crictor* (New York: Harper & Row, 1958).

9. D. Ballesteros, "A language-enhancing classroom," in *Reading, writing and talking with four, five*

and six year olds, ed. E. Jones (Pasadena, CA: Pacific Oaks College, 1988), 129–35.

10. M. Brown, *Stone soup* (New York: Macmillan, 1979).

11. D.L. Norton, "From playing to, to playing with: Interactive music and movement" (master's project, Pacific Oaks College, Pasadena, CA, 1989), 49. Used by permission.

Chapter 3, pages 17–28.

1. E. Jones, & G. Reynolds, *The play's the thing: Teachers' roles in children's play* (New York: Teachers College Press, 1992), 15. Copyright by Teachers College, Columbia University. Quoted by permission.

2. D.J. Cassidy, & C. Lancaster, "The grassroots curriculum: A dialogue between children and teachers," *Young Children* 48, no. 6 (1993): 47–51

3. E. Jones, & E. Prescott, *Dimensions of teaching-learning environments: A handbook for teachers in elementary schools and day care centers* (Pasadena, CA: Pacific Oaks College, 1984).

4. B. Baylor, *Everybody needs a rock* (New York: Aladdin/Macmillan, 1974).

5. Jones & Prescott, *Dimensions of teaching-learning environments*, 32. Quoted by permission.

6. S. Nicholson, "How not to cheat children: The theory of loose parts," *Alternate learning environments*, ed. G. Coates (Stroudsberg, PA: Dowden, Hutchinson & Ross, 1974), 30. Copyright by Van Nostrand Reinhold, New York, NY. Quoted by permission.

7. E. Jones, "Inviting children into the fun: Providing enough activity choices outdoors," *Child Care Information Exchange* 70 (December 1989): 15–19. Reprinted with permission from Exchange Press, Inc., P.O. Box 2890, Redmond, WA 98073.

8. R.L. Stevenson, *A child's garden of verses* (New York: Knopf, 1992).

9. J. Goodman, *Elementary schooling for critical democracy* (Albany, NY: State University of New York Press/SUNY, 1992), 107. Copyright by SUNY. Quoted by permission.

10. Goodman, *Elementary schooling*. Copyright by SUNY. Quoted by permission.

11. E. Prescott, "Is day care as good as a good home?" *Young Children* 33, no. 2 (1978): 13–19.

12. J.J. Tobin, D.Y.H. Wu, & D.H. Davidson, *Preschool in three cultures: Japan, China & the United States* (New Haven, CT: Yale University Press, 1989).

13. J.W. Nimmo, "The privacy behaviors of young children in group care" (master's thesis, Pacific Oaks College, Pasadena, CA, 1988).

14. M. Carter, & D. Curtis, *Training teachers: A harvest of theory and practice* (St. Paul, MN: Redleaf, 1994).

Chapter 4, pages 29–30.

1. D. Kuschner, "Put your name on your painting but . . . the blocks go back on the shelves," *Young Children* 45, no. 1 (1989): 45–56.

2. C. Genishi, ed., *Ways of assessing children and curriculum: Stories of early childhood practice* (New York: Teachers College Press, 1992).

3. V. Vecchi, "The role of the atelierista: An interview with Lella Gandini," in *The hundred languages of children: The Reggio Emilia approach to early childhood education*, eds. C. Edwards, L. Gandini, & G. Forman (Norwood, NJ: Ablex, 1993), 122. Copyright by Ablex Publishing Corporation. Used by permission. For further reading on Reggio Emilia, see several articles in *Young Children* 49, no. 1 (1993): 4–18.

Chapter 5, pages 31–41.

1. E. Jones, ed., *Reading, writing and talking with four, five and six year olds* (Pasadena, CA: Pacific Oaks College, 1988).

2. C. Edwards, L. Gandini, & G. Forman, eds., *The hundred languages of children: The Reggio Emilia approach to early childhood education* (Norwood, NJ: Ablex, 1993).

3. J.W. Nimmo, "The meaning of classroom community: Shared images of early childhood teachers," *Dissertation Abstracts International* 53 (1992): 10A. (Ann Arbor, MI: University Microfilms, no. 9305876).

4. For picture books on *Día de los Muertos* to share with children, see G. Ancona, *Pablo remembers*, English and Spanish eds. (New York: Lothrop, 1993); and D. Hoyt-Goldsmith, *The day of the dead* (New York: Holiday House, 1994). For background information, see E. Carmichael, & C. Sayer, *The skeleton at the feast: The day of the dead in Mexico* (Austin, TX: University of Texas Press, 1992); J. Greenleigh, & R.R. Beimler, *The days of the dead* (San Francisco: Collins, 1991); and J. Strupp Green, *Laughing souls: The days of the dead in Oaxaca, Mexico* (San Diego, CA: Balboa Park San Diego Museum of Man, 1969).

5. J. Gonzales-Mena, *Multicultural issues in child care* (Mountain View, CA: Mayfield, 1993).

6. L. Derman-Sparks, & the A.B.C. Task Force, *Anti-bias curriculum: Tools for empowering young children* (Washington, DC: NAEYC, 1989), 86. Copyright by L. Derman-Sparks. Used by permission.

7. The witch stereotype was used historically, complete with witch burnings, to combat the influence of wise women whose skills with herbal healing were perceived as a threat by men in power, especially in the established church. Many such women wore black because they were widows, a status which gave them relative independence in a patriarchal society.

8. E. Carmichael, & C. Sayer, *The skeleton at the feast: The day of the dead in Mexico* (Austin, TX: University of Texas Press, 1992). Copyright 1991 by the Trustees of the British Museum. Reprinted by permission of the University of Texas Press.

9. J.D. Stone, "A Jehovah's Witness perspective on holiday curriculum" (master's project, Pacific Oaks College, Pasadena, CA, 1991).

10. E. Jones, & G. Reynolds, *The play's the thing: Teachers' roles in children's play* (New York: Teachers College Press, 1992), 62–63, 69. Copyright by Teachers College, Columbia University. Reprinted by permission.

Chapter 6, pages 43–46.

1. W. Corsaro, *Friendship and peer culture in the early years* (Norwood, NJ: Ablex, 1985).

2. S.M. Corbett, "Teaching in the twilight zone: A child-sensitive approach to politically incorrect activities," *Young Children* 49, no. 4 (1994): 54–58.

3. B. Barton, *Bones, bones, dinosaur bones* (New York: Crowell, 1990).

4. D. LeeKeenan, & C.P. Edwards, "Using the project approach with toddlers," *Young Children* 47, no. 4 (1992): 31–35. The authors refer to G. Forman, & F. Hill, *Constructive play: Applying Piaget in the preschool* (Menlo Park, CA: Addison-Wesley, 1984).

Chapter 7, pages 47–52.

1. D. LeeKeenan, & J. Nimmo, "Connections: Using the project approach with 2- and 3-year-olds in a university laboratory school," in *The hundred languages of children: The Reggio Emilia approach to early childhood education*, eds. C. Edwards, L. Gandini, & G. Forman (Norwood, NJ: Ablex, 1993).

2. J. Herndon, *The way it spozed to be* (New York: Simon & Schuster, 1968).

3. G. Boomer, ed., *Negotiating the curriculum: A teacher-student partnership* (Sydney, Australia: Ashton-Scholastic, 1982); L. Katz, & S. Chard, *Engaging children's minds: The project approach* (Norwood, NJ: Ablex, 1989); and C. Edwards, L. Gandini, & G. Forman, eds., *The hundred languages of children: The Reggio Emilia approach to early childhood education* (Norwood, NJ: Ablex, 1993).

4. E. Jones, & G. Reynolds, *The play's the thing: Teachers' roles in children's play* (New York: Teachers College Press, 1992), 43, 51–52. Copyright by Teachers College, Columbia University. Quoted by permission.

5. Jones & Reynolds, *The play's the thing*, 52–54.

6. B. Rankin, "Curriculum development in Reggio Emilia: A long-term curriculum project about dinosaurs," in *The hundred languages of children: The Reggio Emilia approach to early childhood education*,

eds. C. Edwards, L. Gandini, & G. Forman (Norwood, NJ: Ablex, 1993), 192. Copyright by the Ablex Publishing Corporation. Quoted by permission.

Chapter 8, pages 53–58.

1. N. Carlsson-Paige, & D. Levin, *The war play dilemma: Balancing needs and values in the early childhood classroom* (New York: Teachers College Press, 1987).

2. E. Jones, & G. Reynolds, *The play's the thing: Teachers' roles in children's play* (New York: Teachers College Press, 1992).

3. M. Scudder, "Feelings: An integral part of the curriculum," Pacific Oaks Occasional Paper (Pasadena, CA: Pacific Oaks College, 1978).

4. A. Morris, *Bread bread bread* (New York: Lothrop, 1989); R. Krauss, *The carrot seed* (New York: Harper, 1945); and P. Galdone, *The little red hen* (Boston: Houghton Mifflin, 1979).

5. M.R. MacDonald, ed., *Folklore of world heritage* (Detroit, MI: Gale, 1991).

6. B. Nickerson, *Celebrate the sun* (New York: Lippincott, 1969).

7. R.M. Booze, "Incorporating the principles of Kwanzaa into your daily curriculum: A handbook for teachers of young children," Pacific Oaks Occasional Paper (Pasadena, CA: Pacific Oaks College, 1988), 50. Quoted by permission. For a picture book on Kwanzaa to share with children, see D. Hoyt-Goldsmith, *Celebrating Kwanzaa* (New York: Holiday House, 1993).

8. J.W. Nimmo, "The meaning of classroom community: Shared images of early childhood teachers," *Dissertation Abstracts International* 53 (1992): 10A. (Ann Arbor, MI: University Microfilms, no. 9305876).

9. J.T. Gatto, *Dumbing us down: The hidden curriculum of compulsory schooling* (Philadelphia, PA: New Society Publishers, 1992).

Chapter 9, pages 59–63.

1. R. New, "Cultural variations on developmentally appropriate practice: Challenges to theory and practice," in *The hundred languages of children: The Reggio Emilia approach to early childhood education,* eds. C. Edwards, L. Gandini, & G. Forman (Norwood, NJ: Ablex, 1993), 226. Copyright by Ablex Publishing Corporation. Quoted by permission.

2. C. Edwards, L. Gandini, & G. Forman, eds., *The hundred languages of children: The Reggio Emilia approach to early childhood education* (Norwood, NJ: Ablex, 1993).

3. L. Malaguzzi, "History, ideas, and basic philosophy," in *The hundred languages of children: The Reggio Emilia approach to early childhood education,* eds. C. Edwards, L. Gandini, & G. Forman (Norwood, NJ: Ablex, 1993), 64. Copyright by Ablex Publishing Corporation. Quoted by permission.

4. New, "Cultural variations," 222. Copyright by Ablex Publishing Corporation. Quoted by permission.

Chapter 10, pages 65–67.

1. A frequently sung spiritual; in the public domain.

2. E. Jones, & G. Villarino, "What goes up on the classroom walls—and why?" *Young Children* 49, no. 2 (1994): 39. Copyright by NAEYC.

Chapter 11, pages 69–72.

1. J.D. Stone, "A Jehovah's Witness perspective on holiday curriculum" (master's thesis, Pacific Oaks College, Pasadena, CA, 1991).

2. S.G. Clemens, "A Dr. Martin Luther King, Jr. curriculum: Playing the dream," *Young Children* 43, no. 2 (1988): 6–11.

3. E. Jones, & L. Derman-Sparks, "Meeting the challenge of diversity," *Young Children* 47, no. 2 (1992): 13. Copyright by NAEYC.

4. One version of this role play is given in L. Derman-Sparks et al., *Anti-bias curriculum: Tools for empowering young children* (Washington, DC: NAEYC, 1989), 94–95. Teachers considering this activity are advised to give careful thought to its structuring, however, since it is easily, inadvertently, turned into superficial "tourist curriculum." We observed an example of this in a class of Hispanic second graders:
"We're going to play Rosa Parks on the bus," said the well-meaning White teacher. "Who would like to be the bus driver? Who would like to be the little, Black children? Who would like to be the little, White children?" All the children, charmed by the unusual opportunity to get out of their desks and play, volunteered for everything. They had a wonderful time. There was no follow-up discussion. "I'm not sure how I should be doing this," said the teacher in an aside to an observer, "but I thought we should do something for Dr. King's birthday."

5. B.J. Thomson, "This is like that Martin Luther King guy," *Young Children* 48, no. 2 (1993): 46–48.

Chapter 12, pages 73–74.

1. This gospel song, put to use in union-organizing, freedom, and antiwar movements, can be found in several song collections and records. It gets changed by every group that sings it. This Spanish version is one taught me [Betty] by my daughter; other versions have come from the United Farm Workers movement.

Chapter 13, pages 75–80.

1. M. Mead, "Can the socialization of children lead to greater acceptance of diversity?" *Young Children* 28, no. 6 (1973): 329.

2. For further information and resources on quilt making and its use in the classroom, see R. Clark,

& C. Heller, "Quilt connections," *Teaching Tolerance* 2, no. 1 (1993): 38–45.

3. K.R. Stafford, "The story that saved life," in *Stories lives tell: Narrative and dialogue in education,* eds. C. Witherell & N. Noddings (New York: Teachers College Press, 1991), 15. Copyright by Teachers College, Columbia University. Quoted by permission.

4. I.S. Andrews, "Looking back and walking forward hand in hand: What children, parents and teachers can learn from each other" (master's project, Pacific Oaks College, Pasadena, CA, 1992), 87–89. Used by permission of the author.

5. S. Ashton-Warner, *Teacher* (New York: Simon and Schuster, 1963).

6. K.A. Roskos, & S.B. Neuman, "Of scribbles, schemas, and storybooks: Using literacy albums to document young children's literacy growth," *Young Children* 49, no. 2 (1994): 78–85.

Chapter 14, pages 81–84.

1. L. Derman-Sparks, & the A.B.C. Task Force, *Anti-bias curriculum: Tools for empowering young children* (Washington, DC: NAEYC, 1989).

2. L. Read, "Different abilities: A continually emerging curriculum," Pacific Oaks Occasional Paper (Pasadena, CA: Pacific Oaks College, 1993).

3. Derman-Sparks et al., *Anti-bias curriculum,* 16. Copyright by L. Derman-Sparks. Quoted by permission.

Chapter 15, pages 85–90.

1. P. Oken-Wright, "Show-and-tell grows up," *Young Children* 43, no. 2 (1988): 52–57.

2. Ideas drawn from I.S. Andrews, "Looking back and walking forward hand in hand: What children, parents and teachers can learn from each other" (master's project, Pacific Oaks College, Pasadena, CA, 1992), 87–88, 148. Used by permission.

3. K.A. Roskos, & S.B. Neuman, "Of scribbles, schemas, and storybooks: Using literacy albums to document young children's literacy growth," *Young Children* 49, no. 2 (1994): 79, 80. Copyright by the authors. All rights reserved. Used by permission.

4. For a discussion on the issues for children and families who are homeless and on the implications for early childhood educators, see T. Klein, C. Bittel, & J. Molnar, "No place to call home: Supporting the needs of homeless children in the early childhood classroom," *Young Children* 48, no. 6 (1993): 22–31; and L. McCormick, & R. Holden, "Homeless children: A special challenge," *Young Children* 47, no. 6 (1992): 61-67. The picture book by E. Bunting, *Fly away home* (New York: Clarion Books, 1977), which follows a family's search for shelter in an airport terminal, provides a sensitive introduction to the reality of homelessness to older preschoolers.

5. The importance of early childhood teachers accepting and supporting gay and lesbian parents and their families is discussed in S. Corbett, "A complicated bias," *Young Children* 48, no. 3 (1993): 29–31; and E. Wickers, "Penny's question: 'I will have a child in my class with two moms—what do you know about this?'" *Young Children* 48, no. 3 (1993): 25–28.

Chapter 16, pages 91–92.

1. J.W. Nimmo, "The meaning of classroom community: Shared images of early childhood teachers," Pacific Oaks Occasional Paper (Pasadena, CA: Pacific Oaks College, 1992), 240.

Chapter 17, pages 93–98.

1. Book jacket flap excerpt from V.G. Paley, *Bad guys don't have birthdays: Fantasy play at four* (Chicago: University of Chicago Press, 1988).

2. M.W. Piers, review of *Mollie is three: Growing up in school* by V.G. Paley, *American Journal of Education* (May 1987): 499.

3. S. Wasserman, *Serious players in the primary classroom* (New York: Teachers College Press, 1990).

4. E. Jones, & G. Reynolds, *The play's the thing: Teachers' roles in children's play* (New York: Teachers College Press, 1992), 6. Copyright by Teachers College, Columbia University. Reprinted by permission.

5. L. Meckel, "Thinking is the way your mind talks," in *Reading, writing and talking with four, five and six year olds,* ed. E. Jones (Pasadena, CA: Pacific Oaks College, 1988), 152. Copyright by Pacific Oaks College. Quoted by permission.

6. Meckel, "Thinking is the way," 153. Quoted by permission.

7. For a clear statement of the view that food, a precious resource, is only for eating, see B.-G. Holt, *Science with young children,* rev. ed. (Washington, DC: NAYEC, 1989), 156-57.

8. L. Read, "Different abilities: A continually emerging curriculum," Pacific Oaks Occasional Paper (Pasadena, CA: Pacific Oaks College, 1993).

Chapter 18, pages 99–102.

1. "Diana Hop! Advisories for the three year old children," (Reggio Emilia, Italy: Diana Municipal Preschool, September 1990, typescript), subsequently published in *Children's Environments* (see note 2 below). A brief description of 5-year-olds' creation of these very informative "advisories" for younger children entering the preschool can be found in C. Edwards, "Partner, nurturer, and guide: The roles of the Reggio teacher in action," in *The hundred languages of children: The Reggio Emilia approach to early childhood education,* eds. C. Edwards, L. Gandini, & G. Forman (Norwood, NJ: Ablex, 1993), 165–67.

2. Children of Reggio Emilia, "Children in Reggio Emilia look at their school," *Children's Environments* 10, no. 2 (1993): 127. Copyright by Chapman and Hall, London. Used by permission.

NOTES

3. M. Carter, & D. Curtis, *Training teachers: A harvest of theory and practice* (St. Paul, MN: Redleaf, 1994), 189. Copyright by the authors. Quoted by permission.

4. Carter & Curtis, *Training teachers*, 190. Used by permission.

5. N. Carlsson-Paige, & D. Levin, *The war play dilemma: Balancing needs and values in the early childhood classroom* (New York: Teachers College Press, 1987).

6. Carlsson-Paige & Levin, *The war play dilemma*.

7. Carlsson-Paige & Levin, *The war play dilemma*, 56. Copyright by Teachers College, Columbia University. Reprinted by permission.

8. S. Skelding, introduction to "Activities for supporting non-aggressive play," Pacific Oaks Occasional Paper (Pasadena, CA: Pacific Oaks College, 1992), n.p. Quoted by permission.

Chapter 19, pages 103–107.

1. D. Stipek, L. Rosenblatt, & L. DiRocco, "Making parents your allies," *Young Children* 49, no. 3 (1994), 4–9.

2. E. Jones, & E. Prescott, *Dimensions of teaching-learning environments: A handbook for teachers in elementary schools and day care centers* (Pasadena, CA: Pacific Oaks College, 1984), 25. Quoted by permission.

Chapter 20, pages 109–113.

1. M.M. Green, *Everybody has a house* (New York: Wm. R. Scott, 1944).

2. The stories of other quilters turning scraps and throwaways into objects of beauty are shared by M.S. Wahlman, *Signs and symbols: African images in African-American quilts* (New York: Dutton/Penguin USA, 1993).

Chapter 21, pages 115–123.

1. *I centro linguaggi dei bambini* [*The hundred languages of children: Narrative of the possible*], Italian/English ed. catalog of the exhibit "The hundred languages of children" (City of Reggio Emilia, Italy: Department of Early Education, Region of Emilia Romagna, 1987), 70–76. (Assessorato Scuola Infanzia e Asilo Nido, Via Guido da Castello 12, 42100 Reggio Emilia, Italy).

2. G. Petter, "Shadowiness," in *The hundred languages of children: Narrative of the possible*, Italian/English ed. (City of Reggio Emilia, Italy: Department of Early Education, Region of Emilia Romagna, 1987), 74. Quoted by permission.

3. Examples include M. Bang, *Ten nine eight* (New York: Morrow, 1983); M.W. Brown, *Good night moon* (New York: Harper, 1947); R. Hoban, *Bedtime for Frances* (New York: Harper, 1960); and B. Waber, *Ira sleeps over* (Boston: Houghton Mifflin, 1973).

4. R. McCloskey, *Blueberries for Sal* (New York: Viking, 1948).

5. L. Malaguzzi, "History, ideas, and basic philosophy," in *The hundred languages of children: The Reggio Emilia approach to early childhood education*, eds. C. Edwards, L. Gandini, & G. Forman (Norwood, NJ: Ablex, 1993), 41–89.

6. L. Katz, & S. Chard, *Engaging children's minds: The project approach* (Norwood, NJ: Ablex, 1989).

Chapter 22, pages 125–139.

1. E. Jones, ed., *Growing teachers: Partnerships in staff development* (Washington, DC: NAEYC, 1993).

2. Drawn from earlier, informal writing by the author, E. Jones. For another classification of sources of emergent curriculum, see Rebecca New's description of "project-based teaching" in Reggio Emilia in R. New, "Excellent early education: A city in Italy has it," *Young Children* 45, no. 6 (1990): 6–8.

3. D. LeeKeenan, & J. Nimmo, "Connections: Using the project approach with 2- and 3-year-olds in a university laboratory school," in *The hundred languages of children: The Reggio Emilia approach to early childhood education*, eds. C. Edwards, L. Gandini, & G. Forman (Norwood, NJ: Ablex, 1993), 259–67.

4. E. Jones, & E. Prescott, *Dimensions of teaching-learning environments: A handbook for teachers in elementary schools and day care centers* (Pasadena, CA: Pacific Oaks College, 1984).

5. For a stimulating discussion of values and curriculum, see S.A. Kessler, "Alternative perspectives on early childhood education," 183–197; and S. Bredekamp, "Redeveloping early childhood education: A response to Kessler," 199–209 in *Early Childhood Research Quarterly* 6, no. 2 (1991).

6. E. Jones, & G. Reynolds, *The play's the thing: Teachers' roles in children's play* (New York: Teachers College Press, 1992).

7. R. Hart, *Children's experience of place* (New York: Irvington, 1979), 283. Copyright by Irvington Publishers, Inc. Used by permission.

8. L. Derman-Sparks, & the A.B.C. Task Force, *Anti-bias curriculum: Tools for empowering young children* (Washington, DC: NAEYC, 1989).

9. M.N. Bloch, B.R. Tabachnik, & M. Espinosa-Dulanto, "Teacher perspectives on the strengths and achievements of young children: Relationship to ethnicity, language, gender, and class," in *Diversity and developmentally appropriate practices*, eds. B.L. Mallory, & R.S. New (New York: Teachers College Press, 1994), 223–49.

10. L. Delpit, "The silenced dialogue: Power and pedagogy in educating other people's children," *Harvard Educational Review* 58, no. 3 (1988): 280–98.

11. With appreciation to Carol Anne Wien, teacher educator (Faculty of Education, York University, Ontario, Canada), for her way with words—and ideas.

For Further Reading

Teacher-As-Researcher Resources

Researchers gather data and reflect on them. Teachers who behave like researchers, in collaborating in planning and reflecting on their work, can enjoy the challenge of transforming practice into theory. And it is out of their planning and reflection that emergent curriculum emerges. These resources expand on the *teacher-as-researcher* theme in various ways.

Carter, M., & D. Curtis. *Training teachers: A harvest of theory and practice.* St. Paul, MN: Redleaf, 1994.

Clift, R.T., W.R. Houston, & M.C. Pugach, eds. *Encouraging reflective practice in education: An analysis of issues and programs.* New York: Teachers College Press, 1990.

Duckworth, E. *"The having of wonderful ideas" and other essays on teaching and learning.* New York: Teachers College Press, 1987.

Edwards, C., L. Gandini, & G. Forman, eds. *The hundred languages of children: The Reggio Emilia approach to early childhood education.* Norwood, NJ: Ablex, 1993.

Fosnot, C.T. *Enquiring teachers, enquiring learners: A constructivist approach for teaching.* New York: Teachers College Press, 1989.

Genishi, C. *Ways of assessing children and curriculum: Stories of early childhood practice.* New York: Teachers College Press, 1992.

Jones, E., ed. *Growing teachers: Partnerships in staff development.* Washington, DC: NAEYC, 1993.

New, R. "Excellent early education: A city in Italy has it." *Young Children* 45, no. 6 (1990): 4–10.

New, R.S. "Culture, child development, and developmentally appropriate practices: Teachers as collaborative researchers." Chap. 3 in B.L. Mallory & R.S. New, eds., *Diversity and developmentally appropriate practices: Challenges for early childhood education.* New York: Teachers College Press, 1994.

Oja, S.N. "Adult development: Insights on staff development." In A. Lieberman & I. Miller, eds., *Staff development for education in the 90's.* New York: Teachers College Press, 1991.

van Manen, M. *Researching lived experience.* Albany, NY: The State University of New York, 1990.

Witherell, C., & N. Noddings, eds. *Stories lives tell: Narrative and dialogue in education.* New York: Teachers College Press, 1991.

Yonemura, M.V. *A teacher at work: Professional development and the early childhood educator.* New York: Teachers College Press, 1986.

Webbing Resources

On the cover of this book and throughout its pages, the role of *webbing* in emergent curriculum is evident. For those readers who want to explore this approach to planning, the following resources useful may be useful.

Baskwill, J. "Themestorming." *Teaching K-8* 19, no. 1 (1988): 80–82.

Carini, P.F. "Child development: A basis for open classroom curriculum." Conference speech presented at Cortland College, Cortland, New York, May 4, 1973.

Carlsson-Paige, N., & D.E. Levin. "Two sample curriculum webs." App. 2 of *The war play dilemma.* New York: Teachers College Press, 1987.

Cassidy, D.J., & C. Lancaster. "The grassroots curriculum: A dialogue between children and teachers." *Young Children* 48, no. 6 (1993): 47–51.

Gross, A.L., & L.W. Ortiz. "Using children's literature to facilitate inclusion in kindergarten and the primary grades." *Young Children* 49, no. 3 (1994): 32–35.

Jones, E., & G. Reynolds. "Teacher as planner." Chap. 8 in *The play's the thing.* New York: Teachers College Press, 1992.

Levin, D.E. "Weaving curriculum webs: Planning, guiding, and recording curriculum activities in the day care classroom." *Day Care and Early Education* 13, no. 4 (1986): 16–19.

McCracken, J.B. *Valuing diversity: The primary years.* Washington, DC: NAEYC, 1993. (See pp. 68–72.)

Miller, S.A. "Sand and water around the room." *Scholastic Early Childhood Today* 8, no. 6 (1994): 37–45.

Workman, S., & M.C. Anziano. "Curriculum webs: Weaving connections from children to teachers." *Young Children* 48, no. 2 (1993): 4–9.

Information about NAEYC

NAEYC is . . .

. . . a membership-supported organization of people committed to fostering the growth and development of children from birth through age eight. Membership is open to all who share a desire to serve and act on behalf of the needs and rights of young children.

NAEYC provides . . .

. . . educational services and resources to adults who work with and for children, including

• *Young Children,* the journal for early childhood educators

• **Books, posters, brochures,** and **videos** to expand your knowledge and commitment to young children, with topics including infants, curriculum, research, discipline, teacher education, and parent involvement

• An **Annual Conference** that brings people from all over the country to share their expertise and advocate on behalf of children and families

• **Week of the Young Child** celebrations sponsored by NAEYC Affiliate Groups across the nation to call public attention to the needs and rights of children and families

• **Insurance plans** for individuals and programs

• **Public affairs information** for knowledgeable advocacy efforts at all levels of government and through the media

• The **National Academy of Early Childhood Programs,** a voluntary accreditation system for high-quality programs for children

• The **National Institute for Early Childhood Professional Development,** providing resources and services to improve professional preparation and development of early childhood educators

• The **Information Service,** a centralized source of information sharing, distribution, and collaboration

For free information about membership, publications, or other NAEYC services. . .

• call NAEYC at 202–232–8777 or 800–424–2460

• or write to NAEYC, 1509 16th St., N.W., Washington, DC 20036–1426.